Jesus and the Emergence of a Catholic Imagination

An Illustrated Journey

JOHN PFORDRESHER

Paulist Press

New York/ Mahwah, NJ

Art credits are on pp. v-viii.

Cover design by Cynthia Dunne
Book design by Sharyn Banks

Library of Congress Cataloging-in-Publication Data

Pfordresher, John.
    Jesus and the emergence of a Catholic imagination : an illustrated journey / John Pfordresher.
       p. cm.
    Includes bibliographical references and index.
    ISBN 978-0-8091-4453-2 (alk. paper)
    1. Christianity and the arts. 2. Imagination—Religious aspects—Catholic Church. 3. Jesus Christ—Words. 4. Church history. I. Title.
    BX1795.A78P46 2008
    246′.2—dc22
                          2007044672

Published by Paulist Press
997 Macarthur Boulevard
Mahwah, New Jersey 07430

www.paulistpress.com

Printed and bound in the United States of America

Contents

Illustrations and Credits
In Order of Appearance

Chapter 1

Jesus as warrior-god. Mosaic, sixth-century Ravenna. From *The Twentieth Century Atlas of the Christian World*.

Michelangelo Buonarroti (1475–1564), *The Florence Pietà*. Museo dell'Opera del Duomo, Florence, Italy. Alinari/Art Resource, NY.

Chapter 2

The passion and resurrection, early Christian sarcophagus. FreeStock Photos.com.

Hieronymus Bosch, *Christ Carrying the Cross* (ca. 1515). Scala/Art Resource, NY.

Eucharistic image from the catacomb of S. Callisto, third century. Scala/Art Resource, NY.

Dorothy reliquary monstrance. Fifteenth century. Historisches Museum Basel. Photo: HMB P. Portner.

Chapter 3

Torah scroll with staves. German (?), nineteenth century. The Jewish Museum. NY/Art Resource, NY.

Saint Peter called by Christ to be a fisher of people. From *The Twentieth Century Atlas of the Christian World*.

Mystic Lamb. Early Christian ceiling mosaic from San Vitale, Ravenna. Scala/Art Resource, NY.

Jonah and the whale. Early fourth-century ivory relief. From *The Bible in Art (Old Testament)*.

Chapter 4

Fra Angelico and Filippo Lippi, *Adoration of the Magi* (ca. 1445). Samuel H. Kress Collection. Image © Board of Trustees, National Gallery of Art, Washington.

Bartolomé Murillo, *Return of the Prodigal Son* (1667–1670). Gift of the Avalon Foundation. Image © Board of Trustees, National Gallery of Art, Washington.

Baptism. Fresco, catacomb of Saints Marcellinus and Peter. commons.wiki-media.org.

Chapter 5

Salvador Dali (1904–1989), *Sacrament of the Last Supper*. Chester Dale Collection. Image © Board of Trustees, National Gallery of Art, Washington.

Introduction to Part II

A Roman civic basilica. From *The Twentieth Century Atlas of the Christian World*.

Chapter 6

Saint Paul. Mosaic from Archbishop's Palace, fifth-sixth centuries. Scala/Art Resource, NY.

Damascus with Roman city wall. From *The Twentieth Century Atlas of the Christian World*.

Pharisee. KamGlobal.org.

Chapter 7

The following illustrations are from the house-church at Dura-Europos and are taken from Carl H. Kraeling, *The Christian Building: The Excavations at Dura Europos*. Final Report VII, Part II. New Haven: Dura-Europos Publications, 1967. Used with permission.

Floor plan of the house-church. Fig. 1.

The woman at the well: wall fresco. Plate XL.

The good shepherd with Adam and Eve: wall fresco. Plate XXXI.

Women at the tomb: wall fresco. Plate XL.

The healing of the paralytic: wall fresco. Plate XXXV.
The walking on the water: wall fresco. Plate XXXVII.

Chapter 8

Burial niches with fresco of Christ Pantocrator. Catacomb of S. Callisto, Rome, Italy. Erich Lessing/Art Resource, NY.

Romanized Christ as Good Shepherd. Fresco, Catacomb of Priscilla, Rome, Italy. Erich Lessing/Art Resource, NY.

Moses striking the rock. Fresco (late third century), Catacomb of Priscilla, Rome, Italy. Bildarchiv Preussischer Kulturbesitz/Art Resource, NY.

The three Hebrews in the furnace. Fresco (second half third century), Cubiculum of the Velati, Catacomb of Priscilla, Rome, Italy. Scala/Art Resource, NY.

Susanna accused. Fresco, Catacomb of Priscilla, Rome, Italy. Scala/Art Resource, NY.

Adoration of the Magi. Fresco, Catacomb of Priscilla, Rome, Italy. Scala/Art Resource, NY.

Breaking of the bread. Fresco, Catacomb of Priscilla, Rome, Italy. Scala/Art Resource, NY.

The resurrection of Lazarus. Fresco, Cubiculum of the Annunciation, Catacomb of Priscilla, Rome, Italy. Scala/Art Resource, NY.

Chapter 9

Bust of Constantine. From *The Twentieth Century Atlas of the Christian World*.

Interior of Old St. Peter's in Rome. Fresco, S. Martino ai Monti. Scala/Art Resource, NY.

Chapter 10

Iona. From *The Twentieth Century Atlas of the Christian World*.

Celtic cross. Photograph by John Vidmar, OP.

The following illustrations from *The Book of Kells* (TCD MS 58) are reproduced with permission of The Board of Trinity College Dublin:

The arrest of Christ. (Folio 114r.)

Virgin and Child with Angels. (Folio 7v.)

Christ. (Folio 32v.)

"Erat autem hora tercia." (Folio 183r.)

"In principio erat verbum." (Folio 292r.)

Animal interlace. (Folio 250v.)

Chapter 11

The Baptism of Clovis. From *The Twentieth Century Atlas of the Christian World*.

The following illustrations from *The Utrecht Psalter* are reproduced with permission of the Trustees of the University Library, Utrecht, The Netherlands:

Psalm 68(69), Salvum me fac. (Folio 38v.)

Psalm 22(23), Dominus regit me. (Folio 13r.)

Psalm 25(26), Iudica me. (Folio 14v.)

Psalm 23(24), Domini est terra. (Folio 13v.)

Psalm 33(34), Benedicam Dominum. (Folio 19r.)

For
Albert and Virginia Pfordresher
Francis and Margaret Murray

Acknowledgments

This book emerges from the years in which my colleague and friend Jim Walsh, SJ, and I taught a course for Georgetown undergraduates titled "The Catholic Imagination." Many of the ideas here evolved from our shared interest in this topic, and I have learned more than I can adequately acknowledge from working with him. A grant from the then dean of the college, Robert Lawton, SJ, helped us start that course. Like our students, over the years I was able to learn many things important to the topic of the Catholic imagination from our guest lecturers. They included Paul Cioffi, SJ, G. Ronald Murphy, SJ, Bill Samson, SJ, Teresa Sanders, Julia Lamm, Paul McCarren, SJ, and Scott Pilarz, SJ. More recently I have also been teaching another Catholic studies course at Georgetown with Professor Anthony Tambasco, and I know that my understanding of Catholic theology has become richer and more subtle thanks to our ongoing dialogue in and about that course.

I have been twice fortunate in being able to participate in seminars at the Folger Institute in Washington, D.C., during which I was able to extend my reading in and understanding of certain questions relevant to this book, and I am grateful to the leaders of those seminars, Professors Hsia and Eire, for permitting me to work under their direction.

It was my great good fortune to read in several splendid libraries during the years in which I was working on this project, and I would like to thank their staff members and the institutions that permitted me to learn through their generosity. These include the Folger Shakespeare Library, the library at Harvard University's Renaissance Research center I Tatti in Settignano, the Kunsthistorisches Institut in Florence, the Lauinger Library at Georgetown University, and the library of Xavier University of Chicago, Illinois. I wrote much of the body of the book's text while teaching at Georgetown's Villa le Balze in Fiesole. I will always remain grateful to my colleagues and friends Mike Collins, Marcello Fantoni, and Kate Magovern for helping me to write under such fostering and intellectually stimulating circumstances.

I am particularly grateful to friends and colleagues who talked with me about this book, or who read parts or all of the working manuscript and who helped me, each in a different way with their responses to what they read and with suggestions for correction and improvement. These kind people include Bonita Billman, John Langan, SJ, Bess Catherine McCord, G. Ronald Murphy, SJ, Marge Murray, Virginia Pfordresher, Cassandra Potts-Hannas, Lucia Rausch, Daniel Sherman, Anthony Tambasco, and James Walsh, SJ.

It has been my good fortune to be guided, from the early stages of this book, by the help and encouragement of Rev. Lawrence Boadt, CSP, president of Paulist Press. I'm very grateful for his support, for the insightful and generous help of Nancy de Flon, PhD, my editor at Paulist Press, and for the work of Jim Quigley, assistant editor at Paulist Press.

J. Pf., January 2007

Preface

This book considers several important issues that emerge from the following question: How did a Catholic way of imagining the world emerge in the arts of the West?

The ideas in this book and the terms it develops provide a theoretical framework for discussing such questions. The reader can then use the theory to frame further questions and follow up other lines of inquiry.

Part I of this book begins by defining what is meant by *Catholic* and by describing the workings of the imagination. It then examines how Jesus' imagination worked, how he used imaginative strategies to teach, and how the canonical Gospels function as initiating examples of sacred biography and hence of a tradition of Catholic narrative. These early chapters do not read the Bible in terms of contemporary biblical scholarship, though the author is aware of that scholarship and keeps it constantly in mind. Rather, they read the Bible in a traditional way, the way in which ordinary people and some artists used to read it—as a plain and internally consistent account of factual events.

Part II then studies the early historical development of the Catholic imagination by tracing the processes both of creative invention and of cultural adoption and translation that took place as Christianity spread first throughout the Mediterranean basin and later into northern Europe. The six examples analyzed in the book span the period from the age of the apostles to the early ninth century. They permit the close examination of pictures, architectural spaces, lyric and epic poetry, and manuscript illumination. In addition, the discussion of these examples provides an extensive illustration in how the theoretical premises of part 1 work, and in particular how they serve the critic in efforts to discern a distinctive and continuing tradition of Catholic artistic expression.

Today "Catholic studies" is emerging as a new and significant form of intellectual inquiry. This book serves as a contribution to that development. It is written for thoughtful people who may or may not know very much about Catholicism and its historical relationship to the arts but who want to know more. It is the writer's hope that the ideas in this book will open up to the reader fresh opportunities for thought and new ways of experiencing.

John Pfordresher, Professor of English,
Georgetown University

PART I

JESUS AND IMAGINATION

Origins

Creator Spiritus

Jesus and the Arts

The Jesus of the New Testament never says a word about high culture or the fine arts. The written record suggests that Jesus was completely uninterested in painting, sculpture, poetry, music, and architecture. So, for example, when Jesus expresses indignation at the way people are using the Temple in Jerusalem, it's not because he admires this building as the finest work of Jewish architecture, but because it's wrong to do business in a sacred place (Matt 21:12–13).

Given the historical context, this should not be so surprising. As a Jewish man living at a time when Palestine was one of the occupied territories of the Roman Empire, Jesus was a member of an impoverished, subject people who had little time or money for the fine arts. In Jesus' time Judaism as a culture had little to do with certain forms of artistic expression. Jews were forbidden by sacred law from making visual images of people. Other kinds of art were simply never practiced. There was, for example, no Jewish theater in Jerusalem.

And yet the church that Jesus left behind soon became deeply involved in the arts. Why?

From Jesus to Church

The accounts of the last weeks of Jesus' life suggest that he may have anticipated two quite different possibilities for the years after his death.

At times he seems to expect the imminent destruction of the world and the coming of what he frequently referred to as "the kingdom of God." If this was the immediate future of the world, it would make any kind of planning meaningless. The future was about to end.

But at other moments Jesus looks forward to an undefined span of time in which his followers will carry on his teaching. So the Book of Acts tells us that the resurrected Christ, "before he was taken up [into heaven]...gave instructions by the power of the Holy Spirit to the men he had chosen as his apostles" (Acts 1:2 GNB). When his followers ask what was to happen next, Jesus said to them, "It is not for you to know the times or periods that the Father has set by his own authority. But you will receive power when the Holy Spirit has come upon you; and you will be my witnesses...to the ends of the earth" (Acts 1:7-8).

At moments like this Jesus seems to be planning a religious organization—a church. Here again, in everything that is recorded in the Bible about this new church—the sayings of Jesus, the events after his ascension into heaven, and the subsequent coming of the Holy Spirit on Pentecost—there is no record that anyone is thinking about the arts.

There is no talk of buildings, for example. Evidently there were none. The early Christian community continued to practice traditions Jesus had initiated: his followers gathered to pray in private homes; his chosen apostles traveled from place to place spreading the good news of Jesus' life, teachings, and resurrection by preaching—no writing, no pictures—the simplest imaginable religious organization.

Guiding the New Church

During these first decades of Christianity, believers were convinced that God was present with them in two important ways.

First, during his time on earth Jesus had assured them, "I am with you always, to the end of the age" (Matt 28:20), and had described one way in which this would happen: "Where two or three are gathered in my name, I am there among them" (Matt 18:20). Statements like this suggest that early Christians were certain that after he had been taken up into heaven Jesus himself continued to be somehow present in their lives and particularly when they gathered together to talk about and pray to God.

And second, there were Jesus' promises about the coming of a new Holy Spirit of understanding, conviction, and action. The earliest accounts describe this infusion of God's Spirit taking place on the Jewish harvest festival of Shabuoth, which was to become the Christian festival Pentecost. From that day the apostles, inspired with a new confidence and power, began spreading the good news even at the risk of their lives. They began making decisions on their own about church business, evidently feeling sure that what they were doing was inspired and directed by this Holy Spirit.

As things turned out, the "kingdom of God," if by that Jesus meant the immediate end of the world, did not come. Christians had to adjust to a much longer time frame—two thousand years and still counting. The early church expanded from Jerusalem into the gentile world of the late Roman Empire, where it experienced success, persecution, and—later—legitimation. The radically simple church of the apostles began to change. Christians began to express their belief and their membership in community through the arts used by the culture of their time: painting, mosaics, poetry, music; later sculpture, glass making, architecture. The exuberant confidence reflected in these early works illustrates a certitude on the part of those who made them that these forms of artistic expression emerged from a divine creative Spirit living within the church, authenticating and guiding their creation. As the centuries passed, the Catholic Church became the single most influential patron of the arts in the history of Western culture. By the twelfth century, for example, every city, town, and village in Christian Europe had its churches, and in those churches, depending upon the relative wealth of the area, one could find painting, sculpture, stained glass, illuminated manuscripts, ornamented sacred vessels, and so on. Catholic poetry and music celebrated in word and song a living, shared belief. Church commissions alone accounted for patronage in excess of anything ever seen before. If one then includes works on religious subjects commissioned by faithful Catholics, the sheer quantity becomes even more remarkable. Though Jesus never talked about the arts, his followers created a church that became extraordinarily invested in artistic expression.

There are three useful ways of interpreting how and why this happened.

Why Catholic Art Began: Three Explanations

1. *Adaptation.* From the point of view of modern historical theory—a form of analytical thinking based upon *rational materialism*—one can explain the evolution of Catholic art as the adaptive response of a new religion to a changing cultural context. This account sees the evolution of Catholic art as exactly resembling many other such developments in the history of world culture. In this instance, non-Jewish Christian converts coming from a pagan gentile culture simply continued the artistic traditions of the world they knew using those traditions to articulate their new Christian beliefs. So, for example, in the catacombs of Rome, pagan images of Orpheus and Hermes began to serve as symbolic pictures of Christ (Figure 1).

Figure 1. Jesus as warrior-god
Early Christian art frequently portrayed Christ in the image of a pagan god. This sixth-century mosaic from the Archbishop's Chapel in Ravenna shows Jesus as a warrior-god, with the lion and dragon as traditional symbols of the foes to be overcome. His weapon is the cross, and his shield proclaims him as "the way, the truth, and the life."

A pessimistic conclusion that one might draw from this rational/materialist reading of history finds Christianity abandoning the original, pure teaching of Jesus for a misleading mingling of pagan and Christian—a sellout in which Jesus' followers compromised his message in order to successfully convert the pagan world. From this perspective Jesus' challenging insistence upon charity to others at the expense of self—"Sell all that you own and distribute the money to the poor..." (Luke 18:22)—is soon replaced by an indulgence in costly and elaborately sculpted marble tombs for wealthy Roman Christians.

A more optimistic reading of this rational/materialist view of history finds early Christians simply discovering new ways to voice Jesus' teaching. From this perspective the emergence of Christian art is simply a faithful translation of the good news into diverse cultural forms to the enrichment of Christianity as a whole. Indeed, this argument can be pressed further, to suggest that Christianity with its new perspective was able to perceive certain kinds of meaning and possibility in pagan art that had been invisible to pagan minds. So the fourth-century Spanish writer Prudentius takes images and phrases from Roman Latin poetry—from writers like Virgil—and weaves them into poems celebrating a new form of heroism, not of imperialistic Roman conquerors but of early Christian martyrs.

2. *Imitation.* A second explanation for the evolution of Christian art—what we might describe as an *organic, deterministic* explanation—finds in the historical record evidence for a kind of development that was simply inevitable. This reading of history—which will be explained at some length in later chapters of this book—finds in Jesus' own preaching and in the gospel stories of his life and death the generative inspiration for later Christian art. It argues that since the world did not end shortly after Jesus' death, it was inevitable—given how Jesus talked and how he trained his followers—that Catholics would turn to poetry, music, painting, even architecture. From this point of view these developments arise not so much because Christianity

came into collision with pagan culture and awkwardly adapted itself to alien forms, but because what Jesus said and the way that he said it created a dynamic within Christianity that could not avoid using the arts as a further expression of what Jesus had come to say and to do. This explanation works from a paradox: though Jesus himself said nothing about the arts, the way he taught led *necessarily* to the use of the arts in Christianity.

The writer and sociologist Andrew Greeley argues more broadly in his seminal essay, "The Catholic Imagination and the Catholic University," that religion in general "takes its origins and its raw power from experiences, images, stories, community and ritual, and...most religious socialization (transmission) takes place through narrative...."[1] He goes on to point out in his book *The Catholic Imagination* that Catholicism began with storytelling. Catholics instinctively took those stories and translated them into every available mode of expression until, in the end, "few Western artistic traditions were not shaped first in the churches."[2]

3. *Inspiration.* A third explanation for the evolution of Catholic art emerges from the theology of continuing divine presence within the church that I have already described. This interpretation argues that Jesus continues to be actively present whenever his followers gather, to enlighten and move them. The Holy Spirit dwells within the church giving it direction and meaning. Catholic art is thus the simple, direct consequence of the *Creator Spiritus* alive within the church.

Considered in terms of this interpretation, theories of cross-cultural influence, for example, while interesting, are relatively unimportant. A divine creative spirit within the church, active and working, takes people and events where it wills to take them.

This theological idea has a long history. The Jewish authors of Genesis pictured the very first moments in the creation of all things in terms of God's creative Spirit: "The Spirit of God was moving over the face of the waters" (Gen 1:2 RSV). The intangible energy, goodness, intelligence, and purpose of God—the Spirit—hovers here over a chaos, shaping it into substance, order, action, and meaning. When Jesus at the end of his physical life on earth promised his followers that the Holy Spirit would come to inform and direct them, he undoubtedly assumed they would make the connection with this description of creation in Genesis and would understand that with the beginning of his new church God's Spirit would again be at work within the chaos of their own hearts. A new phase in the chronicle of creation was about to begin. In the ensuing centuries, Catholics have understood that *Creator Spiritus* to be continually present, shaping new forms out of the elements of daily life and working, among other things, through Catholic art. That, certainly, is what this book is about.

For nearly two thousand years Catholics have used the arts to present beliefs, to articulate ideas, to express feelings. Indeed, the arts soon came to play a crucial role within the church. It wasn't long before some people found themselves first attracted to Catholicism by the church's use of the arts. It is quite clear that through the centuries the continuing faith, the emotional connection, the sense of collective identity that many Catholics share is given form and energy in large part from works of the artistic imagination—which are, after all, projections or embodiments of theological beliefs that if stated solely in the abstract would touch very few people. To hear a theologian speak about the concept of redemption may satisfy the mind, but looking at a crucifix can stagger the heart.

At crucial moments of its history, such as the period of the Reformation, the Catholic Church has insisted—and as I noted earlier this has nothing to do with any specific statement by Jesus—has insisted that the arts are and must remain a significant dimension of Catholic life.

Contemporary Problems: The Catholic Imagination in the Modern World

That Catholic life, and the arts that emerge from it, have always been tested by the world that surrounds them, a world that doubts faith, mocks commitment, and ignores facts when they're not convenient facts. This is particularly true of our own moment—an era of widespread disbelief coupled with an ideology driven by the frantic desire for self-pleasure. Unhappily, many members of the Catholic

Church are ill prepared to confront this era's scorn for religion and its negation of faith and of goodness. Though millions of people may list themselves as Catholic, the presence of the church in many lives has waned. "Catholic" Europe is today overwhelmingly secular, and one wonders about the "Catholic" Americas tomorrow.

Ignorance contributes to the erosion of individual belief and commitment, and ignorance about Catholicism on the part of educated adults has increased rapidly in recent years—in America particularly because of the unfortunate remodeling of American Catholic higher education along secular lines. Within the span of a lifetime, an educational system once open to the study of topics related to faith, religious history, and religious art has been frequently co-opted by academic faculties dominated by a rationalist/materialist ideology that views religious belief not with sympathy and interest but with hostility.

This is a part of an ongoing drift in the way people think about themselves and their world. Consider this example: I would expect that in reading the first pages of this book you may have been surprised, perhaps even jarred a bit by the argument that a divine creative Spirit is active in the church directing its history. Even suggesting such an idea these days would seem to most college-educated people to be a suspect way of thinking.

Today much of the discussion of Catholic art not only in universities but in many other contexts—art exhibitions, concerts, public lectures, the popular press, television—seeks strenuously to ignore the obvious dimensions of religious belief and feeling that form its essentially Catholic dimension. Instead, attention is consciously and often rigorously directed toward other issues. Michelangelo, for example, is a world-famous sculptor, architect, painter, and an accomplished poet. How do we think about him? How do the experts talk and write about him? As an Italian. As a Florentine of the fifteenth and sixteenth centuries. As a political discontent. As interested in "the Renaissance." As a male. As a (presumably) repressed homosexual. As a businessman (Michelangelo, it turns out, made a lot of money during his career). As a practitioner of the various skills that he used in his work: his knowledge of anatomy, his use of the chisel, his indifference to landscape, and so on. As a theorist interested in philosophizing about art. These are all topics that recent scholarship has considered in thinking about Michelangelo. But, as a Catholic? And his Catholicism not considered as some unhappy bit of bad luck on Michelangelo's part—something that we wish hadn't happened to him—but instead as a central element, perhaps *the* central element, in the makeup of his genius. Take away his religious belief, and where would he have been? Carving table legs for the Medici, presumably. Yet many contemporary people do everything they can to ignore the aspect of his consciousness that inspired Michelangelo for a lifetime— that mattered more to him than anything else, and that touched him the most deeply. When at the end of his life Michelangelo carved the later version of the *Pietà* now in the Museum of the Duomo in Florence, he gave to Nicodemus, the man who lifts up the body of the dead Christ, his own world-weary, pitying face (Figure 2). He pictured his religious faith and his religious emotions in this piece, which he intended for his own tomb. It's one of those facts many modern people would like to forget.

Figure 2. Michelangelo, *Pietà*. Florence, ca. 1550

This book confronts some of these contemporary problems by presenting ways of talking and writing and thinking about Catholic art as *Catholic art*. It begins with definitions of two crucial terms: *imagination* (in the next section of the chapter) and *Catholic*. The definition of *Catholic* uses four descriptive "traits," and the balance of the book explores how people, using their human imaginations as Catholics, created things that we can reasonably call products of a "Catholic imagination." In the service of the emerging field of Catholic studies—a field that aspires to bring back to American higher education topics and ways of thinking now often ignored—the book provides an interpretive structure—concepts and terms, an initial theorizing—that will be useful to the reader as the reader thinks further about the relationship between Catholic history and belief and the arts. It does not offer a full history of Catholicism and the arts: that is an impossible project. But it does offer a series of crucial illustrative examples from the first eight centuries of Christianity that demonstrate the validity and usefulness of the theory when it is applied to specific phenomena.

For the reader who is a believing Catholic, this book serves as a way of expanding and deepening the reader's own background of faith and knowledge. For the reader who is not a Catholic, this book can help in developing an understanding of the specific and particular character of Catholic belief and of some of the cultures that Catholicism has influenced.

In the course of explaining my arguments, I use numerous quotations from the Bible, and I describe some of the liturgical and cultural practices of Western Catholicism. I have made an effort to explain matters in considerable detail, hoping that even for people who know very little about Catholic belief and history this book will make clear, plain, good sense. I ask readers who are already familiar with some of the information I provide to simply skip on to matters that are new to them. I hope that for others, the quantity of information proves useful and interesting.

Imagination

Imagination and Consciousness

We say, "Imagine, flying from New York to Chicago." It's easy to do. One pictures an airport, an airplane, the cabin of the airplane, one's own seat, the plane flying from New York to Chicago. Arriving. One can imagine such a trip even if one has never taken it because the basic operation of the human imagination is to take fragments of memory and reassemble them in new patterns. A person who has never been on an airplane can imagine a flight from New York to Chicago using memories of photographs, clips from movies, and verbal accounts. A person who has never seen or heard about an airplane, on being asked to "imagine flying," would doubtless picture someone moving like a bird through the sky, and that too would be a reassembling of memory fragments. It's impossible to make up something out of nothing. Even the strangest leaps of the imagination remain simply putting things from memory into odd combinations. So when we say, "That's simply a figment of your imagination," we really cannot assert that the thing has no relationship to reality; only that it's something that in this particular combination has never actually existed.

Humans imagine constantly. It's an essential strategy for adapting to life. We use imagination to construct an image of who we are: I imagine myself. I cannot see much of myself most of the time so I imagine where my hands and feet are, how I look, what others are thinking about me, my relative importance in the world at any given moment, and so on. Simultaneously I am imagining the world through which I move. What's on the other side of the door I'm just about to open? It's the door to my own apartment. Before opening it, I already imagine what I will see and I prepare myself for what's coming. We do this every minute of our waking lives.

Because humans imagine themselves and their world all the time, the imagination plays a central role in consciousness and in conduct. One sees the self and the world in the ways one imagines. I imagine I am a brilliant fellow and everyone likes me, and I go to work acting on that image. Or, I imagine I'm a failure and nobody respects me and everyone at the office seems to be frowning.

Imaginative categories shape the way in which humans encounter reality. A biologist and I look at a snake differently. She's identifying the species. I'm scared. It's the same snake.

A number of very different characteristics of any one person enter into how that person's imagination is functioning at any given point in time. The body, for instance: age, gender and sexuality, weight and height, relative good health. The mind, too: intelligence and education. The place where one lives, the kind of work one does, family and friends. These and many other characteristic aspects of being human enter into how an individual imagines self and world.

Religious belief is one such shaping characteristic. Imagine that you are an Italian woman living in a village outside of Rome in 1630. There's a church at the end of the street. You cannot read or write. You are married, you have a family, and you work hard every day. The church is the largest, most expensively ornamented, and most mysterious building you've ever seen. On Sunday the priest there tells you about God, angels, saints, heaven and hell. There are pictures on the walls and statues near the altar; these exactly correspond to what the priest is saying, and they provide you with some memorable visual images that illustrate his words. On particular holidays there are processions, beautiful and costly vestments, incense and music. That church is but one aspect of your life. You may indeed believe more deeply in what a menacing old woman from the edge of town tells you about curses and magic charms, but at the same time to some degree you listen to what you hear and think about what you see in that church at the end of the street, and it enters into how you imagine who you are, the meaning of your work and your pain and your life, and what is going to happen to you after you die. The woman I'm picturing here has an imagination that is female, heterosexual, Italian, seventeenth century, working class, and such, but is also to some significant degree Catholic. She participates, along with many of the other people of her village, in a Catholic imagination.

Catholicism helps to shape the way she imagines herself and her world every day of her life.

Imagination and Religion

Imagination is central to religious experience because belief requires so many deferments in the confirmation of one's expectations. When I stand in front of my apartment door planning to open it, I imagine what I will see, and a moment later I get a confirmation that what I imagined was correct or I get a surprise. By contrast, when the religious believer imagines that after death God will welcome him or her into paradise, that believer may have to wait many years to learn the actual outcome. Imagination plays therefore a crucial part in belief, hope, prayer, and the choice of action. Unavoidably, Catholics imagine God, and they imagine a kind of God who is quite different from the God imagined by other faith traditions. Catholics imagine in prayer what they wish to say to God and how God is responding. They imagine God's wishes for their lives, and they act or refuse to act on those imagined expectations and then they may think of themselves as good or bad in God's eyes and perhaps in their own self-estimation too.

Jesus' Teaching and the Uses of Imagination

Jesus of Nazareth was keenly aware of the crucial importance of imagination in human consciousness and particularly in religious belief. The accounts of his teaching illustrate how he constantly worked with the imagination of his listeners as he endeavored to teach them. Here is a useful example from the Gospel of Luke (11:5–8). Jesus is with his disciples in "a certain place" and they ask him to teach them to pray. He does so, voicing what later came to be called "The Lord's Prayer." Having done this, Jesus goes on to say something further about praying to God.

> Suppose one of you has a friend, and you go to him at midnight and say to him, "Friend, lend me three loaves of bread; for a friend of mine has arrived, and I have nothing to set before him." And he answers from within, "Do not bother me; the door has already been locked, and my children are with me in bed; I cannot get up and give you anything." I tell you, even though he will not get up and give him anything because he is his friend, at least because of his persistence he will get up and give him whatever he needs.

Jesus begins by directing his audience to "suppose"—that is, to imagine. Then through the art of storytelling he creates an entire fictional scene: late at night, a host in need of bread, the cranky "friend" who doesn't want to help, even the sleeping children. When he has set up the situation—when the imaginations of his listeners have pictured everything—he then asks them to do something further with their imaginations: to picture a conclusion to the story.

Jesus entertains two possibilities. Perhaps the friend with the door closed is not really a very good friend—there is a rather bitter, ironic humor running through this part of the story—and he refuses to help at first. What changes the situation? The second possibility: the person asking persists, continues to bang on the door; the kids, we imagine, wake up and begin to cry; and the householder who wasn't motivated by friendship finally hands over the bread because otherwise he won't get any more sleep.[3]

The point of the story now seems clear. If you want something, you've got to keep asking. While high-minded generosity may not motivate your "friend," the selfish need for a night's rest will. It seems like a bit of folk wisdom: just keep asking and you'll get what you want. A story that is a little cynical, a little humorous, and intensely practical and realistic about human nature.

But the shocking aspect of the whole thing is that Jesus tells this story in an effort to describe how people should pray to God. Yes, God is the somewhat unreliable "friend" behind the locked door who at first doesn't want to provide the needed bread and who is finally forced to yield only after the persistent noise-making of the man who needs it. This is an *analogy*, a comparison between two quite different things; here, the ordinary and the earthly compared with the divine. It's a way of thinking Jesus uses constantly.

Jesus' purpose in telling this story is to surprise his hearers into something far beyond a little cynical folk wisdom. His first point is that in the imaginations of many people, God often does seem like the selfish neighbor who won't get up and open the door. Jesus is playing with the natural human exasperation that emerges when one prays to God for something and it doesn't come right away. One may start to blame God. Why won't God do what I want? The story helps Jesus' audience to begin to think about whether that analogy is entirely fair. Is God exactly like the selfish friend? Or is God something more complex than that? Jesus, however, has a further point: the believer needs to persist in praying, comforted by the humorous suggestion that if you insist upon picturing God as recalcitrant and unhelpful, even your kind of God will finally get tired of being asked and will respond to the prayer.

Then, Jesus pushes the question a step further (Luke 11:11–13), using an even more extreme kind of imagining—not a scene people may have actually experienced but rather something out of a nightmare. "Is there anyone among you who, if your child asks for a fish, will give a snake instead of a fish? Or if the child asks for an egg, will give a scorpion? What father among you, if his son asked for a fish, would hand him a snake? Or if he asked for an egg, hand him a scorpion?" Here again we have a tiny dramatic scene. Father, son, a request for food. Something very natural. But Jesus asks us to picture the father responding to the request by handing his child something deadly. Here the imagined picture is not so much funny—the sleepy householder, the friend who keeps knocking—as it is grotesque and frightening: the father hands the child a snake. Again the strategy is analogy, and Jesus makes the parallel clear: "If you then, evil as you are, know how to give your children what is good, how much more will the heavenly Father give the Holy Spirit to those who ask him!" Persistence in prayer is a good thing, yes, but in the end the believer must let God decide what is healthy and what dangerous. At this point Jesus insists that people must reimagine God to the point where they will picture a God who knows more about what is good for them than they do. This God is a Father. He answers prayers but not always in the way we expect them to be answered. God will give what is really needed, and since the relationship is between God as a kind father and believers who are children, the believers must understand that what they get is what is good for them. That's Jesus' point, in abstract language. But what the listener remembers are things of the imagination—two concrete, vivid, dramatic images: not a snake, but bread. The point of the teaching is achieved through imagining and the aim of the teaching is to expand the imaginative grasp of the listener.

Imagination and Artistic Creation

In the scene we have just been considering Jesus is working as an artist skillful in the art of fiction. While he may not *say* anything about the fine arts in the New Testament, the Gospels constantly picture Jesus as a storyteller using his own imagination to invent scenes. He takes bits and pieces of his remembered world—bread, cranky children, closed doors—and makes up a fable. In listening to his words his disciples must reimagine the scene for themselves, using bits and pieces of their own remembered experience. Does their pictured door look like the one Jesus is recalling? Or, is it a lit-

tle different? They enter into the story as active imaginative partici-
pants. Nowhere is this more dramatically obvious than in Jesus'
repeated use of the conditional *if*. He prefaces his narratives with a
moment of uncertainty: "What do you think will happen next?" He
demands that his listeners work imaginatively with what he has
given them so far and carry it further.

Jesus had a highly imaginative consciousness, and throughout
his public life he used a variety of imaginative strategies, as any
artist would, in his efforts to explain to his listeners what he had
come to tell them. The second chapter of this book explores this
topic further.

The inevitable consequence after Jesus had left this earth was
for his followers to imitate his uses of imagination in the various
ways that came naturally to them out of their own imaginative lives.
The story about the householder, the closed door, and the need for
bread is but one way of imagining God's relationship to his people.
Later Catholic artists using words, spoken or written, persisted in
Jesus' imaginative search for viable images of God; so did painters,
sculptors, musicians, and so on. Their work constituted a natural
continuation—what I called earlier an "organic" continuation—of
what Jesus had been doing, and beginning with chapter 3 the rest of
the book considers how that worked. Jesus, who never said anything about the arts, was the first Catholic artist, and Catholic art
grew from how Jesus imagined and how he talked.

Imagination, then, is crucial. But, what do we mean by
Catholic?

CHAPTER TWO

Catholic Belief

Defining *Catholic*

Problems with Terms

The historical record seems unquestionable. A group of people claiming to be followers of Jesus of Nazareth began enrolling new followers in Jerusalem shortly after Jesus' death, and that group soon spread throughout the Mediterranean basin. Like most religious groups, they quarreled among themselves about what exactly it was they were believing and about who was in charge.[1] That has gone on for two thousand years now. The history of their quarrels is tragic, particularly because the Jesus they wish to follow had instructed his first disciples to love each other, and at times there seems to be so little love between Christians.

In this book I use the words *Catholic* and *Christian*. Many readers will hear a painful difference between them.

The word *catholic*, which means "universal,"[2] was first used, so far as we know, in the year 110 by Saint Ignatius of Antioch in a letter that he wrote to Christians in Smyrna urging them to "follow the lead of the bishop, as Jesus Christ followed that of the Father....Where the bishop is, there is the Catholic Church."[3] Ignatius was the third bishop of Antioch, a large and politically important city of the period and a place where Saints Peter, Paul, and Barnabas had all taught. We must presume that Ignatius's ways of thinking could be very close to those of the apostolic church.[4] Concerned about heresy and the mounting persecution of Christians—Ignatius was martyred in Rome shortly after writing this letter—he sought to strengthen loyalty and obedience by stressing the importance of church hierarchy.[5] But in using a word that means "universal," Ignatius clearly tries to assert that the church once led by Saint Peter is for everyone, everywhere. During the early fourth century, as soon as the official Roman persecutions of Christianity ceased, the word *catholic* became a part of some of the earliest formal statements of Christian belief, such as the Nicene Creed (drafted in 325), and it is in those formulations that the official, public proclamation of belief in and membership in "the Catholic and apostolic Church" seems to have first been defined.[6] So the term *catholic* refers to membership in a group that aspires to include all people—a universal church. But of course it has never achieved this aim. Rather, as Richard P. McBrien argues in his magisterial book *Catholicism*, to be Catholic is to be a specific kind of Christian, one who belongs to a specific eucharistic faith community within the universal church: the Body of Christ, which encompasses *all* forms of Christian faith.[7]

The term *Christian* refers to a form of religious belief. As a noun it means one who follows the teaching and the life example of Christ; or, as the *Oxford English Dictionary* has it, "One who believes or professes the religion of Christ; an adherent of Christianity," and "One who exhibits the spirit, and follows the precepts and example, of Christ; a believer in Christ who is characterized by genuine piety." According to the Acts of the Apostles, it was "in Antioch" where Paul and Barnabas worked for over a year instructing "a great number of people...that the disciples were first called 'Christians'" (Acts 11:26).

The differences in meaning between these words will be useful in this study. *Catholic* stresses church, membership in a specific ecclesial form of Christianity, and its goal of universality. *Christian* stresses belief and membership in a far broader and larger faith community that strives to live in terms of a vital personal and collective relationship with Christ.

As I have already noted, these two words present a problem. While some Christians were happy to be called Catholics as well, differences in the way people conceived of and defined what they believed soon led to painful ruptures within the Christian community. From early in its history, the Christian church has faced differences of thought and opinion on matters of faith and morals as well as on matters of ecclesiastical order and authority. What seemed heresy to some seemed genuine and necessary reform to others. For the first millennium, however, it's fair, for all practical purposes, to say that most of the people who considered themselves Christians thought of themselves as Catholics. This book studies that period, in the hope that many readers who are not now members of the Catholic Church as such can find on these pages a record of what Christians thought, felt, and believed in the earliest centuries of the faith.

There is a further problem, though, that has emerged from the divisions of the second millennium of Christianity. Many of today's readers will hear in the word *catholic,* Rome, or "Roman Catholic."

It is a fact that the leadership of the Christian community migrated early in its history from Jerusalem to Rome and that ever since then the bishops of Rome have continually exercised—or tried to exercise—their influence upon the world Christian community, sometimes for good, and sometimes for ill. But the Roman pope and the administrative staff that he directs are not, according both to tradition and to official church teaching, the Catholic Church. Rather, they serve that church. When I use the term *Catholic* I mean to suggest that there has been an historically continuous community of Christian believers that is the Catholic Church, a community located in many places but continuing to share in certain specific beliefs, to commit themselves to certain shared ethical values, and to follow certain shared liturgical practices. This community evolved a way of imagining the self, the world, and God. It is this community that I am describing as "Catholic," and it is *the shared imagination of this community* that this book considers. Usually the Roman popes and those who represent them participate in this imaginative community, and on occasion they make valuable contributions to its vision of what it is to be human. For those contributions everyone should be grateful.

Inclusion versus Precision

My goal in developing a theory of Catholic imagination is inclusiveness but coupled with precision. In framing such a theory I wish to be able to consider contributions by lifelong Roman Catholic Church members like Michelangelo, but to include as well at least a consideration of work by those formed in youth by Catholicism but who in some ways may have moved away from it during their adult lives, like Beethoven; and even those artists once Catholic who later chose to consciously and actively reject Catholicism, like film director Alfred Hitchcock, whose rejection was so intense that he refused to see a priest as he lay dying, but who nevertheless remained so deeply marked by his Catholic youth that as he made his films he could never successfully shuck off some of the ways in which the Catholic imagination envisions the world. In several of the examples from part 2 of this book, thoughtful people might indeed question the degree to which a specific work is thoroughly imbued with a Catholic imaginative take on reality, and to wonder whether at times, for example, the Roman catacomb frescoes are "too Jewish" or the illustrations to the *Utrecht Psalter* "too pagan." At the appropriate moment we will discuss those issues. Clearly, however, the most inclusive sense of Catholicism, what Georgetown theologian Anthony Tambasco insists upon as its "both/and" openness, rather than narrow and categorical orthodoxy, is the most useful attitude to adopt simply because it permits the consideration of the largest number of instances.

The examples studied in this book, as noted earlier, all come from a period of time when Christianity was to some degree unified. Thus this study avoids a whole complex of problems that begin with the division of Eastern from Western Christianity in "the Great Schism" of 1054 and that got much worse with the era of the Reformation. But, how to deal with those problems? It would be nice to say that this book is about a "Christian imagination," and indeed anyone interested in Christianity and the arts is interested in the artistic work of all Christians and in trying to understand its relationship to belief, tradition, and forms of imagination. It would be foolish never to consider the work, for example, of Johann Sebastian Bach, saturated as it is with a profound Christian faith. At the same time it would be imprecise to ignore the fact that Bach's faith emerged from the Christian communities of Lutheran Germany, and that in substantial ways Lutherans of the era envisioned the role of the arts in the exercise of their Christian beliefs in quite a different way from the concept of the relationship between religion and the arts that held sway south of the Alps.

Definition means setting boundaries and limits. One cannot claim a universality for a certain kind of Christianity that it simply does not enjoy. For example, a thoughtful, deeply spiritual person who insists that it is categorically wrong to make pictures of God, as did John Calvin, is simply not a part of that kind of Christianity that we define as typical of Catholic belief and tradition—as indeed John Calvin would be the first to insist. Catholics look at, rely upon, and make pictures of God all the time. It's one of the ways they are Catholic. To ignore the importance of the physical image in their imaginative lives is to ignore one of the roots of their religious belief. Similarly, many people who are in love with Jesus refuse to join any religious community and find their way to the divine exclusively through individual prayer and private meditation. That too is a way foreign to Catholicism. Catholics come together in community to celebrate sacraments, and they feel a communal obligation to help others, which they believe was given them by Jesus himself. That is another way they are Catholic.

It is important for the success of this study to define what Catholic is and what it is not. Otherwise a discussion of "Catholic imagination" will unravel into aimless generalizations. If the Catholic Church is indeed a community that has evolved a way of imagining the self, the world, and God, then what's needed is a short list of traits that help to define and distinguish the beliefs of that church and the way of imagining that it evolved—traits that are interdependent, historically based, but independent of local specifics, shared by citizens of São Paulo, Boston, Dublin, Lisbon, Vienna, Seoul, and Manila. To find them, let us adopt a quite specific strategy and turn to the source text for both Christian and Catholic identity—the New Testament—and to subsequent Catholic understanding of what the New Testament means. Since the New Testament has been from the start the central and defining text for Catholic belief, nothing will better serve as a basis for defining a Catholic way of imagining.

Reading the New Testament

At the start, let us be clear on what the New Testament can mean and what it cannot mean. Believing Christians regard the Bible as a source of true statements on which they can rely. For many centuries believing Catholics read the New Testament as a unified historical record: the four Gospels telling the life story of

Jesus, the Acts of the Apostles and the Epistles filling in the subsequent early history of the church, and Revelation describing in advance the end of the world and the paradise of eternity.

Figure 3. The passion and resurrection
As the central event in Christian belief, the passion, death, and resurrection of Jesus caught the imaginations of artists from a very early stage, as this series of carvings on an early Christian sarcophagus attests.

A more recent understanding, and one that makes good sense, is that the New Testament Gospels offer four short narratives recounting what early Christians had remembered some forty to seventy years after the death of Jesus and what they had come to believe crucial about his life, each of these narratives reflecting a somewhat different way of imaginatively reconstructing that life. The New Testament is the work of Jesus' fledgling church. It has been passed down within that church ever since. It has been interpreted and used by that church in ways that church members consider to be guided by the Holy Spirit. The New Testament is not the direct writing of Jesus, and it is not in our modern sense a work of biography or of history. It is a collection of texts that function as statements of belief. The "search for the historical Jesus" that has fascinated so many scholars and writers over the past century will never succeed. The historical Jesus was lost at his death. What the New Testament records is the Jesus of the church. That Jesus is the subject of this book. For two millennia Catholics read the New Testament as a valid record of Jesus' life and teaching transmitted, mediated, and understood by his church. It is the source of their shared imagination. For the purposes of this study, the scientific discoveries of modern biblical scholarship, while of enormous importance in themselves, are of little use. What matters in defining and exploring the Catholic imagination is how in quite a simple, almost naïve way, Catholics received, read, and used the New Testament over the course of the centuries—and how it led to the formation of Catholic imagination.

Characteristic Traits of Catholic Belief

Incarnation: How Catholics Imagine God's Nature and God's Relationship to the Material World

From the start, Catholics have believed in a single God. Like the Jewish people, from whom they stem, they are monotheists. However, departing from Jewish faith and tradition, they believe that this God took flesh in the form of one man: Jesus. This is how John's Gospel puts it: "In the beginning was the Word, and the Word was with God, and the Word was God" (John 1:1).

IMPLICATIONS FOR THE CATHOLIC IMAGINATION

These beliefs have a profound effect upon the characteristic qualities of the Catholic imagination. Consider four of them:

1. *There is a God.* For Catholics, there is a constant divine presence in their world and in their lives. They are never alone. They are never hidden from view. As the psalmist sings, "O LORD, you have searched me and known me. You know when I sit down and when I rise up....Where can I go from your spirit? Or where can I flee from your presence? If I ascend to heaven, you are there; if I make my bed in Sheol, you are there" (Ps 139:1–2,7–8).

Catholics can never dream of being the most important or the most powerful thing in the universe. They are always in relationship with something greater.

2. *This God cares about creation.* Catholics know that they are never unloved. They are always the focus of a concerned plan for their well-being. Not only they, but all things, are the subject of this concern and this love. For this reason they must deal with a world that is made and loved by God and that therefore merits their love and concern.

3. *This God acted within time at a specific historical moment.* In doing this he gave a particular kind of meaning to time and to history. This God became a man. While other religions had already imagined the divine crossing the metaphysical barrier between transcendent and created, this new form of understanding saw God as in every way human. God embraced his friends, pared his nails, got angry, cried, urinated, was battered, bled, and was killed. God did those things. So implausible is this belief that in the early centuries of Christianity one explanation after another tried to deny its force. There were two Jesuses, some theorized, one a body, the other a God. Or, what people saw was only a ghostly shadow but not an actual body. And so on. Again and again the church insisted upon the most audacious and implausible explanation: This man was God incarnate.

4. This implies, among many other things, that *the divine has intersected with the created and that it can do so again.* The divine may be found within the material and the temporal.

Because this is so, the gospel accounts are factual and reliable accounts of God himself. They are true statements about God. We can now say some things about what was once unutterably remote and inexplicable. As John's Gospel puts it, "No one has ever seen God. It is God the only Son, who is close to the Father's heart, who has made him known" (John 1:18). God has come out of the thunder cloud and the terrifying gloom of the temple. He has joined us for dinner. He lets us know how he feels and what he wants.

The belief in incarnation distinguishes Catholicism from, on the one hand, all forms of atheism, which deny the existence of any divinity, and on the other hand from some of the great and profound religious traditions of the world, such as Judaism and Islam, which insist upon a more remote, utterly transcendent God. As Paul puts it, Christian monotheism is a message that is "a stumbling-block to Jews and foolishness to Gentiles…" (1 Cor 1:22).

THE CONTINUING INCARNATION

The concept of incarnation leads to radical metaphysical innovations. The transcendent can intersect with the material. It can inhabit, or be "in" the material. Historically, Catholics believe, this was the case in the life of Christ. God took on a human body.

But not just then. As we have already seen, the promises of Jesus led his followers to conclude that after his death and resurrection the divine continued to intersect with time and space thanks to the continuing presence of Jesus and the Holy Spirit within the church. In a way that is different but nevertheless valid, God continues to be present "in" people. Not metaphorically but literally.

First, for individuals. As Paul argues, "I have been crucified with Christ; and it is no longer I who live, but it is Christ who lives in me. And the life I now live in the flesh I live by faith in the Son of God, who loved me and gave himself for me" (Gal 2:19–20). The assertion is that Christ, God's only Son, lives through the believer. God is in people. The concept of what it means to be human is here being reimagined.

Second, collectively. Again, Paul addressing the early church: "Now you are the body of Christ and individually members of it" (1 Cor 12:27). And, "For just as the body is one and has many members, and all the members of the body, though many, are one body, so it is with Christ. For in the one Spirit we were all baptized into one body—Jews or Greeks, slaves or free—and we were all made to drink of one Spirit" (1 Cor 12:12–13). Just as God is in the individual believer, so God is in all Christian believers as a collective whole, a living organism, that *is* the continuously present body of Christ on the earth. The concept of the social organization known as church is here being reimagined.

The argument goes even further. Jewish belief and spirituality for a long time had understood that traces of God could be discerned in his creation. "The heavens are telling the glory of God," sings the Psalmist, "and the firmament proclaims his handiwork" (Ps 19:1). After all, Genesis insists that in creating the world God found what he made to be "good" (Gen 1:10). Traces, at least, of God can thus be found everywhere in God's creation.

Further still, the great traditions of the Jewish chronicles had discerned in the experiences of that people God's direct wish and intervention. God chose the people of Israel, told them what he wanted of them, helped them toward that goal, and chastised them when they failed him. Thus for Jewish tradition God expressed himself not only in nature but in history. Hence, one could know about God from studying history.

Catholic belief carried forward these ways of discerning a divine and transcendent God within that God's creation. Paul argues that everyone ought to believe in God because "ever since the creation of the world his eternal power and divine nature, invisible though they are, have been understood and seen through the things he has made…" (Rom 1:20). In 1259, Saint Bonaventure (1217–1274) elaborated on this in his book *The Soul's Journey into God.* All things, for Bonaventure, can be seen as

> shadows, echoes, pictures of that first, most powerful, most wise, most perfect Principle….They are vestiges, representations, spectacles proposed to us and signs divinely given so that we can see God….The creatures of the sense world signify *the invisible attributes of God,* partly because God is the origin, exemplar and end of every creature….Every creature is by its nature a kind of effigy and likeness of the eternal Wisdom…. (Bonaventure 77)[8]

Here the meaning and significance of every existing thing is being reimagined.

To sum up: Jesus, for Catholics, is God in human flesh. He remains present after his death and resurrection in different ways in each of those people who believe in him, in the church, and in every created thing. Creation is not God. But it participates in different ways with the never-ending presence of its maker and it constantly reflects aspects of its maker.

From the point of view of Catholic imagination, it's likely that God is shining through everyone and everything in one way or another.

A very pretty picture, but not the whole picture.

Redemption: How Catholics Imagine Moral Categories; The Meaning of Time

A FALLEN WORLD

Why was incarnation necessary?

The picture of God's creation sketched out in the last few paragraphs suggests a world filled, as the poet Gerard Manley Hopkins exclaims, "with the grandeur of God."

Saint Paul, writing of the people with whom he worked, finds a very different world:

> They were filled with every kind of wickedness, evil, covetousness, malice. Full of envy, murder, strife, deceit, craftiness, they are gossips, slanderers, God-haters, insolent, haughty, boastful, inventors of evil, rebellious towards parents, foolish, faithless, heartless, ruthless. They know God's decree, that those who practice such things deserve to die—yet they not only do them but even applaud others who practice them. (Rom 1:29–32)

This is not the world as God created it—a good world. Something terrible has happened to it, and now it is full of individual and collective wrongdoing and full of ugliness, deformity, sickness, pain, and death. Indeed, much of the time the world we live in can seem to be the creation not of a good God but rather of some malign power bent on torturing people—as in the grim, pagan vision of Gloucester in Shakespeare's *King Lear*: "As flies to wanton boys are we to th' gods—/They kill us for their sport" (*King Lear* IV, i, 37–38).

This is the second important characteristic of the Catholic imagination: seeing ours as a damaged and fallen world full of evil and moving toward death—and therefore a world profoundly in need of God's help.

Evil can seem to be an active presence, something alive and sentient, consciously warring against goodness. "But woe to the earth and the sea," cries the Book of Revelation, "for the devil has come down to you with great wrath, because he knows that his time is short!" (Rev 12:12).

From a Catholic perspective, the power of this active evil is so great that on their own people cannot win the struggle against it. In an analysis of the human condition of great penetration and insight, Paul voices this sense of powerlessness. "I do not understand my own actions. For I do not do what I want, but I do the very thing I hate." Indeed, it seems "that when I want to do what is good, evil lies close at hand" (Rom 7:15,21). Unaided, it would appear, the only possibility for human beings is despair.

REDEMPTION

This is why the incarnation was necessary. Only God himself could save a world so damaged, so perversely driven toward what is wrong. "While we still were sinners Christ died for us," Paul argues, and "now that we have been justified by his blood, will we be saved through him from the wrath of God" (Rom 5:8–9). "God put [Jesus] forward as a sacrifice of atonement by his blood, effective through faith…to prove at the present time that he himself is righteous and that he justifies the one who has faith in Jesus" (Rom 3:25–26).

The concept of redemption carries the idea of incarnation to a new, even more audacious limit. Not only did God become a human being, but he did so with a specific purpose in mind: to suffer and die. This is God we are talking about. Built into this concept is a seemingly insoluble paradox: Jesus had to become weak and vulnerable to the point of death in order to conquer the otherwise overwhelming power of evil in the world. In being a victim he became a conqueror. "Death," exults Paul, "has been swallowed up in victory. 'O death, where is your victory? O death, where is your sting?' The sting of death is sin, and the power of sin is the law. But thanks be to God, who gives us the victory through our Lord Jesus Christ" (1 Cor 15:54–57).

Thanks to the saving act of redemption, the fundamental nature of all human life and of the world in which human beings live has been changed. It still looks the same much of the time. But in reality people no longer need fear the death that they must suffer because now it leads to a joyful reward. The challenges of a fallen world are now just that: not reasons for despair but rather bracing invitations to struggle. Now life and the world fill with hope.

IMPLICATIONS FOR THE CATHOLIC IMAGINATION

These ideas have had a profound effect upon the characteristic qualities of the Catholic imagination. Consider seven of them:

1. *The world as Catholics see it, even after Jesus' redeeming sacrifice, is still damaged:* full of evil, pain, death. The vision of the eighteenth-century idealist, that this is "the best of all possible worlds," is not a Catholic way of seeing things. Catholic art throughout the centuries has been keenly alert to the reality of evil, to its menacing power, and to the desperate human need evil creates. In Catholic art there is often a somber, even seemingly cruel insistence upon pain and wrongdoing. This is a consequence of the candor and accuracy of Catholic reporting on what life is really like.

2. *God cares about evil and death.* The God of Catholicism does not turn away, indifferent to human suffering. Jesus insists that those who wish to follow him must share in his sympathy for others. When we speak about divine love, we define it in terms of the terrible wrongs it works against.

3. *God chose to suffer and die to rescue humanity from its fallen condition.* In so doing he gave a new and transcendent meaning to suffering and death. As a consequence, all Catholics are called to act in analogous ways: to help others in need by whatever means they have at their disposal, even if that means their own indignity, suffering, and death. For Catholics, passivity is not an option.

4. *The world was changed by God's action.* It no longer justifies despair.

5. *Reality is now a place of struggle between the forces of evil and good.* Jesus warns his disciples, "See, I am send-

ing you out like sheep into the midst of wolves; so be wise as serpents and innocent as doves. Beware of them, for they will hand you over to councils and flog you in their synagogues...and you will be hated by all because of my name" (Matt 10:16–17,22). Catholic conscious-ness includes a sense of difference and conflict, of the endangerment that comes with commitment. There is an enemy out there, a strong one, and working actively against what is good. At the same time, there is the con-fidence that comes from knowing without question that no matter how terrible the interval, in the end the victory will be God's.

Figure 4. Hieronymus Bosch, *Christ Carrying the Cross*, ca. 1515
Many of the works of the Dutch painter Hieronymus Bosch (ca. 1450–1516) depict sin and moral failing. This painting of *Christ Carrying the Cross*, show-ing Christ's face surrounded by a gallery of grotesques, is an example of Bosch's use of half-human animals and demons to portray human evil, and of the Catholic artistic tradition's response to the narratives of Christ's passion.

6. *For the ultimate outcome is sure: divine redemption.* As one of God's angels reports God's will: "Do not fear what you are about to suffer. Beware, the devil is about to throw some of you into prison so that you may be tested, and for ten days you will have affliction. Be faithful until death, and I will give you the crown of life" (Rev 2:10).

7. And the implication emerging here is that history is not a random chaos of chance events, a series of grotesque jokes played on humanity by cruel gods or impersonal forces. Rather, *history is filled with meaning, a meaning given it by God when he chose to redeem his people.* Now everything can be understood to have a purpose, a purpose given to it by God's plan.

Belief in redemption distinguishes a Catholic vision from a number of modern philosophical stances. It opposes the argument that evil does not exist as an active presence, or the argument that there is no real meaning to the categories of good and evil, all choices being equally meaningless or at least morally neutral. It also opposes the idealism of eighteenth-century rationalism and its nineteenth-century descendants such as Marxism, which hoped that somehow through human effort alone evil could be eliminated from the world. At the same time Catholic vision refuses to accept the opposite position, that there is no hope for the future and that cynicism, selfishness, and ultimately nihilistic despair are the only options available to us.

Redemption anchors the Catholic imagination in hope and trust, even as it acknowledges how bad everything can seem to be.

Sacramentality: How Catholics Imagine a Continuing Presence of the Divine in Daily Life

What happened after Jesus left?

The great themes of the gospel narratives—incarnation and redemption—had all been achieved. Jesus ascended into the heavens and yet he still remained within his followers and within their church as an active, guiding presence. The church had become his living body on earth. But, what would it do? And, in particular, what would it do once people had accepted the good news and joined in membership?

SACRAMENTS

Daily Catholic life is dominated by sacramental experience.[9] For Catholics the sacraments bracket life: baptism initiating church membership, the sacrament of the sick preparing people for death. In between, crucial stages in life such as reaching maturity (confirmation) and marriage or entrance into the priesthood are similarly marked by a sacramental moment. Weekly, even daily, Catholics are called to join in the Eucharist and to purge their sins by confession. While incarnation and redemption define the parameters of Catholic reality, the sacraments create the texture of ordinary experience and give to the days, the seasons, the phases of each life order and meaning.

Catholics believe that Jesus began these practices, and the New Testament directly pictures him creating the practice of Eucharist, authorizing the forgiving of sins, and sending his apostles out to baptize others.

For Catholics the sacraments are formulated rituals that have real, literal consequences. They emerge from a contract or understanding between God and humanity: when people do certain things—say specific words, act out specific gestures—God will do his part and something real will happen. In the Eucharist, for example, when the celebrant acting as a representative of the believers gathered together at that moment says a specific verbal formula, the bread he holds will be transformed, literally, into the body of Christ. The Catholic Church has insisted upon this even though during the Reformation it meant the angry separation of whole nations of devoutly religious Christians from membership in its ranks.

For Catholicism, the sacraments continue the miracle of the Incarnation on a daily basis. God continues to enter the world at specific moments in concrete ways.

CHARACTERISTICS OF CATHOLIC SACRAMENTS

Catholic sacramental rituals have significant characteristics that have had a powerful influence in the formation of the Catholic imagination.

First, there is nothing secretive or mysterious about them. During their enactment, plain words are openly and plainly said by ordinary people. They are not carried out in remote, mysterious places, and they do not employ complex, inexplicable movements or verbal formulae. For the sacrament of the Eucharist, the only thing the celebrant needs to say is, "This is my body." That's all.

Second, the Catholic sacraments make use of plain, cheap, ordinary things—indeed, for people from the Mediterranean region, the most common things around: water, bread, wine, oil, salt. That's about it. The sacraments emphatically do not require things that are expensive or rare, though during centuries of development the piety of some led to putting plain bread and plain wine into vessels of gold encrusted with rare gem stones. Such practices had nothing to do with the nature of the sacrament itself.

Third, the sacraments can be celebrated anywhere, anytime. While traditions within Catholicism have found certain places on this earth to be special—Rome, Jerusalem, pilgrimage sites—this practice, like the golden chalice, is a later and quite dispensable development. Essentially, for Catholics, there is no particularly and specifically sacred place on earth. Any place can be sacred. The sacraments are universal in the sense that it is suitable to perform them wherever believing Catholics gather. All times can be sacred.

As with the incarnation, the Catholic vision of the sacraments is resolutely concrete, plain, matter of fact, and ordinary. Just as God became a Jewish man, so God continues to help people through water, bread, and a few simple words that everyone can understand. Catholics believe God is really there, really doing things through these simple means. Confess your sins: they are gone. Forgiven. Take the communion bread in your mouth: God is literally in you. Pour the water of baptism: that person is saved from death. Simple as that. No strings. No payment. It's all free.

IMPLICATIONS FOR THE CATHOLIC IMAGINATION
Consider seven:

1. *The divine is constantly entering the material world.* God is dropping in all the time. He is easily accessible. Indeed, he is urging us to come to the party. The divine presence emerges through ordinary people using ordinary things.

2. *The divine enters when human beings act.* Sacraments take place because people do them. While God will come—he will keep his side of the agreement—people must initiate things. They've got to want to come to the party.

3. While sacraments can take place anywhere, any time, it is nevertheless the case that *the moment of the sacrament is different from other moments.* In that place, at that time, something utterly different from the ordinary is taking place. The sacred enters this world in a specific and unique way.

4. *The sacraments are all communal events.* Not one of them can take place through the solitary action of a single person. They each embody in a different form the relationship of the individual with the community life of the Christian Church. Baptism: enrollment as a new member. Eucharist: community with Christ and all believers. Confirmation: enrollment as an adult member of the community. Confession: reconciliation after estrangement from the community. Marriage: joining with another to build community through family life. Ordination to the priesthood: vowing to serve the community. Sacrament of the sick: preparation for entrance into the community of heaven.

5. And yet *the sacraments are quite intimate.* The touch of the baptismal water, the taste of the Eucharist, the utterance of promises by a couple or a new priest, the confession of sins, the soothing oil of confirmation and the last rites—Catholic sacramental experience is profoundly physical and profoundly personal. Sometimes the Mass may be held for thousands of people in large churches or even sports arenas but finally, centrally, someone hands the eucharistic bread to each person singly, and each person takes that bread within themselves. It's hard to imagine anything more interpersonal or more intimate.

6. *The Catholic sacraments do not require skill, training, or expertise of any sort.* There is no need to study for years, to discipline the body, to outperform others, to become a member of a spiritual elite. Quite the opposite. The most

simple, ordinary people, very imperfect and sinful people, people who might seem to others to lack much in the way of education and high culture, are all eligible—indeed are warmly welcomed to participate.

7. *The Catholic sacraments are clean, portable, simple.* Try to imagine a pagan temple during the era in which Jesus lived: an enormous, costly building in the center of a metropolis built for the ritual slaughter of animals like goats and bulls, which meant herds of eligible beasts, manure, weapons for slaughtering, a priesthood trained and skillful in killing, blood, the stench of bowels and intestines torn open, the carving up of bloody meat and its distribution, the burning of the offered portions in fires that must have had a foul stink and given off obnoxious, greasy smoke. That's what was going on in Rome and Athens at the most sacred sites. The Catholic sacraments replaced that with a morsel of bread, a sip of wine, the friendly touch of a hand upon a forehead.

Figure 5. Eucharistic image from the catacomb of S. Callisto
The third-century fresco from the catacomb of Saint Callistus in Rome depicting a basket with bread, fish, and a glass of wine symbolizes the eucharistic banquet, which was prefigured by the miracle of the loaves and fishes.

The sacramental life distinguishes Catholic experience from religious traditions in which solitary prayer and meditation serve as the sole suitable link between people and God. In its resolute insistence upon the material factuality of what is happening it distinguishes Catholicism from religions that see what people do in religious ritual as solely symbolic in character. In its use of the most ordinary things, words, people, and places, the Catholic sacramental life differs from those traditions of the sacred that prize the secret, the mysterious, the remote, and the specially privileged. It makes the sacred democratic and universal.

There is, of course, still the "both/and" of Catholic history. In the very first centuries, devotion to the martyrs led to the prizing of certain burial sites as somehow peculiarly sacred locations. Pilgrims from a great distance would come to touch the clothing, even the mummified remains of the saint, hoping for special spiritual benefits. Particularly ardent Christians went out into the Egyptian desert to pray alone, and the tradition of the hermit began. Later, bands of men and women gathered apart from ordinary people in monasteries and

Figure 6. Dorothy reliquary monstrance
The veneration of relics has always been an important part of devotion to the saints. This reliquary monstrance, from fifteenth-century Switzerland, was owned by a prominent family from Basel and intended to hold a relic of the fourth-century martyr Saint Dorothy.

nunneries to follow specific prayer rituals. Enormous churches rose, filled with objects of incalculable value. There were times when the ritual of the Mass took place behind screens so that ordinary believers scarcely saw what was happening; and there were periods when the faithful were fortunate to receive holy Eucharist once a year. The opposite of almost every characteristic of Catholic sacramentality described previously has existed within the church, and perhaps some readers of this book have experienced some of these opposites. Catholicism is open, inclusive, and sometimes welcomes the "both/and." Nevertheless, I think that the account that I have given accurately reflects the biblical origins of sacramental life and captures certain immutable characteristics of Catholic sacramental experience that have had a powerful creative effect upon the Catholic imagination.

Community: How Catholics Imagine the Self in Relationship to Others

JESUS AND COMMUNITY LIFE

When Jesus' human body left this earth, what did he leave behind?

The short answer is, Nothing. Pious belief in the centuries following Jesus' death discovered the cross upon which he died, the veil Veronica used to wipe his face as he struggled toward Calvary, the winding sheet in which he was buried. But the New Testament makes it clear that Jesus himself did not intentionally leave relics. Indeed the angel at the tomb on the morning of the resurrection is a trifle curt with the devout believers seeking the remains of Jesus' body: "Why do you look for the living among the dead? He is not here, but has risen. Remember how he told you, while he was still in Galilee, that the Son of Man must be handed over to sinners, and be crucified, and on the third day rise again" (Luke 24:5–7).

No relics of himself, no things filled with the magic of his former presence, and no sacred places: volcanic fissures in the earth, oak groves, mountain tops, magic rocks that fell out of the sky—the usual holy places to which believers flock.

Nor did Jesus himself write down anything that might serve as a formulation of his ideas as have many great leaders and visionaries of the past. Indeed, other than one questionable passage in John (8:7), the Gospels never show Jesus writing at all.[10]

What he did, as the four New Testament accounts make clear, was start a church. He thought in terms of community. Gathering people together is just about the first thing Jesus did when he began his public life—collecting disciples, teaching and instructing them, and preparing them for the time after his death.

The narrative rhythm of the New Testament is quite interesting on this point. It portrays Jesus leaving his followers from time to time to be alone in order to pray, as if the burden of leadership was sometimes more than he could bear, and yet he always returns to his followers. The New Testament presents a Jesus who lived in community with others.

This Jesus moves through a landscape full of people who need him. To each who asks he gives a healing response. Jesus' earthly life as the Gospels picture it is a life of care for others: "Then Jesus went about all the cities and villages, teaching in their synagogues, and proclaiming the good news of the kingdom, and curing every disease and every sickness" (Matt 9:35).

It is characteristic of Catholic consciousness, rooted in this story, to imagine the self in relationship, as Jesus did, relationship to the God to whom he prayed and relationship to that community of others that Jesus encountered from day to day throughout his life, and that we still encounter today.

BEING GOOD

Jesus stated the ethical implications of this way of constructing consciousness and identity with simplicity and clarity: "'You shall love the Lord your God with all your heart, and with all your soul, and with all your mind.' This is the greatest and first commandment. And a second is like it: 'You shall love your neighbor as yourself.' On these two commandments hang all the law and the prophets" (Matt 22:37–40).

Note that he defines being good in terms of one's relationship with others, in terms of loving. Jesus is not interested in self-discipline, esoteric meditation rituals, secret cabals, even martyrdom as ends in themselves. His command is much simpler: Loving is everything.

Jesus defines what this kind of loving means in very practical terms in a scene from Matthew in which he describes the end of the world. There he will be on his throne with "all the nations…gathered before him." Then, he will divide everyone into two groups, the saved and the damned. Why will some be saved? "I was hungry and you gave me food, I was thirsty and you gave me something to drink, I was a stranger and you welcomed me, I was naked and you gave me clothing, I was sick and you took care of me, I was in prison and you visited me." When the people who did these things express incredulity because they never thought they were doing a kindness to Jesus himself he replies, "Truly I tell you, just as you did it to one of the least of these who are members of my family, you did it to me" (Matt 25:32, 35–36, 40). Here we see an aspect of incarnation discussed earlier in this chapter. Jesus, the Son of God, is in the least important of people, and particularly people in need. To love neighbor is nothing abstract or elevated: it is direct, pragmatic, and simple. A glass of water, a sandwich, when needed. Such actions precisely match the way Jesus is himself described as living in Palestine. The scene in Matthew makes it quite clear that Christians—indeed all people—have no choice in this particular matter. Either one lives in community with others, caring for those in need, or one "will go away into eternal punishment" (Matt 25:46).

The Catholic stress upon community life differentiates it from religious traditions that urge people to live apart from the world seeking solitary spiritual perfection. Catholics can live this way only if they understand that through it, somehow, they will be helping others. For example, when Saint Teresa of Avila (1515–1582) and her fellow sisters lived apart in a small Carmelite nunnery in Spain, it was to pray all day long for other people leading more "ordinary" lives. Teresa and her friends were connected, immediately, with others.

The stress upon care for those in need has always and will always create a tension between Catholicism and those more extreme formulations of capitalism that stress the success of the individual at the expense of the other. The Catholic vision of membership in community provides a critique for any ideology that seeks to argue that the self and its desires are all and that the other person is of no consequence. By contrast, it argues that one can only be oneself, one can only be fulfilled, one's life can only have meaning, in terms of others and the happiness and well-being of others. At the same time, this understanding of what it means to be good is profoundly different from the collectivist thinking that dominated twentieth-century fascism and communism and that argued that virtue means disregarding the rights and the needs of individuals for the sake of some idealized concept of "the people." Jesus' vision of an individual loving and caring for another individual works against notions that individuals can and should be sacrificed for the sake of some general good that will come to the collective and not to the particular. In this sense it is anarchic, ignoring social and political structures and constructing instead narratives, such as the man who needs a loaf of bread, in which one person simply encounters and helps another.

IMPLICATIONS FOR CATHOLIC IMAGINATION
Consider three:

1. *Self and self-consciousness exist only in relationship.* Radical—that is to say, absolute—individualism is impossible, because we all live in relationship to God and to other people, and seeking to achieve it would be profoundly immoral.

2. *Goodness is a consequence of love and care for others.* Goodness is not power, money, physical glamour, fame, and so on. Picturing heroism means imagining self-sacrificial generosity.

3. *The church is a living, active presence in people's lives.* Church is defined as the caring community of believers through whom Jesus continues to work. People live for others and find God through others. That is where holiness resides.

Summary

Put in short, simple terms:

1. The Catholic imagination sees a world made by God and reflecting God in the way that it is; this closeness of God to creation intensified immeasurably when God became a man: Jesus, the incarnation.

2. However, it also sees the world as damaged by evil and death. Jesus came and transformed the world through his crucifixion and his consequent resurrection: redemption.

3. The Catholic imagination sees daily life shaped by the sacred through the continuing divine presence in the sacraments.

4. It defines personal identity and goodness in terms of relationship to community.

The reader will have noticed that this short list of traits, typical of how Catholics imagine the world, says nothing about specific aesthetic embodiments. While it describes a kind of Catholic consciousness, the list is extraordinarily open to various forms of aesthetic invention and expression. In the two thousand years since the coming of Christ, some possibilities for development have dominated. As we shall see, the belief in incarnation, for example, led to an almost constant use of visual images in Catholic art. But the traits themselves continue to invite almost limitless variety in creative effort, an invitation being accepted in the early twenty-first century by a new generation of artists that includes the novelist Ron Hansen, the composer James Macmillain, and the filmmaker Lars Von Trier.

All of this began with the mind of Jesus himself, and it is to that seminal topic we now turn.

CHAPTER THREE

The World of Jesus' Imagination

The Gospels present the reader with a complex portrait of Jesus as teacher, spiritual leader, miracle worker, and prophet. But here we consider a different aspect of Jesus: Jesus as an artist in language. We have already seen that when Jesus tells the story of a householder begging for a loaf of bread, he is using the art of storytelling to teach. Stories like this one demand the listener's imaginative involvement. That imaginative involvement in what Jesus said, how he said it, and the narratives of how he lived—the Gospels—became the generative source for the Catholic imagination, an imaginative "take" on reality that developed organically from Jesus as starting point. In the present chapter we consider what we can learn about Jesus' use of language and of the imagination, and the different ways in which his artistry helped create a Catholic imagination. Later, in chapter 5, we turn to a consideration of the Gospels as biographies and, looking at them from that different angle, we will see how they too contributed to the creation of a Catholic imagination.

Jesus' Voice and Jewish Literary Tradition

New Testament Sources

The only source for information about the way Jesus spoke is the Christian community that emerged after his death and resurrection. For the first forty years of its existence, it seems, the members of this community simply talked about Jesus. They told and retold stories about him: what he said and what he did. Then, as the first apostles began to die, Christians started writing down these stories in the form of narratives; four of them became the Gospels of the New Testament.

In the following pages I refer frequently to "the imagination of Jesus" and "the sayings of Jesus," and so on, but the reader must always be aware that this imagination, these sayings, are what Jesus' followers chose to recall and, eventually, to write down; and it is this Jesus who is the source of the Catholic imagination.

How Jesus Speaks

One day, Luke writes, the disciples of John the Baptist come to Jesus asking him if he is the promised Messiah. Jesus answers their question by listing the good things he is doing for the people—a list that matches some of the Messianic expectations of the Jewish prophets. John's disciples leave. Then Jesus turns to his own followers and, speaking to those who have heard John preach, he asks, "What did you go out into the wilderness to look at? A reed shaken by the wind?" (Luke 7:25).

If one pauses to think about the suggestive power of the *image* of a reed in the wind—which is the concrete picture evoked by Jesus' words—it can carry our imaginations in several different directions. When people went out into the wilderness, did they literally hope just to see a landscape that included dry reeds? Were they, perhaps, enthusiastic eco-tourists? Or, if we interpret the reed as a *metaphor,* did they go to see a man who was like a reed, easily swayed by every passing wind of thought or feeling and therefore unreliable? Or, reading the metaphor in a diametrically opposite way, did they seek someone in whom the spirit of God—pictured as the wind of inspiration—was moving, stirring his mind and feelings, preparing him to make a prophetic utterance?

The Gospels present us with a Jesus who instinctively tends to speak this way. It's the way a poet speaks:

1. He uses highly evocative, specific, concrete imagery.

2. He uses figurative (that is, nonliteral) expressions such as metaphor. And

3. He leaves it up to his audience, using their imaginations, to decide how they will understand what he says.

Even after Jesus finally answers this rhetorical question—it was a prophet you went out to see—the uncertain, suggestive power of the image remains. Was this prophet simply part of the landscape, a madman, or one of God's inspired messengers? Or did John's prophetic role make each of these characterizations apt each in its different way?

Here is a second example. During the years of his public life Jesus seems to have led a rootless existence. He wandered from place to place with his followers, staying at the houses of sympathetic friends. When a new disciple volunteers to join the group, this is how Jesus describes his mode of life: "Foxes have holes, and birds of the air have nests; but the Son of Man has nowhere to lay his head" (Luke 9:58). Jesus could have said, "Look, we don't have much money so we more or less depend on someone taking us in." Instead, he makes comparisons and he exaggerates—what we call *hyperbole*. Jesus did sleep. But somehow it seemed as if he never had a real home. The sadness of this self-description is underscored by the way he names himself. Jesus doesn't refer to himself as "I"; instead he uses a well-known phrase from the Hebrew Bible: "the Son of man." This comes from the tradition of Jewish prophecy and identifies Jesus as a messianic leader and at the same time as someone particularly vulnerable and human. By using a conscious *allusion* to biblical tradition, Jesus expresses himself *typologically*; he implies through the name "Son of man" that the great Hebrew prophets centuries earlier were already preparing the way for his coming and that the symbolic name they used was an anticipation, a *type*, for his own ultimate appearance.

The would-be follower has received quite a complex reply to his expression of interest. If this is someone without imagination the initial response might be, "What's all this about foxes and birds? I was just interested in following you. And what do you mean by this 'Son of man' phrase? I thought your name was Jesus." A perfectly reasonable reaction, really. Jesus can only be understood by a listener who imaginatively enters into what he is saying.

Jesus never speaks in abstractions. The technical languages of philosophy, theology, and history are completely foreign to him. He never refers to God as "the uncreated ground of being"; rather, he calls God "Father." Though he lived in a province of the Roman Empire in which many educated Jewish people were strongly influenced by Hellenic ideas, and though he may himself have known some words of Latin and Greek,[1] Jesus never gives any indication that his mind or his manner of speaking have been even slightly influenced by the high intellectual culture of his day. Once or twice he refers to "Caesar," but whichever Caesar currently rules seems monumentally uninteresting to him.

Jesus' teaching is never systematic. He doesn't reason to basic principles or organize what he has to say in terms of interdependent arguments. Indeed he makes no use of logic or of factual evidence as a political scientist or an economist might. Jesus never seeks to prove anything.

Rather, as Matthew puts it, "he taught them as one who had authority, and not as their scribes" (Matt 7:29). Michael Grant describes this Jesus of the Gospels as "tremendously confident and self-assured." His use of the affirmative word *Amen* preceding a statement—indicating that what follows is beyond question—is, as Grant points out, "something unparalleled in Hebrew literature."[2]

Jesus and Jewish Literary Tradition

Just how much did Jesus actually know about "Hebrew literature"? Could Jesus even read? One day, Luke tells us:

> He came to Nazareth, where he had been brought up....He went to the synagogue on the sabbath day, as was his custom. He stood up to read, and the scroll of the prophet Isaiah was given to him. He unrolled the scroll and found the place where it was written: "The Spirit of the Lord is upon me, because he has anointed me to bring good news to the poor. He has sent me to proclaim release to the captives and recovery of sight to the blind, to let the oppressed go free, to proclaim the year of the Lord's favor." And he rolled up the scroll, gave it back to the attendant, and sat down. The eyes of all in the synagogue were fixed on him. Then he began to say to them, "Today this scripture has been fulfilled in your hearing." (Luke 4: 16–21)

This is the only scene in the New Testament in which Jesus is specifically pictured as literate (see Figure 7). Though brief, it suggests not only that he could read but also that his education had given him a thorough knowledge of the scriptures. His use of specific biblical allusions when he talks confirms this. We can be sure he was familiar with the central stories of the Pentateuch—the first five books of the Hebrew Scriptures—because he refers to Adam, Noah, Abraham, Isaac, Jacob, and Moses. He refers as well to the later historical books with their stories of Saul, David, Solomon, and the Queen of Sheba, to the Book of Jonah, to the major prophets Isaiah and Ezekiel and minor prophets like Malachi. He knows the apocalyptic tradition as it is found in the Book of Daniel and he quotes freely from the Psalms. All of this suggests that the Jesus who stood up in the synagogue in Nazara was well aware of Jewish scriptural traditions.

Figure 7. Torah scroll with staves
This Torah scroll from nineteenth-century Germany is probably not much different from ones that Jesus would have read from in the synagogues in his homeland.

It is from these traditions—indeed, from the art of Jewish writing and teaching—that Jesus learned many of the expressive strategies he uses in his spontaneous and instinctive manner of quasi-poetic utterance. It is through Jesus that this complex art of expression eventually evolved into the Catholic imagination. Understanding how he spoke, and what his manner of speaking suggests, is therefore central to understanding where Catholic imagination came from.

Jewish tradition offered Jesus not only a repertoire of literary and historical allusions such as those listed but also a vocabulary of images—wind, fire, water, growing things—that already had strong symbolic resonance and that he could use and amplify as he wished. It offered him symbolic figures such as the good shepherd, Psalm 23, singing, "The Lord is my shepherd, I shall not want" (Ps 23:1). The tradition also offered him a range of literary forms in which to express himself: *chriae*—short, pointed wisdom statements; *parables*—concise fictional narratives of daily life that have a moral or theological implication the listener must figure out; *prophetic utterances*—urging people to reconsider their lives; *apocalyptic prophecies*—which envision events at the end of time; and so on.

As all of these examples illustrate, the central art form in the Jewish culture of Jesus' day was literature. Indeed language—written or spoken—enjoyed a uniquely valued position in the history of the Jewish people. Through the centuries they had evolved—audacious as it may sound—a complex theology exploring the different ways in which God himself was understood to use language. It was a theory Jesus clearly knew, and the art of his utterance is dependent upon its principles.

A Jewish Theory of Language

As we noted in chapter 1, the opening pages of Genesis describe God as a kind of poet. God speaks, and God's words cause created things to come into existence. Creation is the utterance of God. When we listen to what creation is telling us we hear what God means to say. God also speaks through events. Jewish tradition understood victory or defeat in battle, famine, plague, and prosperity as in their different ways God's writing his will in time and space.

In Genesis God also talks to people: to Noah, to Abraham, and in Exodus to Moses. Sometimes God's speech is quite practical, as in his instructions to Noah on how to build the ark (Gen 6:14–16). At other times God's speech can be highly poetic. Talking with

Abraham he says, "Look toward heaven and count the stars, if you are able to count them." Then he said to him, "So shall your descendants be" (Gen 15:5). God writes as well, inscribing the Ten Commandments on stone (Exod 32:16).

The God of the Hebrew Scriptures also speaks through messengers, and their speech too can be poetic, as when an angel tells Hagar, the slave made pregnant by Abraham, about the child she is to bear: "He shall be a wild ass of a man,...and he shall live at odds with all his kin" (Gen 16:12).

The Hebrew prophets continue the tradition, speaking at God's command the words he wishes them to utter. This is symbolized when the heavens open and God himself instructs Ezekiel to preach to the people of Israel:

> "But you, mortal, hear what I say to you; do not be rebellious like that rebellious house; open your mouth, and eat what I give you." I looked, and a hand was stretched out to me, and a written scroll was in it. He spread it before me; it had writing on the front and on the back....He said to me, "O mortal, eat what is offered to you; eat this scroll, and go, speak to the house of Israel."...So I opened my mouth, and...I ate it; and in my mouth it was as sweet as honey. (Ezek 2:8–3:3)

It's easy to see parallels with the scene that pictures Jesus in the synagogue at Nazara. Just like the prophet Ezekiel, at the start of his public life Jesus begins to speak for God, as Luke suggests through the typological parallels—the scroll, the prophetic message, the special name "Son of man."

This is the culture in which Jesus was formed, a culture in which language and the art of language had a divine authority. Jesus' use of words and literary traditions makes it clear that he fully understood this tradition, and the scene at Nazara shows him dramatically inserting himself into that tradition. There he declares that he *is* what the prophets spoke about. Writing has become real. The prophet foresaw Jesus' coming. The text now, at this moment, becomes a living man. The climax of this idea comes at the beginning of John's Gospel: "In the beginning was the Word, and the Word was with God, and the Word was God....And the Word became flesh and lived among us, and we have seen his glory, the glory as of a father's only son, full of grace and truth" (John 1:1,14).

Fully alive to the complexities of the Jewish tradition, John the Evangelist declares that Jesus was from all time the creating word of the first page of Genesis; he was the word of the Law inscribed upon the tablets; later, he was the word uttered by prophets like Ezekiel. He is the divine utterance of the divine will that in time becomes a man.

Jesus often spoke poetically because he came from a culture in which poetic speaking was understood to be an opening up to the divine—a connection to the *Creator Spiritus*. He used language and the various strategies of artistic verbal expression in order to voice himself and the divine message he had come to deliver.

But how did Jesus' way of speaking and teaching fit and amplify what he came to say? In what ways do his characteristic forms of imagining and talking correspond to and further develop the content of what he has to say?

Jesus and Imagination

The World of Jesus' Imagination

In chapter 1 we saw that human beings constantly imagine themselves and their world and that they use the way in which they imagine in order to think and act. How did Jesus imagine? By going back into the way Jesus talks, and particularly into the images his discourse generates, we can begin to reconstruct the world as he pictured it—the world of his own imagination. While this kind of investigation is interesting in and of itself, it is crucial for the present study because the world of Jesus' imagination is also the originating source for two millennia of Catholic art.

So, let us enter into the images Jesus uses and the pictures they evoke in our minds. What do we see?

We see: an old cloak with a new patch; old skins that hold wine; a lamp set out in the open; salt; a cup of cold water; a coin; a mill stone; a sword; a fisherman's net; a yoke. These are ordinary things, everyday objects, concrete and particular things, the things people see and touch and use.

A second list: a fig tree; a mustard seed tree; a mulberry tree; flowers in the fields; sparrows, vultures, crows; an ox drinking water; a camel; a lost sheep; wheat growing up and weeds tangled in between; vineyards. This is a landscape full of living things: plants, trees, animals, birds, enmeshed in the rhythm of the seasons, the cycles of birth, growth, and death.

A third list: people in the landscape: a farmer sowing seed, casting it in every direction; farmers at harvest time threshing the chaff from the wheat; a vineyard and the workers harvesting the grapes; a shepherd looking for a lost sheep; some fishermen out on a lake hauling in their catch (Figure 8). This is an agricultural world almost as old and simple as time itself, a world that existed centuries before Jesus and still exists today, a world of hard work done by hand, of people dependent upon the land, the weather and the seasons, alert to animals and birds and fish and living in harmony with them.

Figure 8. Saint Peter called by Christ to be a fisher of people
Fishermen and boats were important everyday elements in Jesus' time. The Gospels show him calming stormy waters and, as depicted in this early mosaic, calling fishermen to be his apostles.

A fourth list: villages and towns: children in the marketplace shouting to one another; a solitary woman working yeast into bread dough; a wealthy man arranging for a big wedding feast; a neighbor asking for a loaf of bread; a man planning to build his house; a man fearful that robbers will break in on him; a traveler robbed and beaten and left for dead by the roadside. Ordinary people doing ordinary things, feeling ordinary emotions of elation, anxiety, camaraderie, loneliness, danger and risk and fear.

A fifth list: ordinary people in socially defined relationships: a pupil and his teacher; a master and his servant; a shifty and dishonest servant and his indignant master; a businessman calling in a loan; a clever administrator who knows how to cut a good deal; faithful servants staying up late waiting their master's return; a judge confronted by a widow begging him for a decision; a generous father forgiving his intemperate son.

A sixth list: we move on to the city of Jerusalem and there we see: opponents arguing on their way to court—one of them may be thrown into jail; a Pharisee and a tax collector praying in the Temple; other people offering gifts at the Temple altar; teachers of the Law in long robes shoving into the best seats at the table; a king planning for a future battle; a king giving a wedding feast.

While these lists are suggestive rather than complete, they offer a fairly accurate sketch of the world as Jesus sees it. These are the images his imagination uses day by day.

The Poet of Everyday Life

This is a world of concrete particulars: objects, living things, and the landscape. Jesus thinks about nature in terms of an agricultural economy, and yet there are moments when he can still gaze at the lilies of the fields and wonder at "how they grow; they neither toil nor spin; yet I tell you, even Solomon in all his glory was not clothed like one of these" (Luke 12:27).

Jesus knows about work: the tools needed, how you get a job done, pragmatic considerations that practical people must consider if they want the wheat to grow or they don't want the foundations of a house to be washed away by the next heavy rainstorm.

Jesus is interested in ordinary people and particularly people in terms of their interpersonal relationships. Rather than speak of individuals by personal names, he speaks in terms of the roles people play: servant or master, judge or petitioner, father or child. He's aware of how social systems create interdependence. Servants must obey but masters must forgive.

In the end, one is particularly impressed by Jesus as a realist. Though his speech is almost always poetic in its expressive strategies, his imagery is almost always that of a concrete, factual, emphatically ordinary world. He is a poet of everyday life.

What Jesus does not imagine helps to clarify this point further. Jesus never makes reference to the history of the ruling order of his day: Rome. He never mentions Greco-Roman gods or pagan mythology. He does not use the form of the beast fable—stories in which personified animals speak and act like people. He is not interested in tales of wonders: ghosts, prophetic foresight, magical objects. Only once does Jesus tell a story that pictures the afterlife (Luke 16:19–31), and he never provides concrete descriptions of what God or God's angels might look like. Twice, in Matthew's Gospel, he refers to pearls, and there are a few times in Luke when he tells stories about kings. But almost all the time Jesus does not talk about and evidently doesn't try to imagine the very wealthy and the very powerful; instead he describes the kind of local rich people he would himself have usually encountered. All of which is to say that Jesus as a realist limits himself to what he and his listeners have themselves seen and what they know from firsthand experience.

It's difficult to calculate the extent of the influence of Jesus' way of seeing. Two thousand years of readers and listeners have hovered over his words, picturing the images they evoke. Jesus' people, like the good Samaritan, the prodigal son; Jesus' landscapes, like the sower scattering his seed over good and bad ground; Jesus' workers and villages and tools and birds and beasts necessarily entered into the minds and the feelings of every generation of Christians. How could they avoid weaving them into their own imaginative picture of human life? Those field flowers more beautiful than Solomon in all his glory: we find them widely scattered—in garlands decorating the Roman catacombs, carved into the capitals of twelfth-century French Gothic cathedrals, spotted about the edges of sacred scenes in paintings by early Renaissance Italian artists, ecstatically celebrated as a metaphor for the Virgin in the motet *Gaude gloriosa* by the Renaissance composer Thomas Tallis, and spilling across the sky in the Victorian poet Hopkins's "The Wreck of the *Deutschland*." That innocent lamb once lost and now found rests on the strong shoulders of a good shepherd in a third-century Roman sarcophagus; as a mystic embodiment of Jesus it caps the sixth-century mosaic ceiling of San Vitale in Ravenna (Figure 9), stands at the center of an adoring paradise in the fifteenth-century Van Eyck *Ghent Altarpiece*, and is shot in the head by a Nazi soldier in Roberto Rossellini's film *Open City* (1945).

Figure 9. Mystic Lamb
This sixth-century ceiling mosaic of the Mystic Lamb from the church of San Vitale in Ravenna takes its inspiration from the image of the lamb from the Book of Revelation: Christ is the lamb who was sacrificed and is now worthy to receive honor, glory, and blessing.

From the earliest years of Christianity, the immediate realism of Jesus' imagination lent itself to the seemingly endless invention of artists.

But they didn't just take up Jesus' images, they took up their meanings as well. There is a logical coherence across how Jesus imagined, how he spoke, and what he had to say. It's customary for practical people to regard poetic utterance as a form of nonessential decoration. From this point of view, there are facts and then there are pretty but essentially untrue ways of saying facts. That is not the case here.

Jesus used Jewish poetic and imaginative traditions not because they were pleasing or ornamental but because they were the only viable way of saying what he had come to say. Jesus spoke the way he did because it was *the only possible way to speak about reality as he understood reality to be.* He was a poet because he could not speak accurately in any other way.

Imagination and Meaning

THE IMPORTANCE OF INTERPRETATION

"Consider the ravens," Jesus says one day, "they neither sow nor reap, they have neither storehouse nor barn, and yet God feeds them. Of how much more value are you than the birds!" (Luke 12:24). His point is that one must not simply look at the concrete things around us, one must understand what they might imply. Ravens are not simply birds; they are also a kind of sign from God that, if correctly read, can tell us to trust in God's care and put aside anxiety about unimportant matters. Jesus makes it clear to his listeners that he expects them to read and interpret what they see not simply literally but also analogically.

Central to Jesus' imagination, and to the Catholic imagination that followed, is a *double vision.* Nothing is simply itself; everything has a second meaning. This is naturally the case because all of creation is a form of divine writing in which God has inscribed "shadows, echoes...vestiges, representations" of himself and his intentions, as Bonaventure suggested. Everything is more than it appears to be. The material density of the world of Jesus' imagination is matched by a parallel density in meaning. Indeed it's delightful that Jesus pictures for us ravens, vineyards, and fishermen, but because the whole of creation is full of divine meaning each one of his images is a doublet. It's a raven, yes, but it's also a sign of God's care for all that God has made.

ANALOGY

The double vision of the Catholic imagination frequently operates through *analogy:* making a comparison in which a meaning true in one case is seen to be true as well in a parallel case. For example, here is Jesus on false prophets: "You will know them by their fruits. Are grapes gathered from thorns, or figs from thistles? In the same way, every good tree bears good fruit, but the bad tree bears bad fruit" (Matt 7:16–17). Two analogies here: false prophets are analogous to thorns or thistles, plants that do not bear fruit; or, false prophets are analogous to rotten trees and can only bear rotten fruit. They are either sterile, or their yield will be worse than worthless—it will be destructive. In these examples there is a double wisdom in operation. The statements Jesus makes are folk truisms—a kind of simple, universal knowledge based upon material facts everyone shares without thinking. Sure—bad tree, bad fruit. This kind of wisdom is then used to define something perhaps not so immediately obvious—here something intellectual, spiritual, and moral. A bad teacher will give you bad ideas. Consume them and they'll poison your soul.

The Gospels frequently portray Jesus' listeners, even his most devoted disciples, as failing to grasp the meaning of his analogies; the implication of their failure is that they don't think imaginatively about what Jesus is saying to them. At one point Jesus is warning his followers about "the yeast of the Pharisees and Sadducees" and almost comically they think he's talking about baking. In exasperation he replies, "How could you fail to perceive that I was not speaking about bread?" (Matt 16:6,11). Cursed with excessive literalism, Jesus' own followers seem to have been unable ordinarily to understand the double meaning of his utterances.

The world as Jesus sees it is an endless network of analogies, and Jesus' speech constantly uses analogies in trying to explain to people the double nature of the reality in which they live.

PARABLE

A perfect example of a literary form that articulates this double vision is the *parable*. Parables had already been a part of Jewish literature for centuries; you can find examples in the Second Book of Samuel (2 Sam 12:1–4) and the prophets Isaiah (Isa 5:1–7) and Ezekiel (Ezek 17:1–10). During Jesus' era they were popular with Jewish teachers as a way to explain and interpret passages from the Bible. Jesus' innovation, which is yet another suggestive instance of the authority of his voice, was to make up parables not linked to a biblical text; rather, he uses them to articulate his own ideas.[3]

Parables are fictions: short stories developing an analogy that in Jesus' hands usually describe incidents from the ordinary life of his day. They can be very short: "He told them another parable: 'The kingdom of heaven is like yeast that a woman took and mixed in with three measures of flour until all of it was leavened'" (Matt 13:33).

And they can be quite long; the parable traditionally titled "The Prodigal Son," which reads like a short story, is twenty-two verses long and fills the better part of a page (Luke 15:11–32).

The gospel accounts of the way people responded to Jesus' parables indicate frequent bafflement, and there are scenes in which Jesus later takes his disciples aside and explains to them what he really meant (for example, Matt 13). But there are other instances in which it seems as if the Gospel writers themselves permitted various interpretations to stand simultaneously. The famous parable of the lost sheep has two quite different conclusions. In Matthew's Gospel it appears at a point where Jesus is talking about the sin of leading little children into evil, and then he tells of the lost sheep and the shepherd who seeks him and concludes, "So it is not the will of your Father in heaven that one of these little ones should be lost" (Matt 18:14). Luke retells the same parable, but in his account Jesus concludes, after describing the return of the lost sheep, "I tell you, there will be more joy in heaven over one sinner who repents than over ninety-nine righteous people who need no repentance" (Luke 15:7). One evangelist hears in the parable a story about misleading innocent children, another hears in the same tale a comforting message for adult sinners: that they will always be welcomed back.

We should not be surprised at these divergent interpretations. Jesus created parables as analogies that are intentionally made to be open and that challenge different people to find in them diverse implications, because the human imagination can go in quite different directions. Rather than insisting that there is a single correct interpretation of a parable, which is to insist that one's own imaginative response is the only acceptable response, we are encouraged to consider parables as a form to incite thought, introspection, questioning, and creativity of mind. The openness of parables is liberating, and through the centuries there is a rich history of alternative responses to them, suggesting that they are indeed fertile ground for imaginative growth.

PARADOX

In John's Gospel, Jesus says to the Pharisee Nicodemus, "Very truly, I tell you, no one can see the kingdom of God without being born from above." Nicodemus said to him, "How can anyone be born after having grown old? Can one enter a second time into the mother's womb and be born?" (John 3:3–4). This is a paradox—what appears to be an impossibly contradictory statement. In the scene Jesus seems to delight in puzzling his listener. The solution to the paradoxical problem posed by his statement emerges from the double nature of reality. In terms of simple physiology, Nicodemus cannot reenter his mother's womb. But in terms of the spiritual life, rebirth is a real possibility. On the spiritual plane to be born again, or to become like a child a second time, is to achieve a spiritual innocence that offers a person a second chance at goodness. The paradoxes of Jesus always work out of two different kinds of meaning or two different levels of reality. A statement that is literally impossible becomes valid on a spiritual level of meaning. Thinking with paradoxes was soon to become central to the emerging Catholic imagination, and it has remained one of its most pronounced characteristics for two millennia.

IRONY AND IRONIC JOKING

Rhetorical irony—saying one thing but meaning its opposite—emerges naturally as a consequence of paradoxical thinking. "Blessed are you who are poor, for yours is the kingdom of God" (Luke 6:20). The "beatitudes" of Jesus such as this one work out of contradictory logic. How can one feel fortunate or blessed by poverty? That's a paradox. It's also ironic. The people who think they are fortunate because they enjoy worldly wealth and power and glamour are actually the unfortunate ones, since it is the poor who will come into "the kingdom of God."

Jesus likes to create stories in which a situation is ironic. People think one thing to be the case, but the opposite is the reality. He also has a penchant for rather grim jokes. In Luke he describes a man who has become so rich that he decides to build new, larger barns in which to store all his things. Smugly he says to himself, "Soul, you have ample goods laid up for many years; relax, eat, drink, be merry." But God said to him, "You fool! This very night your life is being demanded of you. And the things you have prepared, whose will they be?" (Luke 12:19–20). The irony of this situation is clear: the man thinks and plans in terms of earthly values but there is another level of reality, which is God's divine plan, and when these two kinds of plans are in conflict, the human will always lose. Jesus intends his hearers to react to this story with laughter at the expense of the rich man who is, in God's own words, a "fool."

DIVISION

Seeing the world in terms of two different orders of reality leads Jesus, at times, into employing figurative language and parable in order to insist that people are going to have to choose between one kind of reality and another, and he pictures his own mission and the kingdom that he has come to proclaim as demanding this kind of choice and hence as dividing people. "Everyone therefore who acknowledges me before others, I also will acknowledge before my Father in heaven; but whoever denies me before others, I also will deny before my Father in heaven" (Matt 10:32–33). This way of seeing reality, in which one must declare for one or the other of the two orders or levels of reality—here described as "human beings" versus "my Father in heaven"—leads to a series of dramatic and menacing images. A dragnet brings in fish of many kinds, and the fishermen "when it was full…drew it ashore, sat down, and put the good into baskets but threw out the bad. So it will be at the end of the age. The angels will come out and separate the evil from the righteous and throw them into the furnace of fire, where there will be weeping and gnashing of teeth" (Matt 13:48–50). And, "Every plant that my heavenly Father has not planted will be uprooted" (Matt 15:13). Jesus' imagination favors the construction of a world of antagonistic opposites and repeatedly foresees a future moment when one half wins while the other loses, irrevocably.

TYPOLOGICAL PARALLELS

Jesus uses his knowledge of the Hebrew Scriptures to establish parallels between well-known events of Jewish history and the significance of his own life. For a Jewish audience in particular, these comparisons have a powerfully emotional meaning because they are so directly connected to some of their favorite stories. For example, unhappy with the crowd's demand for a "sign" to prove his authenticity, Jesus says, "An evil and adulterous generation asks for a sign, but no sign will be given to it except the sign of the prophet Jonah. For just as Jonah was for three days and three nights in the belly of the sea monster, so for three days and three nights the Son of Man

will be in the heart of the earth" (Matt 12:39–40; see Figure 10).
Perhaps we can forgive Jesus' listeners for finding this saying puzzling, since it constitutes a direct prediction of his future death as
well as his future resurrection three days later. The point of the parallel Jesus creates is that (1) in the wonders of Jewish history there
is already the story of an extraordinary sign, a man who seemed to
be dead—Jonah—who returned to the world of the living after three
days, and now (2) Jesus' own life will repeat that wonder, or "sign,"
but in a much more remarkable and important form. He won't simply be spewed out of the belly of a sea monster; he will die and come
back to life. Looking back on Jewish history, Jesus reads in the story
of Jonah an anticipation or foreshadowing of what will happen in
his own life. Jonah becomes a prototype of Jesus.

Figure 10. Jonah and the whale
This early fourth-century ivory relief of Jonah and the whale depicts the whale
as resembling a serpent—an interesting example of early iconography of "sea
beasts."

Underlying the use of typological parallels is yet another kind
of doubleness. We see a comparison between two different moments
in time: Jesus and Jonah. The underlying logic of the comparison is
that God in working through history establishes *in advance* specific
signs—or types—that anticipate later events. After Jesus' coming, it
becomes possible to read back in Jewish history and to discover for
the first time another, deeper meaning in earlier historical events.

Summary

Jesus' unusual way of speaking emerges from the Jewish literary culture in which he was raised, and he uses poetic forms of

utterance—simile, metaphor, hyperbole, typological allusion—in explaining how he imagines or pictures the world. He must speak this way because he sees reality existing on two levels: the material/human/ordinary level, and the transcendent/divine/eternal level. These coexist in time and space, and the differences between them lead to Jesus' frequent use of paradox, irony, images of division, and typological comparisons.

All of this was soon to become the basis for Catholic art.

CHAPTER FOUR

Jesus' Teaching
and Catholic Belief

Jesus' way of imagining, his modes of expression, and his understanding of the complexity of reality as depicted through the record of the Gospels were to enter into the minds and the creative imaginations of the generations that followed. In the subsequent chapters of this book we will trace just a few of the many ways in which this happened.

To begin that project, we turn now to investigate how gospel accounts of Jesus' own sayings during his life as a teacher helped to formulate those ways of thinking about God and creation that were to be foundational for Catholic belief.

Our question is simply this: In what ways do the Gospels present Jesus during his public life as already talking about incarnation, redemption, sacraments, and community?

Incarnation

The world as Jesus imagined it is concrete, particular, and ordinary. He talked about that world through specific material images of things, people, and the acts of daily life. His world and his way of speaking about that world fit perfectly with his analogical way of talking about God. Jesus finds God in what we see and hear every day, and he explains aspects of God's nature through imagined scenes of ordinary life. In all of these ways Jesus' imagination is deeply incarnational. He keeps finding suggestions of the divine in everyday life.

Figure 11. Fra Angelico and Filippo Lippi,
***Adoration of the Magi* (ca. 1445)**
This painting, thought to have originated with the saintly Dominican friar Fra Angelico and completed by Fra Filippo Lippi, is a sumptuous example of fifteenth-century devotion to the earthly aspects of Christ's life. While it contains a number of symbolic elements, its festive colors also make it simply a delight for the eyes.

There is, further, a crucial double meaning to the scenes pictured by the Jesus of the Gospels, a meaning that originates in what may have been the difficult rhetorical position he faced during his public life. As he traveled through the countryside Jesus taught and healed the people he encountered. The Gospels do not, however, picture him getting up on a stump and proclaiming, simply and directly, "I am God." Almost certainly no one would have believed him if he had tried talking that way. The gospel narratives make it clear that Jesus' own chosen disciples consistently misunderstood who he was, why he had come, and what he was trying to tell them. Indeed, ultimately one of the deepest mysteries about Jesus is the nature of his own inner consciousness of himself. Was he, as suggested by John the Evangelist, always aware that he was the Son of God and was only adapting his utterances to the limitations of his audiences? Or did Jesus only obscurely sense who he was and what his destiny was to be? Did Jesus have to discover his own divinity through the experiences of his death and resurrection? There is no way of knowing. The gospel writers began their work grounded in the belief that had transformed their own consciousnesses after the resurrection that Jesus was divine and our redeemer. When they wrote their four accounts, this belief suffused everything they did; thus, each of the four Gospels depicts Jesus as being aware, to a greater or lesser degree, of his own divinity and of his destiny. This is the Jesus of the Gospels whom this chapter discusses, and, as we have already noticed, this representation of Jesus must cope with the utter novelty of his coming. So of necessity the Gospels show a Jesus who had to use various ways of indirectly suggesting his divine nature. For example, he makes typological allusions to traditional messianic prophecies in which he adopts as his own the special name "Son of man." At other times he forgives a person's sins, and when doubters asked how he could claim this divine power, he heals physical ailments to indicate that he had the authority from God to do what he was doing (see, for example, Luke 5:17–26). But the ultimate, clinching proof of his own divine nature was to come only with Jesus' death and resurrection.

Anticipation

For this reason the gospel narratives, in their descriptions of Jesus' public life, must work in terms of anticipation. The evangelists writing several decades after Jesus' death know that their story will end in Jesus rising from that death and that he will come thereafter to be recognized as God the Son. But they are describing events that took place before Jesus' real nature was known to ordinary mortals. How can they show Jesus talking implicitly or, as we just said, through forms of "double meaning," about his own divine nature and in particular about himself as the incarnate Son of God? The strategy they often use is to have Jesus actually talking about himself when he is speaking about his heavenly Father. In the Gospels it turns out that Jesus' description of God the Father usually applies to Jesus too—Jesus while he is still living his life on earth. In this sense, then, it is crucial to understand that the Gospels present the man Jesus as a *living analogy* to the God who is in heaven and that statements about that God become simultaneously statements about Jesus.

Consequently the analogies between ordinary earthly things and God that we are about to look at are, first, statements about God the Father, but they are equally valid as statements about God the Son. They permit the Jesus of the Gospels to talk about himself indirectly, and therefore with a becoming modesty and caution to talk about the fact that he is, indeed, as the gospel writers believed, God incarnate in human flesh.

Here are some of Jesus' favorite analogies for God that become simultaneously analogous descriptions of Jesus' own nature as the Son of God incarnate as a real man.[1]

THE DADDY

Instructing his disciples to pray, Jesus tells them to address God as "Abba" (Luke 11:2), a name that suggests that God is "a caring, provident, gracious, and loving parent."[2] In using this intimate, familial word, Jesus imagines God as approachable and ready to help. The parallel works here: Jesus' own teaching—the virtues he recommended and the wrongs he warned about—and his life—what he did for others—both illustrate that as a man and as the Son of God incarnate he was indeed caring, approachable, and ready to help.

THE LEADER

"Do not be afraid, little flock, for it is your Father's good pleasure to give you the kingdom" (Luke 12:32). Here God the parent is generously giving his "kingdom" to Jesus' followers, imagined as individually small and hence vulnerable. "Flock" suggests they are like sheep, proverbially meek and in need of direction. Jesus' image of God and of himself as the leader of his disciples here reinforces the "Abba" of the prayer in Luke 11.

THE PRODIGAL FARMER

Listen! A sower went out to sow. And as he sowed, some seeds fell on the path, and the birds came and ate them up. Other seeds fell on rocky ground, where they did not have much soil, and they sprang up quickly, since they had no depth of soil. But when the sun rose, they were scorched; and since they had no root, they withered away. Other seeds fell among thorns, and the thorns grew up and choked them. Other seeds fell on good soil and brought forth grain, some a hundredfold, some sixty, some thirty. (Matt 13:3–8)

This parable can be read a number of different ways: it can describe the creator-God's superabundance in filling the earth to the full with possibilities for life and growth, and it can describe Jesus as teacher scattering the good news of his kingdom to anyone who will listen. The point in either reading, and in others as well, is that God and Jesus are prodigally generous, throwing good things in every conceivable direction and never holding back out of a fear that what they offer might not be accepted. Theirs is a generosity beyond pragmatism and even beyond logic, driven by an excess of love.

THE FORGIVING FATHER

The story in Luke usually called "The Prodigal Son" tells of a young man who asks his father for his future inheritance and goes out and wastes it all, finally coming home begging to be taken back as a servant. The father's response exemplifies the same prodigality as that of the sower: he pardons the son, welcomes him into the family, and celebrates his return with a party (Luke 15:11–32). The parable suggests God's ready inclination to forgive anything to the person who confesses past errors.

THE MASTER

The God Jesus imagines is profligate and tireless in his love but he is not indiscriminate. He warns his followers to "be like those who are waiting for their master to return from the wedding banquet, so that they may open the door for him as soon as he comes and knocks. Blessed are those slaves whom the master finds alert when he comes; truly I tell you, he will fasten his belt and have them sit down to eat, and he will come and serve them" (Luke 12:36–37). Jesus' God has authority and power and merits faithful and subservient service. Hence those who fail him will face rejection. For those who stay awake, there is a very surprising reversal in store: the master will paradoxically begin to serve them.

Figure 12. Murillo, *Return of the Prodigal Son*
The *Return of the Prodigal Son* by the seventeenth-century Spanish artist Bartolomé Murillo is an outstanding depiction of a scene from one of Jesus' most beloved parables.

THE INVESTOR

Jesus tells the parable of a wealthy man about to go on a trip who leaves money behind with three of his servants. He expects each of them to find a way of investing the money. When he returns, two of the servants have cleverly doubled what he had given them and he praises them as "good and trustworthy." The third hasn't done anything with what was given to him, and the master commands his servants to "throw him into the outer darkness, where there will be weeping and gnashing of teeth" (Matt 25:14–30). God gives, as in other parables, but here he expects something in return. When he doesn't get it, the man who fails is tossed out of the party.

Jesus imagines a God who combines kindness—"Abba"—with a certain severity: people must live up to the challenges offered them. God expects his investments to work for him.

THE JUDGE

We have already seen parables that offer analogies between God and less-than-admirable human beings. Here is one more.

> In a certain city there was a judge who neither feared God nor had respect for people. In that city there was a widow who kept coming to him and saying, "Grant me justice against my opponent." For a while he refused; but later he said to himself, "Though I have no fear of God and no respect for anyone, yet because this widow keeps bothering me, I will grant her justice, so that she may not wear me out by continually coming." And the Lord said, "Listen to what the unjust judge says. And will not God grant justice to his chosen ones who cry to him day and night? Will he delay long in helping them?" (Luke 18:2–7)

Here Jesus combines divine justice with divine mercy. Even the corrupt Judge will finally take pity on the widow; and so it is all the more likely that God, who loves his creation, will temper justice with mercy.

If we link all these figures together, we find ourselves building a composite portrait of how Jesus imagines God by means of analogies with human beings, and since this portrait exactly reflects the ways in which Jesus himself taught and acted, Christians have read these analogies as speaking of how Jesus imagines himself, a self-description of Jesus as God's son incarnate. And what is he? A caring parent, a tireless leader, a reckless lover, someone who forgives and welcomes back the penitent but who expects in return alert service and hard work, a judge who will finally admit or expel each person from the party but who is ready to give in to his own innate sympathy and inclination to forgive. It is a human portrait, of course, because each analogy comes from a specific kind of human situation, but the point of Jesus' teaching is clearly that this is the way to glimpse aspects of the otherwise transcendent and unknowable God.

Redemption

The concept of redemption can be usefully considered in terms of three chronological phases:

1. There is a fallen and evil world.

2. Jesus comes to sacrifice himself as an atonement for past sin.

3. And so he saves and transforms the world, giving all who will follow him hope for future salvation.

The great events of redemption were still in the future while Jesus lived his public life. But looking back on those years after his death and resurrection, his followers could remember how Jesus' own ways of imagining and of teaching formulated the terms that would describe his redemptive act, anticipating what was to come. Let us consider each phase in turn.

EVIL

The world as Jesus imagines it is a damaged, fallen world.

Nature has become hostile. While the sower may generously fling his seeds in all directions, some fall on rocky ground, others are devoured by birds or scorched by the sun, and many of those that sprout are choked with thorns and weeds (Matt 13:4–7).

Far worse are people themselves. The householder must always be wary of the burglar (Luke 12:39). Enemies will sneak up and plant weeds in a farmer's fields to spoil his crop (Matt 13:25). Bandits on the road to Jericho rob, strip, and beat a man, leaving him for dead (Luke 10:30).

Jesus' vision can be very dark indeed.

SELF-SACRIFICE

Into this fallen world come people of remarkable personal generosity who reach out to help those in need. The prodigal father welcomes home an errant and foolish son who has nearly been killed by the evils of the distant city and calls for a banquet. The victim bleeding and dying on the road to Jericho is saved by a Samaritan, a man he would ordinarily despise; this Samaritan goes to extraordinary lengths to help, not only soothing and binding up the man's wounds but taking him to an inn where he pays in advance for all the victim's expenses (Luke 10:34–35). The shepherd leaves the flock to rescue a stray (Luke 15:4–7). In an evil world these acts of kindness redeem, at least, the moment.

But, what about the ultimate saving act, Jesus' death and subsequent resurrection? We have already seen the Jesus of the Gospels hinting at this in his obscure reference to "the sign of Jonah," where, interpreting an old story typologically, he intimates his return as the resurrected savior (Matt 12:39–40). Speaking to his disciples alone, Jesus was quietly even more specific, making references to his arrest, condemnation, crucifixion, and resurrection (for example, Matt 20:18–19) that they clearly did not understand at the time. Grasping what he meant seems to have been possible for Jesus' disciples only after the actual events had taken place. But by the time the evangelists wrote down the gospel accounts, such statements were seen to be Jesus' own way of describing the redemptive process soon to occur.

SALVATION

While Jesus imagines the world in terms of evil and suffering, he also frequently pictures it in terms of growth and renewal. His parables of the kingdom, such as the woman kneading yeast into dough (Luke 13:20–21), or the mustard seed "that someone took and sowed in the garden; it grew and became a tree, and the birds of the air made nests in its branches" (Luke 13:19), are stories of irreversible goodness spreading everywhere. Jesus' personal fascination with nature and with life and growth leads him to images filled with an optimism that seems to envision a future in which his kingdom will thrive perhaps on earth, perhaps in a paradise after death.

Adopting traditions of Jewish apocalyptic prophecy, Jesus also talked about the end of this world and the conclusion of his work of redemption, when "the Son of Man is to come with his angels in the glory of his Father, and then he will repay everyone for what has been done" (Matt 16:27). Then "many will come from east and west and will eat with Abraham and Isaac and Jacob in the kingdom of heaven..." (Matt 8:11). The enormity of the one vision, seeing God, the angels, Jesus throned in judgment, and all the peoples of the earth, gives way once again to the intimacy of Jesus' favored picture of the party, here hosted by the patriarchs of Israel, who welcome not only Jews but people from all over the world.

Thus Jesus' ways of talking voiced a rich repertoire of redemptive imagery, all of which was later to be taken up and used by his followers.

Sacrament

In the first three Gospels to be written—those of Mark, Matthew, and Luke—Jesus is already seen during his own days of teaching to be anticipating the sacraments adopted by his church after his death.

We find a clear suggestion of baptism, the sacrament that consecrates a person's decision to join Christ, in Jesus' assertion that "everyone therefore who acknowledges me before others, I also will acknowledge before my Father in heaven…" (Matt 10:32). Indeed here the theology of sacramentality, that a human act on earth is matched by a divine action in the transcendent world, is already being defined.

Figure 13. *Baptism*
Much of the earliest Christian imagery was to be found on the catacombs. This fresco on the catacomb of Saints Marcellinus and Peter in Rome depicts the rite of baptism. Note the prominence of the pouring of water.

Jesus' words also begin to shape the paradoxical and hyperbolic language that the church was to use with baptism: "Those who find their life will lose it, and those who lose their life for my sake will find it" (Matt 10:39). The new life in the spirit that comes with the sacrament of baptism can only be achieved when one drops the old life of sin, selfishness, and doubt.

Jesus frequently suggests the future eucharistic celebration in his pictures of feasts at which the guilty have been pardoned and all who are eligible are warmly welcomed. In one such story, when those first invited all refuse to come, the host tells his servants, "Go therefore into the main streets, and invite everyone you find to the wedding banquet" (Matt 22:9). After Jesus instituted the consecration of bread and wine as the elements of the eucharistic banquet, his followers recalled how many of his stories focused upon farms and vineyards, wheat and wine, and saw in this predilection for certain kinds of images an anticipation of the sacraments to come.

Jesus liked to tell stories about people who were guilty but who found forgiveness, sometimes because they repented, as in the story of the prodigal father, and sometimes simply because the person who had authority over them decided to pardon them, as in this tale:

> "A certain creditor had two debtors; one owed five hundred denarii, and the other fifty. When they could not pay, he cancelled the debts for both of them. Now which of them will love him more?" Simon answered, "I suppose the one for whom he cancelled the greater debt." And Jesus said to him, "You have judged rightly." (Luke 7:41–43)

The generosity of the creditor and the responding love of those in his debt shape anticipatory images of the sacrament of reconciliation that was to come.

In the Gospel of John, the last of the canonical Gospels to be written, Jesus speaks in a very different way. There he takes the symbolism of the sacraments and points out that he himself and the life he is leading are already becoming sacramental. "I am the bread of life" he says. "Whoever comes to me will never be hungry, and whoever believes in me will never be thirsty" (John 6:35). And John pictures Jesus proclaiming, "Let anyone who is thirsty come to me, and let the one who believes in me drink. As the scripture has said, 'Out of the believer's heart shall flow rivers of living water'" (John 7:37–38). In these passages the elements of the Catholic sacraments are seen as coming from Jesus' own body; that is, through his incarnation and redemptive death he becomes Eucharist and baptismal water— in the latter statement the water that burst from the spear-wound in Jesus' dead body becomes the water for future baptism. In John's Gospel, Jesus' own language leaves no doubt that the sacraments will be an element of his continuing presence among his people.

In chapter 2 we found that the sacraments of the Catholic Church are remarkably plain and simple in the things they use, the gestures and language of their rituals, and the presumptions of eligibility upon which they are based. This sacramental system emerged directly from Jesus' way of imagining the world in similar terms: from his constant focus upon ordinary, humble particulars; from the stories he told of daily life; and from his constant stress upon choosing to follow him. The Jesus who insisted upon the paradox that to enter his kingdom meant becoming a child prepared the way for the kinds of sacraments that emerged from the church that followed him.

Community

That church, as a believing community, is already anticipated in the way Jesus imagines the human relationships he prizes most. "My mother and my brothers," he says, "are those who hear the word of God and do it" (Luke 8:21). Jesus lived in community throughout his public life surrounded by his followers, meeting with new people, both those who rejected him and those who came to trust and follow him.

It's easy to join him, and everyone is welcome right up to the last minute. Jesus tells the story of a vineyard owner hiring people to harvest grapes. Some begin at dawn, some at midday, but even late in the afternoon still more are hired. When at the end of the day the owner pays everyone equally, those who have worked all day long complain. His response is, "Friend, I am doing you no wrong; did you not agree with me for the usual daily wage? Take what belongs to you and go; I choose to give to this last the same as I give to you. Am I not allowed to do what I choose with what belongs to me? Or are you envious because I am generous?' (Matt 20:13–15).

The crowning imagined picture—we have seen it many times—is the banquet at which everyone who chooses to come is welcome.

These are all images of church as Jesus is already imagining church. The followers treading the dusty roads of Palestine. The vineyard workers who arrive at the last minute and get paid just like everyone else. The festive partygoers welcomed by the king or bridegroom to the filled table where everyone is celebrating.

The first Christians gathering to celebrate the Eucharist remembered these invitations, which they recalled in the stories that Jesus had told. Following his example they welcomed others into their midst and waited for the time when they would join a heavenly banquet and be reunited with the Jesus who so generously kept inviting them to come.

CHAPTER FIVE

The First Christian Narratives

Four Biographies of Jesus

Christian Narrative and Biography

Christianity began with storytelling. As the many examples of Jesus' own teaching already quoted illustrate, he constantly used the literary form of the parable to teach. The evangelists love to picture him surrounded by people—some sympathetic, some hostile, and perhaps only a few really understanding what he is saying—but all of them drawn imaginatively into the narratives he was inventing.

Spreading the good news about Jesus also began with narratives, and narratives of a particular sort. As Pierre du Bourguet points out, "Christianity is less a doctrine than a person, that of Christ. Christian dogma derives as much from his being as from his teaching."[1] Consequently the central texts of Christianity take the literary form of biographical narratives—four of them.

It is important to stress that this was something new for Mediterranean religions. Pagan Greece and Rome had no specific sacred texts. Judaism was, as we have seen, richly literary, but the books of the Bible (even the tales of Jewish heroines like Judith and Esther) are not life stories presented within a specific and authentic historical moment. Christianity emerges from the story of a real man; a man who, Christians came to believe, was God's son.

At the same time it's important to keep clearly in mind that the gospel writers did not set about writing biography in the way a modern writer would. What mattered to them was the proclamation of Christ's death and resurrection, and the evangelists chose what to include and what to exclude on the basis of its relationship to their resurrected Savior. While modern scholarship tries to determine those elements of these narratives that could conceivably have the kind of factual basis we would look for in biography as we understand that term, the loosely chronological narratives of the Gospels are far less interested in where, when, and who than in announcing the good news of Jesus' life and death as Son of God and as redeemer.

The Kernel

After Jesus' death his disciples began telling other people about him using very brief biographical summaries of what they took to be the central events of his life. In a striking, early example that may be typical of the earliest preaching of the apostles, Peter, made bold by the Holy Spirit on Pentecost, bursts out to the streets of Jerusalem to preach publicly, and this is what he says:

> You that are Israelites, listen to what I have to say: Jesus of Nazareth, a man attested to you by God with deeds of power, wonders, and signs that God did through him among you, as you yourselves know—this man, handed over to you according to the definite plan and foreknowledge of God, you crucified and killed by the hands of those outside the law. But God raised him up, having freed him from death, because it was impossible for him to be held in its power.... (Acts 2:22–24)

Here is almost certainly one of the first brief, crucial summaries of belief—the first creeds—of the emerging Christian faith. Central to this message is the paradox of Jesus: first, the Son of God, who acted according to "the definite plan and foreknowledge of God," has died, and died a terrible death. The proclamation begins with the emphatic assertion of what reasonable, worldly, material-minded people would regard as failure. Jesus has been killed by his enemies. This is followed by a second assertion, again something that any sensible person would laugh at: Jesus came back to life. This is the narrative kernel, the seed of Christianity, and from it all Christian narrative has grown.

Surrounding these two assertions we can already see certain kinds of amplifications emerging, details about the humiliation and physical suffering Jesus had to endure, the injustice of what happened to him, and how he became a victim first of his own Jewish kinsmen and then later of the gentiles who were ruling Jerusalem.

What followed these early kernel statements was the compiling of further accounts of Jesus' sayings and teachings as well as the events of his life into narratives called "good news," or gospel. The church chose to accept four such narratives for its sacred scriptures.

The Story of Jesus and the Catholic Imagination

Important consequences emerged from the fact that Christians were storytellers and that the story of redemption and salvation they were telling was a biography located in a specific place at a specific historical moment. A number of the formal characteristics of biography as a genre, and of this biography in particular, were to have a foundational influence on the way that Christians thought and felt, and on the emergence of a Catholic imagination. So deeply embedded in Western culture are these characteristics that at first they may seem so self-evident as not to merit consideration, but thinking about them *as* foundational helps in our analysis of how Catholics imagine.

Time

Time and history were from the start crucial structural characteristics of Catholic imagining. In the story of Jesus, time takes on meaning. There is a period when Jesus teaches and heals and encounters a mixture of opposition and acceptance. Then, there are a series of pivotal events: his torture, death, and resurrection. The nature of reality was different before these events took place: the world was damaged by evil beyond the power of any human effort to make it better. The nature of reality then, at one historical moment, altered fundamentally. After the saving events of Jesus' final days, each human person could hope in salvation.

Jesus' life, then, from a Catholic perspective, changes fundamentally the nature of all the rest of history.

TYPOLOGICAL THINKING: REREADING THE PAST

Looking back on everything that preceded Jesus, Christians
now found that the past took on a whole constellation of new
meanings. For example, all the utterances of the Jewish prophets,
vague and incoherent as some of them might have seemed, could
now be explained as anticipating Jesus' life and death. Additionally,
crucial events from the earlier history of the Jewish people could be
understood as types anticipating his coming. When at God's command Abraham takes his son Isaac up onto a mountaintop and prepares to kill him in sacrifice, only to be stopped at the last minute
by the intervention of an angel, he becomes a type of the later narrative of the life of Jesus, in which God himself does not halt the
killing and permits *his* son to die the sacrificial death on Calvary. In
this way, all of the past can now be restructured and reimagined.
The story of Abraham and Isaac seen from a Christian perspective
plays a new and different role in sacred history.

Such thinking proved deeply repugnant to believing Jews
then and today, but it became fundamental to how Christians read
the Bible and understood history.[2]

PROPHETIC THINKING: IMAGINING THE FUTURE

In much the same way, the gospel narratives, joined later by
the prophetic Book of Revelation, reformulate human understanding of the future. With individual and group salvation now possible,
Christianity looks forward with certitude to how history will come
to an end. Jesus himself in extended apocalyptic statements describes
the final days, and Revelation amplifies what he has to say and then
provides a detailed description of the heavenly paradise.

The traditional formulation of historical dates created by the
Catholic Church using the Gregorian calendar (adopted in 1582)
distinguishes these two historical eras as BC (before Christ) and AD
(*anno domini*, in the year of our Lord), and thus reflects this early
Christian understanding of the meaning of history.

All of this implies that Catholics find meaning in time and that
they think and imagine in terms of time and of history. They make
distinctions between different eras and understand what was hap-

pening at one time and place in terms of its relationship to the larger structures of salvation history. An event before Jesus' life occurred in a world fundamentally different from an event that happened after his resurrection.

Preceding Catholicism, Jewish religious thought had already evolved a theory of sacred history that narrated God's choice of the Jewish people, his divine care for them (which included finding them a homeland), and his promise to send a messiah as their leader. In Greece, rational, scientific historical writing had begun in the fifth century BC, with the work of Herodotus and Thucydides. Catholicism was to inherit and to use aspects of both traditions in its own distinctly historicist way of seeing and understanding every human event.

Narrative Structure

The narratives of Jesus' life have a distinct shape, a shape repeated in all four Gospels. Jesus begins his public life of teaching and healing. He encounters opposition. The conflict intensifies until his enemies arrest and kill him. Three days later he rises from death and rejoins his followers. Like all good stories (as Aristotle tells us in *The Poetics*), the Gospels have a beginning, middle, and end. They enjoy a tight, self-contained aesthetic wholeness. They have led Christians to value unitary narratives, to look for beginnings and for conclusions, and to expect structure and meaning in life events rather than randomness and senselessness. The Gospels appear headed toward tragedy, but in the miraculous last pages they switch suddenly to the genre of comedy. The narrative, as it turns out in a moment of paradoxical surprise, was not about failure, death, and destruction but about new life and joyous celebration. The interplay between tragedy and comedy was to become central to the formulation of Christian storytelling and a Christian understanding of history and of individual lives.

Characters

Clustered around the figure of Jesus are characters who take on distinctive roles. There is Peter, the leader of the disciples, impulsive but ardent. There are the sons of Zebedee, unhappily ambitious. There is John, emotional, passive, and yet unlike all the others nervy enough to stand at the foot of the cross. And then there is Judas, twisted by false values, ultimately betraying his master. At the beginning of two versions, Matthew and Luke, one reads about Mary, the mother of Jesus, who then appears intermittently throughout the story. In the Gospel of John she arrives, with extraordinary bravery one suspects, at the foot of the cross. There are Jesus' enemies, the Pharisees and Sadducees, bringing him up short, challenging what he has to say, mocking him in public.

As this list illustrates, the characters and events from the narratives of the life of Jesus evoke strong emotions. We laugh at Peter stepping off the boat, out onto the surface of the water, as Jesus comes walking toward him on the waves and suddenly discovering that as an ordinary mortal he's sinking. We watch with mounting alarm Judas turning against Jesus. We respond with sympathy and admiration to Mary's stoic loyalty and suffering.

But all of these other characters fade into supporting roles when one considers the narrative portrait of Jesus that each Gospel develops. The Jesus of the Gospels is anything but simple. He is full of what appear at first to be contradictions, a man at times tender and yielding, at other times angry and confrontational. Though he speaks candidly and at length, mystery obscures his inner thoughts and the reach of his intentions. The Gospels portray other people as baffled by Jesus, and two thousand years have not been enough time to figure him out. This Jesus is a man of strong feelings. He weeps openly at the death of a friend, speaks cuttingly of those who oppose him, tenderly caresses the children who seem attracted to him, and in the end is so afraid of what lies ahead that he begs God the Father to release him from his imminent death. The Jesus of the Gospels is deeply involved in the material world. Meeting two blind men, he mixes his own spittle and mud and puts it on their eyes (Matt 9:29). He takes the hand of a dead corpse and brings a little girl back to life (Matt 9:25). He deals with people suffering from leprosy, people who are crippled, and victims of diabolical possession. He sails on boats, rides donkeys, gets hungry and tired. Physically tough, he endures crucifixion for hours, and the Romans have to finish him off by piercing his heart with a lance.

Setting

The gospel narratives carry the listener or reader through the Palestine of Jesus' day. They show us the villages at twilight, the diseased and impoverished crying out to Jesus for help. A woman who cannot stop bleeding secretly snatches at the hem of his robe hoping for healing. We see Jesus and his disciples, many of them fishermen, sailing on the Sea of Galilee, and we see crowds gathering on a remote hillside hoping he will speak to them. We watch Jesus entering Jerusalem for the last time, teaching in the Temple itself, joining his followers in a private upper room for the Passover supper, and later praying in an olive garden. We follow him as he is dragged into the barracks of the Roman soldiers, brought before the local Roman official for judgment, paraded on a platform before jeering crowds, forced to march through the streets, and finally crucified on a hill while his enemies mock him.

Implications for Catholicism and the Arts

There are important implications for the future of the Catholic imagination in all of these matters.

Realism

The same sort of material concreteness, particularity, and realism that were so crucial to the way in which Jesus spoke and the way in which he imagined the world reappear in the way the evangelists wrote down these biographical narratives of his life. As I hope my lists and summaries suggest, they have all the elements of an excellent work of literary narration. They frame Jesus in terms of historical time and place. They put him in the context of Roman-occupied Israel and the political and religious conflicts of his day. They observe Jesus as typical of the Jewish culture of his era, showing him teaching in synagogues, deeply knowledgeable about Jewish beliefs and customs, and widely read in Jewish sacred writings. They depict his family, friends, and enemies. They picture him in well-known settings: countryside, village, city. They build up out of hundreds of details a complex portrait of Jesus as a man, a portrait as richly convincing as one would expect in the best works of fiction or the most insightful biographies.

These stories indelibly validated for Catholics the importance and the meaning of the material world, of individual people, of particular places and times. They led to a nearly incessant drive for concreteness and signification in the Catholic imagination.

For painters, sculptors, the makers of mosaics and glass, these narratives provided an inexhaustible fund of subjects for depiction. From the first pictures sketched out on the walls of the catacombs to Salvador Dali's dreamlike *Sacrament of the Last Supper* (Figure 14), these narratives have endlessly revivified the art of picturing. The same thing is true for poets like Rilke, ready to explore the emotional overtones of particular gospel scenes and of the episodes from Jesus' life.

Figure 14. Salvador Dali (1904–1989),
Sacrament of the Last Supper.

Narrative

In succeeding centuries the Gospels would provide materials for plays, narrative poems, stories, and novels. The way in which the Gospels are written, their emphasis on the narrative elements listed previously, is one of the reasons *why* they have proven such a rich resource for the arts. At least at one level, it is *because* the evan-

gelists, like the Jesus whose life they tell, were themselves so completely alive to the art of writing narrative that their work has
become perennially inspirational to later generations of artists. It is
a central reason why the art of narrative grew as it did in a Western
culture dominated by Christianity.

And it's important to understand that the nature of this inspiration does not lie only in providing specific scenes, situations, or
stories that later artists adopted and revoiced. While there are innu-
merable paintings of the Annunciation, the power of the Gospels to
provoke the imagination does not stop there. In addition to inspiring
literal retelling, the characteristics of gospel stories— the kinds of
people, conflicts, narrative movement, and closure they employ—
were to reemerge in endless variations on the basic tale in narrative
poems, plays, novels, stories, and movies. The Gospels shaped the
instinct in Christians to look at, think about, and use material particularity. They led Christians to value individual personality, emotion,
moral choice, and to try to understand why specific people make certain decisions and live in certain ways. They established a paradigm
for a kind of heroic story, and they raised the problematic narrative
tension between tragic and comic closure. Catholic fictions about
people struggling to discern God and God's will in many different
contexts—such as political and religious oppression in a novel by
Graham Greene (an alcoholic priest in Mexico in *The Power and the
Glory* [1940]), or the uncertainties of justice versus mercy in a
movie by John Ford (a cowboy goes off in search of a young woman
kidnapped and raped by Comanches in *The Searchers* [1956]), or
the nature of guilt and true repentance in a poetic narrative such as
Sir Gawain and the Green Knight (to save his life an otherwise
faultless knight must lie [late fourteenth century])—ultimately all
trace their source back to the gospel narratives of Jesus.

A Continuing Witness

This, certainly, was not the reason that the evangelists wrote
their narratives. They were setting down the facts of the history of
salvation. In doing so they knew they were providing a paradigm
for living a good life. The story of Jesus was intended to bring faith
and to galvanize people to live as Jesus had lived, to transform the
inner being of the listener or reader. What we have been considering

in the last few pages is a later, perhaps an unexpected series of con-sequences. And yet the minute that we think again about the theory of the *Creator Spiritus,* that the Spirit of God present in the church directs what people do through the centuries, we must reverse the implications of that last sentence. The question of the conscious intentions of the evangelists is secondary at best. Those writers worked at the highest pitch of their art to present, powerfully and convincingly, the essential elements of the life of Jesus. As the church they helped to initiate grew and evolved, the same spirit of belief, the same power of insight that animated them filled the minds and imaginations of later Catholics, such as Dante and Michelangelo and Beethoven, and their works in many different artistic media continued, in a wide variety of ways, to bear witness to the life story that the evangelists first set down in language.

The next seven chapters examine at length early examples of this process. They look at some of the ways in which Catholic art emerged within a variety of different contexts from the intersection of existing cultures and the developing Catholic imagination.

PART II

THE EMERGENCE OF CATHOLIC ART

Expansion, Accretion, Synthesis

Introduction to Part II

"Fundamentally, all art is religious, or, if that is
considered too sweeping, all religion, which occupies
the middle ground between the visible and the
invisible, unfolds, perhaps unconsciously, on the
esthetic plane."[1]

The Working of the *Creator Spiritus*

When the apostles began spreading the good news of Jesus
Christ, there were no Christian pictures or statues. There were no
books or buildings. There was no music, no ritual. What existed
and was already vividly real and deeply felt were the imaginative
forms of expression familiar to the earliest Christians from their
own past experiences and histories, whether Jewish or pagan. The
members of the early church worked their way forward through
time, adopting, adapting, discarding, and, as time went on, developing new forms as individual members of its highly varied communities participated in the communal exercise of imagination
inspired and inspirited by the imagination of Jesus.

We have already considered the essential elements of Jesus'
imagination. We have looked at how he used imagination to teach.
We have seen how Jesus' followers shaped the telling of his life into
the biographical narratives known as Gospels. Now we are ready to
take a look at a few selected examples of the first Christian pictures,
buildings, and texts. In studying them we can trace some of the
ways in which the germinal energy of Jesus' imagination was at
work within the early church. The examples we consider span the

first eight hundred years of Christianity. They come from the ever-expanding radius of Christian peoples. We are particularly interested in what happened with those later converts whose cultural imagination was further and further removed from the Mediterranean world that Jesus knew.

Our examples begin with the first surviving writings by a Christian convert from modern-day Turkey and then continue with third-century Syrians living near the Euphrates River on the easternmost border of the Roman Empire. After this come third-century citizens of the center of urban Rome, a fifth-century Spaniard living near what is now Barcelona, ninth-century Celtic Irish monks from tiny islands off the coast of Scotland, ninth-century Frankish artists working at Reims in what is now north central France, and, from the same era, a Saxon poet writing in the monastery at Fulda in northern Germany. As each new cultural group adopted the Catholic imagination they adapted it as well, integrating it with the experiences that were a specific aspect of their own lives. In the process of adoption and adaptation, they found new meaning in old instances, extending the original Christian vision. This, as the next seven chapters suggest, was a process not of distortion but of fuller discernment and progressive development, a vital phase in an evolving understanding of the meaning of Jesus.

What the imagination of Jesus and the constitution of the early church offered these new members of ever more remote communities was a synthetic vision: a way of seeing God, the created world, the human community, and the self in a distinctive way. We might summarize the vision this way:

1. Catholic belief in *incarnation* established *a metaphysic*: a way of seeing, understanding, and working with the world—a world understood to be God's creation, a reflection of God's will, and after the coming of Jesus a world transformed because God had taken on the body and the life of a man. From this metaphysic emerged a Catholic way of seeing and of representing.

2. Catholic belief in *redemption* established a primal or kernel *narrative*, and this story had the power to structure time, experience, action, and choice along distinctly

Christian lines. It served to establish a narrative paradigm for how to live and thus gave meaning to every aspect of life. Since the originating story tells of a fallen world, the appearance of a redeemer, and salvation through self-sacrifice, now each new Christian could recognize the call to define his or her own self in parallel: I am like Jesus; I am Jesus in this moment; my life should resemble his. My story should relive the kernel narrative. From this narrative emerged a way of telling the story of life and of salvation.

3. Catholic belief in *the sacraments* established *a rhythm* in Christian life, structuring the timing and the character of human encounters with the divine and with the community according to the hours of the day, the seasons of the year, the phases of human life. From this rhythm were to emerge the rhythms of Christian poetry, music, and dance.

4. Catholic belief in the centrality of *community* established *a context* for living, giving structure and meaning to the self in terms of others. If redemption led to the understanding that the self always exists in an interpersonal relationship with Jesus, then community led to the inevitable parallel conclusion that the self always exists in an interaction with other people, an interaction defined by love and by the need to care for the other. Within this context Christians soon came to shape the physical character of their surrounding world: constructing buildings of many types and even at times altering the face of the earth itself to correspond to their communal needs.

Creative Challenges for the New Christian Community

Du Bourguet, author of the magisterial historical study *Early Christian Art*, argues that "all religion," since it "occupies the middle ground between the visible and the invisible," must unfold "on the esthetic plane."[2] This was to be particularly true for Christianity, because the very fact of the incarnation necessarily led to a desire for representation. With Jesus, God became a man, and his followers saw him, spoke with him, and touched him (see the First Letter of John 1:1). It was unavoidable that after his death they began telling stories about him, reenacting certain crucial moments of his life in sacramental rituals, and as time passed fashioning images of him for those who had never seen him. Because Jesus had taken on human flesh, flesh had become deified. Picturing that flesh became an act of sacred witness. Because his life on earth became the subject of stories, and perhaps even more important because Jesus was himself a storyteller, Christians told stories too, about Jesus, and about many other things as well within the context of a Christian vision. Those stories took on a sacred dimension. Because Jesus had used things and gestures in his teaching and healing, and particularly because just before his death he instructed his followers to used bread and wine in remembering him, Christians soon generated sacred rituals and objects used in those rituals. Because Jesus told his followers to love one another and to pray together, they soon required buildings in which to care for those in need and in which to worship. These became places where the sacred actions of Jesus' life could be reenacted by those who followed him. The invisible truths that Christians believed soon led them to use the arts of the physical worlds from which they came and hence to work on what du Bourguet calls "the esthetic plane." It was the Catholic imagination that animated and gave a spiritual generative power to that process.

All of this suggests that the early Christian communities found themselves facing what might strike us now as a challenging list of artistic demands. They were setting out to fill that "middle ground" between the visible and the invisible with useful and valid forms.

In this process, they had to be cautious. The cultures from which they came, Judaic or Greco-Roman, already had highly successful and very influential ways of writing, picturing, building, and worshiping. The first Christians had to distinguish carefully between elements from those cultures that they could usefully adapt to their own purposes and elements that might lead them, perhaps unawares, in dangerous directions. There is a useful example of this in how the earliest Christians designed their churches. When the Roman persecutions finally ended and fourth-century Christians could build in the open, they consciously chose not to adopt the plan of the Roman temple. Instead they chose a very different model, the basilica, a large hall in which people assembled to do business but which had a semicircular apse at one end to hold a sacred image (see Figure 15). Early Christians did not want any kind of architectural link with the Roman temple. They wished to express dramatically the distinct difference in their beliefs. They may even have feared that if they were to erect new versions of the old sacred buildings, they might be tempted to revert somehow to pagan practices. Instead they chose to use a form that was free of any strong religious associations. That kind of decision faced Christians wherever they began extending the aesthetic expression of their beliefs.

Figure 15. Roman civic basilica
The basilica in Pompeii (shown here in a restored state) was the oldest and most important public building in the city. After AD 62, when an earthquake caused the roof to fall in, it served as the seat of the judicial system and for business-men's meetings. The basilica evolved into the most significant form of Christian architecture.

As we noted in chapter 5, Christianity is fundamentally narra-tive in character. In his study of the relationship between art and rit-ual, S. G. F. Brandon puts it this way:

> That much of the art of the Christian Church has been of a narrative kind is surely due to the essentially historical character of its original tradition...[since] the faith [was] derived from historical persons....The earliest records...were written in narrative form....The very doctrine of the Incarnation... made narrative art a natural form of expression.[3]

There was, however, an absence of formal precedents. The Hebrew Bible did not offer a model for sacred biography. That had to be invented. So too did Christians have to invent religious autobiography—personal narratives describing the growth in belief of individual people. The Hebrew Bible is rich in poetry, however, and Christians adopted wholesale the Jewish hymns, making the Psalms central to their own prayer life. But as time passed, Christians wished to voice belief and the feelings provoked by belief in other poetic forms, and they found themselves adapting the expressive strategies of pagan writing to fashion new Christian lyric and epic poems.

Making pictures presented early Christians with a myriad of problems. There were no handy pictorial traditions for representing the events of the New Testament. The nativity, the calling of the disciples, Jesus' working of miracles, the last supper, the crucifixion, the resurrection—these were all new scenes never depicted before. The way the Gospels are written made the job even harder because they are so sparing in their use of visual description. Jesus, for example, is never described, and so we don't know anything about his appearance: how tall he was, the color of his hair and eyes, and so on. All that had to be imagined. Jewish religious tradition had forbidden the picturing of God and the sacred persons from Jewish history.[4] As a result, the same problems that faced people wishing to make pictures of Jesus faced people wishing to make pictures of Noah and the flood, Abraham and Isaac on the mountain, Moses parting the Red Sea, and so on. What early Christian painters did find available was a superabundance of pagan images. Here, again, they had to use caution.

Christian ritual and sacramental life, rooted as it was in Judaic practice, had to find its own way. The sacred ritual of the Mass, while emerging from the Jewish Seder, had to be sufficiently different to mark it as a departure from earlier practice. Amplifying and enriching that and other ritual activities necessitated the invention of new prayers, songs, patterns of ritual movement, ornaments, and costumes to express what was innovative and novel in their new religion.

As they worked with each one of these artistic challenges, early Christians took what they could from the past, adapted it, and made it their own, finding in the process a growing enrichment in their understanding of themselves and their beliefs. At times, ingeniously, they were able to draw out of earlier cultures latent meanings that had perhaps never been noticed before—elements that had been implicit, but unrecognized, until Christian adaptation brought them into the light.

Overview

Here are the examples of the evolving Catholic imagination to be considered in the following chapters:

CHAPTER 6: Autobiography
The earliest efforts to construct a personal, autobiographical account of what it means to be a Christian, found in the Epistles of Saint Paul, written probably before 67.

CHAPTER 7: Architecture and Fresco Painting
The only surviving Christian house-church at Dura-Europus in eastern Syria, ca. 230.

CHAPTER 8: Architecture and Fresco Painting
The structure of and images from the Catacomb of Priscilla in Rome, made sometime after 210.

CHAPTER 9: Lyric Poetry
From eastern Spain, the book of poems by Prudentius titled *Cathemerinon*, before 405.

CHAPTER 10: Abstract Decorative Themes
The elaborate illuminations for the Irish-Celtic *Book of Kells*, ca. 800.

CHAPTER 11: Picturing Poetry
From Reims, the illustrations for the Psalms found in *The Utrecht Psalter,* ca. 820.

CHAPTER 12: Epic Narrative

From the Saxons of northern Germany, an epic poem now called *The Heliand,* describing the life of Christ, written around 830.

That's the menu. Now, here comes the feast.

CHAPTER SIX

Saint Paul
and Autobiography

Paul's Letters

Characteristics and Significance

In the epistles of Saint Paul we encounter the earliest known Christian writings. Some, perhaps most, of his letters to Christian communities may have been written before the gospel narratives were set down. They are full of surprises.

Paul, a devout Jew, began his public life persecuting the followers of Jesus. But famously, on the road to Damascus something extraordinary happened to him, and he not only converted but soon became one of the most effective Christian missionaries in history. In his letters we can see for the first time the impact of the Catholic imagination on a stranger, and right here at the start we see how flexible and adaptive the Catholic imagination would be to the experience, the worldview, the imaginative consciousness of others. Paul adopts what he learns of Jesus' teaching and of the preaching of the early church, but he internalizes everything, makes it a part of his way of thinking and of perceiving, and as he begins to write what we find is a Pauline Catholic imagination at work. Paul was no ordinary man. His was a powerful, independent, creative personality. He accepted the Christian faith, yes, but in so doing he helped to develop, even to transform it. He is one of the very first examples of the *Creator Spiritus* at work within a man and within history. His letters, among other things, constitute the first written Christian theology—that is, they are the first conscious intellectual effort to make theological sense out of Jesus, to imagine in quasi-abstract and general terms the meaning of the salvation Jesus had won for all people and to trace the pattern of salvation history.

Paul writes to communities he had converted, and the letters have a pastoral intent. They are full of the business of the early church. In them Paul works at resolving disputes among the early Christians, he gives them instructions about ethics and religious belief, and issues warnings about the danger of false teaching coming from opponents of his, people who, he thinks, "proclaim Christ from envy and rivalry..." (Phil 1:15).

Figure 16. Saint Paul
After the Byzantine emperor Justinian I invaded Italy and conquered Ravenna, Ravenna became the seat of Byzantine government in Italy. Among the city's famous sixth- and seventh-century Christian mosaics is this depiction of Saint Paul from the vault mosaics in the Archbishop's Palace.

Paul writes in a highly personal way. His letters come from an intensely particular man given to strongly voiced views and high emotion aimed directly at the reader. They are rich with references to himself. He understands that selfhood in terms of relationships: his relationship to the Christ he follows and his relationship to the people he has converted. In both cases the relationship is full of love. His address to the people of Thessalonica is typical: "We were gentle among you, like a nurse tenderly caring for her own children. So deeply do we care for you that we are determined to share with you not only the gospel of God but also our own selves, because you have become very dear to us" (1 Thess 2:7–8).

Paul's letters entered the canon of sacred Christian writings and thus became the subject of constant subsequent reading and reflection by virtually every believing Christian. They are second only to the Gospels in their formative impact on Christian thinking and belief. As with the teaching of Jesus, it will be very useful in our explorations of the Catholic imagination to consider the nature of Paul's imagination. To do this we look only at those epistles that modern biblical scholarship attributes to Paul's hand: the Letters to the Romans, 1 and 2 Corinthians, Galatians, Philippians, the First Letter to the Thessalonians, and the Letter to Philemon. For many centuries other early Christian letters were also thought to be by Paul and thus were accepted into the Christian canon. But there is more than enough information in the letters mentioned for us to begin an exploration of Pauline imagination. The analytical strategy we will use at first resembles the way we tried to get at Jesus' imagination: by looking at how Paul pictures his world.

A Pauline Imagination

PAUL AND JESUS

Perhaps the biggest surprise in Paul's writings is how little they have to say about the Jesus of the Gospels. Though the Gospels may not have been written down when Paul sent his letters, the stories on which the Gospels are based must certainly have been circulating throughout the early Christian communities, and Paul must have known them. But in his epistles we hear little or nothing about the many well-known details of Jesus' life. For example, Paul doesn't write about the calling of the apostles, about Jesus' miracles, about Jesus' encounters with enemies and friends. The barest minimum of the kernel story of redemption seems to be sufficient for him—what Paul calls the "clear picture of Jesus Christ crucified" (Gal 3:1 NJB). And another surprise: Paul makes no efforts to refer to the parables of Jesus, nor most of the time does he make specific reference to Jesus' teaching through direct allusion or quotation. One might imagine that virtually any early Christian in writing about faith and salvation would refer to the comforting image of the good shepherd. But not Paul.

Paul's imagination too is strikingly independent of Jesus'. Even the parallels reveal their differences. We began our consideration of Jesus' world with lists of objects, people, places, and activities that Jesus talks about. If we turn to Paul's epistles we get much shorter lists. Elements of daily life, for example: Paul refers to things people make and use such as clay pots, gongs, mirrors, a flute, a bugle. He employs images of elements from nature: light and dark, the stars, day and night. Paul uses even these images sparingly.

Paul does imagine the simple, country life that Jesus pictures, a world of agricultural work and the cycles of organic life. But such images are always being used as analogies in the process of teaching abstract theological and ethical ideas. The image of the seed, for example, so favored by Jesus, becomes in Paul's writing an analogy for conversion. Paul writes of his teaching, "I planted, Apollos watered, but God gave the growth" (1 Cor 3:6). Explaining the resurrection he uses the seed analogy again. "What you sow does not come to life unless it dies. And as for what you sow, you do not sow the body that is to be, but a bare seed, perhaps..." (1 Cor 15:36–37). The difference from Jesus' use of such images is dramatic. Speaking in parables, Jesus created a fictional world that his listeners could enter into imaginatively, and Jesus expected them to find the implications of his stories on their own. Paul uses similar images, but as illustrations of theological ideas that he is simultaneously driving home though abstract argumentation. His mind thrives on ideas and on the generalization of idea into theory. He leaves little or no space for imaginative work in the minds of his readers.[1]

Paul's references to seed, wheat, and breadmaking seem to emerge less from a familiarity with country life and more from an existing Christian sacramental practice. In Paul's letters it is already clear that bread and wine have become dominant religious symbols. Here, for example, is Paul writing about the eucharistic celebration: "The cup of blessing that we bless, is it not a sharing in the blood of Christ? The bread that we break, is it not a sharing in the body of Christ? Because there is one bread, we who are many are one body, for we all partake of the one bread" (1 Cor 10:16–17). The churches he serves not only have a defined, ritualized sacramental practice, but Paul is reading symbolic theological meaning into its details, such as the one loaf illustrating the unity of the believing community. This kind of imagining is very different from Jesus' spare storytelling.[2]

COMBAT

If we turn to other Pauline images we get another kind of difference. Jesus, as we saw, sometimes imagines human relationships and human social systems in terms of division and conflict. He has any number of stories about separating wheat from chaff and sheep from goats. Such stories can be full of ominous warning. Believers had better join the kingdom or they risk being thrown into the outer darkness. This way of imagining life choices and the future is even more pronounced in Paul. His imagination is full of conflict with enemies: the pagans, the Jews, teachers of false Christian doctrine, converts who are falling away from the faith, even devils. This leads to a Pauline fondness for images of struggle and combat. He imagines belief in terms of warfare: "Put on the breastplate of faith and love, and for a helmet the hope of salvation" (1 Thess 5:8). He sees his own Christian witness this way: "For the weapons of our warfare are not merely human, but they have divine power to destroy strongholds. We destroy arguments and every proud obstacle raised up against the knowledge of God, and we take every thought captive to obey Christ" (2 Cor 10:4).

Even when Paul isn't writing about warfare, there is a sense of tension and endangerment in his world. Jesus imagined his final return to this world through stories about a bridegroom or a householder. Paul warns his readers, "You yourselves know very well that the day of the Lord will come like a thief in the night. When they say, 'There is peace and security', then sudden destruction will come upon them...and there will be no escape!" (1 Thess 5:2). While

Jesus issued similar warnings, this sinister image is foreign to Jesus' mind. So too is Paul's frequent use of images of competition. He thinks of his life and his work in terms of a foot race or of boxing: "Do you not know that in a race the runners all compete, but only one receives the prize? Run in such a way that you may win it" (1 Cor 9:24); and "I do not run aimlessly, nor do I box as though beating the air; but I punish my body and enslave it, so that after proclaiming to others I myself should not be disqualified" (1 Cor 9:26–27. Winning is his aim: "Not that I have already...reached the goal; but I press on to make it my own" (Phil 3:12).

Figure 17. Damascus with Roman city wall
Saint Paul—then known as Saul—was headed to the great Roman city of Damascus, shown here with its Roman city wall, to persecute the followers of Jesus. It was on the road to Damascus that he had his dramatic conversion experience.

Paul's imagined world is the world of ancient Rome—the army as a profession, the imperial wars, the stadium back home with its Greco-Roman sporting events and its competitive athletes vying for the laurel wreath. This is a world foreign to the farms and small towns of Jesus' typical imaginings. Paul's life had been lived in a different world. Though he was a Jew and rigorously trained in Jewish belief and tradition, he had been born and raised in a Jewish community resident not in Israel but in Tarsus of Cilicia (what today is southeastern Turkey), and pagan Hellenistic culture was as familiar to him as Judaism. In Paul's writing we see for the first time the Catholic imagination expanding and diversifying, acquiring the flexibility to welcome the urban pagan by seeing things from a quite different perspective. Paul finds a further, Christian meaning in some of the root values of pagan culture—for example, that the life of virtue can be a battle or a race. This kind of analogy came to have powerful resonance for later Christians, especially when faced with persecution. Jesus had insisted upon his vision against many kinds of opposition, but in the end he accepted the cup of death from his Father. Paul gives bracing authentication to Jesus' nonviolent passivity through his use of certain pugnacious, aggressive images that helped prepare early Christian martyrs for the trials of endurance they faced.

A Pauline Theory of History

Paul had been a Pharisee, and his writings make it clear that he was deeply read in the Hebrew Scriptures. He absorbed that Jewish tradition in which he had been reared and went on to help formulate the concepts of incarnation and redemption and to frame them in terms of time. In the process Paul imagined history in terms of a specific form, a specific paradigm. Paul saw history in linear terms. It is Paul who first declares Jesus' redemptive act to be the central event in the chronicle of humanity (an issue we touched upon in chapter 5). This he then worked into a much broader conceptual panorama.

Paul imagines a beginning of time, the moment when all of creation came from an act of God. He argues that the consequences of that act continue to clearly reflect and bespeak the God who originally made all things (Rom 1:20).

Then came Adam's sin and humanity's fall. That is why "God gave them up in the lusts of their hearts to impurity, to the degrading of their bodies among themselves, because they exchanged the truth about God for a lie…" (Rom 1:24–25).

At various points in his letters, Paul makes reference to the subsequent history of the Covenant: God's call to Abraham and his progeny, the Jewish people. He then comes to Jesus, who

though he was in the form of God, did not regard equality with
God as something to be exploited, but emptied himself, taking
the form of a slave…and became obedient to the point of death—
even death on a cross. Therefore God also highly exalted him and
gave him the name that is above every name, so that…every
tongue should confess that Jesus Christ is Lord.…" (Phil 2:6–11)

This vision climaxes in Paul's articulation of the theology of
Christian redemption—the first time[3] this concept appears in written form: "Since all have sinned and fall short of the glory of God;
they are now justified by his grace as a gift, through the redemption
that is in Christ Jesus, whom God put forward as a sacrifice of
atonement by his blood…" (Rom 3:23–25).

Now Paul and his converts wait for the Second Coming confident
that "the testimony of Christ has been strengthened among you—so that
you are not lacking in any spiritual gift as you wait for the revealing of
our Lord Jesus Christ. He will also strengthen you to the end, so that you
may be blameless on the day of our Lord Jesus Christ" (1 Cor 1:6–9).
On that final day in history, "in a moment, in the twinkling of an eye,
the trumpet will sound, and the dead will be raised imperishable, and
we will be changed. For this perishable body must put on imperisha-
bility, and this mortal body must put on immortality" (1 Cor 15:52–53).

This historical paradigm, so familiar in Christian cultures for
two thousand years, was something new when Paul wrote his letters
to former pagans who before their conversion had scarcely believed
in an afterlife at all and who had often conceived of history in terms
of repeating cycles or as a steady decline from an earlier age of gold
to the current age of lead.[4] Paul's moving Christian optimism was to
remake the way in which people imagined past, present, and future.
Its theoretical ambitiousness, like his use of traditional imagery for
the sake of theological exposition, indicates how he drew from Jesus
and from earlier Jewish historical narratives latent or implicit ideas
and developed them into his own conceptual formulations.

Typology

Paul did repeat two ways of speaking and thinking that are
already present and significant in Jesus' teaching. Each is anchored
in the way both Jesus and Paul imagined the nature of reality itself.

We have seen that in his references to Jonah, Jesus uses typo-logical examples: stories from Jewish tradition are seen to be antic-ipations—or types—of what was later to happen in Jesus' life and death. Paul too uses typological thinking and at times delights in elaborating on it at great length: "And all were baptized into Moses in the cloud and in the sea, and all ate the same spiritual food, and all drank the same spiritual drink. For they drank from the spiritual rock that followed them, and the rock was Christ" (1 Cor 10:2–4). In this complex passage Paul draws parallels between the Jewish people fleeing the Egyptians and passing from almost certain death into a new life by crossing the Red Sea, and Christians who leave their old lives, pass through the cleansing waters of the sacrament of baptism, and enter into a new life. If in the desert the people of Israel were fed by God's direct aid, so now Christians are fed by the sacrament of the Eucharist. When there was no water in the desert, God directed Moses to strike a rock, and saving water gushed forth. For Christians, Christ becomes the new rock from whom the water of baptism and the wine of Eucharist come flooding.

Paul here not only elaborates on the symbolic parallels between Jewish history and Christian faith, but he also asserts, audaciously, that the Jews themselves centuries before the coming of Jesus were already dependent upon the salvation only Jesus could win. Even in those former times Christ was already the sacred rock from which flowed the waters of salvation. Indeed, in another epistle Paul is so brash as to insist that the Jewish people were unable, up until his own day, even to understand their own sacred scriptures, because the crucial event of their history, Jesus, had not yet occurred. "Their minds were hardened. Indeed, to this very day, when they hear the reading of the old covenant, that same veil is still there, since only in Christ is it set aside" (2 Cor 3:14). Only through typological interpretation, Paul asserts, can the real meaning of Hebrew Scripture be discerned. This assertion emerges directly from the way Paul imagines history. Since Jesus' coming is the central event of all time, it redefines the meaning of everything that preceded it as well as everything that would come later. It is the single event that gives the ultimate, revelatory meaning to every other event within the framework of historical time.

Paul's habit of typological reading of the Hebrew Scriptures, perhaps inspired by the few instances in which Jesus does the same thing, was to become in the early centuries of Christianity one of the central ways of imagining the life of Christ and of the church. We follow how this works a little later on (in chapters 7 and 8) when we consider the first surviving Christian pictures that almost constantly employ this typological form of thinking.

Paradox

Paul, like Jesus, also delights in the paradoxes that emerge, as we saw in chapter 3, from the double vision of the Catholic imagination. Writing of the Christian belief that he shares with his converts, Paul insists that "God chose what is foolish in the world to shame the wise; God chose what is weak in the world to shame the strong; God chose what is low and despised in the world, things that are not, to reduce to nothing things that are, so that no one might boast in the presence of God" (1 Cor 1:27–29). Those people who, measured by worldly standards, seem smart, powerful, and worthy, are in the paradoxical inversions of God's plan far less important than the people who seem to worldly minds stupid, weak, and contemptible. From the double perspective of Christian paradox, the fools are the only people who are truly wise.[5]

In his use both of typology and of paradox we can see Paul taking up forms of thinking and a manner of expression that are rooted in Jesus' teaching and making them his own, even perhaps pushing the development of certain ideas harder than Jesus was inclined to do.

Missionary, theologian, church leader, biblical scholar, and propagandist, Paul's diverse skills, exuberant personality, and energy are everywhere on the pages of his letters. From a literary point of view, one of their most pronounced characteristics is how personal they are. In fact, Paul's presentation of himself through writing constitutes one of his most important contributions to the Catholic imagination.

Saint Paul and Autobiographical Narrative: A Life in Christ

Paul is constantly making reference to the story of his life in his letters.[6] He appears to assume that the main elements of this narrative, the highlights of his life, are already known to his readers.

Rather than tell the whole story straight through, he simply alludes to episodes, expecting his readers to understand what he is writing about.

Yet it is clear that for Paul the importance of this story is not simply anecdotal. On the contrary, Paul repeatedly points out to his converts that his own life should be, for them, exemplary, a distinctive paradigm that they ought to follow. In what may be his first epistle he writes to the people of Thessalonica, "You know what kind of people we proved to be among you for your sake. And you became imitators of us and of the Lord, for in spite of persecution you received the word with joy inspired by the Holy Spirit, so that you became an example to all the believers" (1 Thess 1:5–7). Note Paul suggests here that the conversion to Christianity these people have experienced is a conversion based upon a model of living exemplified by both Jesus *and* Paul in their lives. Later, in writing to the Colossians he says even more ambitiously, "For though you might have ten thousand guardians in Christ, you do not have many fathers. Indeed, in Christ Jesus I became your father through the gospel. I appeal to you, then, be imitators of me" (1 Cor 4:15–16). The faith Paul writes about is *his* faith, a living thing that he has passed on to those he has taught in the way that a parent passes life on to a child. This faith and the life that demonstrates it should become a pattern for other lives to follow. His message to the people of Philippi is much the same: "Brothers and sisters, join in imitating me, and observe those who live according to the example you have in us" (Phil 3:17). How could Paul be so bold? How could he tell others they should imitate him, rather than saying they should imitate Christ? How could he claim a kind of parallelism and even equality between Christ's life and his own?

The answer brings us back to our discussion of the incarnation from chapter 1. There we noted that one of the many ways in which Catholics understand God to be Incarnate within our existing physical world is within each believing Christian, and we noted Paul's words, "It is Christ who lives in me." This Pauline development in the concept of incarnation is one of the central elements of Catholicism. It means that Paul's own story as pattern and model of conduct turns out to be, in literary terms—that is to say, in terms of the aesthetic expression of a theological belief—the same kernel story of redemption that we have already found in the story of Jesus' life. In turn, it also parallels the paradigm of Christian world history as Paul was beginning to work out that paradigm—which is another one of the ways in which God's will becomes incarnate in human space and time. It is the same story for Jesus, for Paul, and for all of humanity. It becomes the universal Christian story of God incarnate. Repetition, not originality, proves its validity. In a simplified form we can divide it into four stages, as shown in Table 1 following.

Table 1. The Story of God Incarnate			
Stage	Jesus	Paul's Personal History	World History
1	Sinless savior in fallen world	Fallen existence	Adam's fall
2	Public life as a model of love	Commitment to others	Church active
	Opposition by his enemies	Opposition, persecution	Opposition
	Hope in coming Kingdom	Expectation of Kingdom	Expectation
3	Redeems all through his death	Is redeemed by Jesus	Jesus saves world
4	Resurrection	Hope in resurrection	Apocalypse

Narrative proves crucial to the formulation and expression of Christian belief. Christianity begins as biography, repeats itself in the individual lives of faithful followers—who sometimes recount their own lives in autobiography—and repeats itself as well in the collective historical accounts of all who believe.

Paul's Autobiography

It's useful to piece together Paul's own narrative, not only because it is the first self-portrait by a believing Christian, but also because it became, as Paul hoped and expected, a primary model for the later literary genre of Christian autobiography and indeed, until the Renaissance, for all autobiography written in the West. For centuries it constituted one of the principle models for believing Christians in imagining the self, which is to say imagining what it is to be a human being. It is one of Paul's central contributions to Western culture.

INDIVIDUALISM AND CHOICE

Christianity puts a distinctive stress on the individual and on the value of each individual person, and it puts a parallel stress on the choices people make in their lives and on how some choices determine what a person becomes. Individualism and the significance of individual choice are central to how Jesus, Paul, and Catholicism generally imagine human nature, and they become constitutive in how that Catholic imagination understands incarnation, redemption, and membership in community. They were also, interestingly, related to the fact that at its beginning Christianity was a "new" religion—a sect, a tiny band of outsiders.

In many cultures the human person is imagined not as an individual but rather as one member of a larger, aggregate whole. Strong movements in current thought argue that people are determined by such factors as gender, race, and economic circumstance and are relatively powerless to do anything about these given elements in their lives. Forms of collectivist thinking such as twentieth-century fascism and Marxism stressed nationality or race or class status and attempted to force people to live and to think of themselves almost exclusively in terms of group needs and group demands. Indeed, for many centuries and in many societies, people thought of the self as having meaning insofar as the individual fit into and cooperated with existing social institutions and structures, including religious belief. Thus, for the young Paul in the first century, being human and being good meant being Jewish—accepting the religion and culture of his ancestors. In this he was like most of the people of his day, Jew or pagan.

But when Christianity suddenly appeared, it confronted people like Paul with a new choice. To join the Christian community, Paul had to make a difficult decision that involved leaving the religion of his ancestors. A decision of this significance could be made only after thinking carefully about who he was and what he wanted from his life.

It turns out that in his teaching, and in his way of dealing with his friends, Jesus had already considered these issues. A crucial element in Jesus' teaching, as reported in the Gospels, is an emphasis upon the individuality of each person and God's minute awareness of each individual as an individual. With a kind of humorous impatience quite typical of him, Jesus upbraids his followers for being worried about the material details of daily life. "Are not five sparrows sold for two pennies? Yet not one of them is forgotten in God's sight. But even the hairs of your head are all counted. Do not be afraid; you are of more value than many sparrows" (Luke 12:6–7). God knows in fine and exact detail everything about us and cares about these details even to the hairs on our heads. There couldn't be a much greater emphasis upon individuality and the value of the individual than this.

To this stress upon individuality the gospel narratives connect the idea that God and Jesus choose each person, inviting them to join in an active personal relationship as members of the Christian community. The Gospels repeatedly show Jesus offering specific invitations to particular people to join him. At the same time the Gospels make clear that this call must be followed by the free and conscious decision on the part of each individual person to accept and act upon the invitation. Each can follow or stay behind. Choice is central. However, "whoever does not take up the cross and follow me is not worthy of me. Those who find their life will lose it, and those who lose their life for my sake will find it" (Matt 10:38–39). The analogy of the cross suggests the challenge that being a Christian brings with it. At the same time Jesus' typical use of extreme paradox—of dying in order to live—extends an offer full of hope for the transformation of one's life.

AUTOBIOGRAPHY AND DECISION MAKING

The art of literary autobiography naturally emerges from this way of imagining God, the self, and choice. If each person matters enormously to God, then each individual has a story well worth telling and well worth hearing. After all, God is listening already. When Jesus extends the invitation to join with him, it becomes necessary for each person to scrutinize the self, to examine where they have come from, who they are now, and what they want out of the rest of life. This self-assessment is the act of autobiography. To write down the thoughts that are a part of this act is to write an autobiography.

Paul's autobiographical remarks in his letters are thus a simple outgrowth and consequence of the process of choice he went through in deciding to become a Christian. Telling his converts about that process was instinctive and natural, since he had been in many cases the missionary who had first extended Jesus' offer of salvation to them, and they had made their own self-scrutiny and their own choices under Paul's direction. He knew very well that his story was their story.

What does that narrative look like? This is how Paul tells it.

RIGHTEOUSNESS AND GUILT

Coming into a fallen world and guilty himself, Paul describes his early life in highly negative terms. In the Epistle to the Philippians this takes a distinctly ironic turn: "circumcised on the eighth day, a member of the people of Israel, of the tribe of Benjamin, a Hebrew born of Hebrews; as to the law, a Pharisee; as to zeal, a persecutor of the church; as to righteousness under the law, blameless" (Phil 3:5–6). One of Paul's favorite paradoxes is the false sense of moral righteousness felt by people who mistakenly think they can be good, indeed can be perfect, if they just keep to

Figure 18. Pharisee
Pharisees were fervently devoted to every letter of the Mosaic Law. Saint Paul was an ardent Pharisee before his conversion.

the traditional Mosaic Law. As a young man he preened himself on being "faultless," and hence was ironically even more full of wrong-doing than most people. This was dramatically exemplified in his persecution of the emerging Christian Church: "You have heard, no doubt, of my earlier life in Judaism. I was violently persecuting the church of God and was trying to destroy it" (Gal 1:13). Excess, Paul suggests, is an essential aspect of his character, and when he viewed moral issues from the false perspective of the old law his excessive-ness took the form of a ferocious attempt at destroying what he now recognizes to be "the Church of God." He portrays this phase of his life as that of a man surrounded by a fallen world—a world ruined by excess: "Now the works of the flesh are obvious: fornication, impurity, licentiousness, idolatry, sorcery, enmities, strife, jealousy, anger, quarrels, dissensions, factions, envy, drunkenness, carousing, and things like these" (Gal 5:19–21). How could any person extri-cate themselves from a situation in which the world only aids and confirms their own false self-righteousness and cruelty?

BEING SAVED

Paul's answer is that alone no one could succeed. The descrip-tion of his life puts particular stress on the sudden, unexpected, and unmerited invitation he received from God. "For I did not receive it from a human source, nor was I taught it, but I received it through a revelation of Jesus Christ" (Gal 1:12). It is in the Acts of the Apostles that we read two accounts of Paul on the road to Damascus suddenly illuminated by a heavenly light, thrown to the ground, hearing a voice demanding, "Saul, Saul, why do you persecute me?" (Acts 9:4). There follows the story of his blindness, his study of Christianity and his baptism by Ananias, the return of his sight, and his new sense of Christian mission. In the second telling of this story, Paul has been set upon by an angry mob in Jerusalem and is rescued by a Roman tribune who does not understand what is happening. Turning to the crowd, Paul addresses them in Hebrew and tries to justify to them his role as the last of the apostles by recounting this crucial conversion story. In one of his letters Paul defines the signifi-cance of this call from God. Speaking of Jesus, he says, "Last of all, as to someone untimely born, he appeared also to me. For I am the least of the apostles, unfit to be called an apostle, because I perse-cuted the church of God. But by the grace of God I am what I am, and his grace toward me has not been in vain" (1 Cor 15:8–10). The claim here is first one of sight—Paul, blinded, saw Jesus. A typical Pauline paradox, and the reader quickly recognizes its assertion that there are two kinds of seeing, and only when Paul was able to see with spiritual eyes could he observe what was right in front of him all along. The second claim is election: Jesus chose Paul to be an apostle even though he had been "untimely born." There is no question of Paul's meriting election. Paul chose to accept this invitation. But his spiritual growth did not end there.

INEFFABLE VISIONS

Paul's autobiographical remarks indicate that his mystical contact with Jesus intensified in the years following his conversion. He seems to have had visionary experiences. Here is how Paul, struggling with language, tries to describe what they were like.

> I know a person in Christ who fourteen years ago was caught up to the third heaven—whether in the body or out of the body I do not know; God knows. And I know that such a person—whether in the body or out of the body I do not know; God knows—was caught up into Paradise and heard things that are not to be told, that no mortal is permitted to repeat. (2 Cor 12:2–4)

In this peculiar passage full of hints, denials, and evasions, Paul seems to be remembering a transformative moment when he himself, considered here objectively as "a person," found himself lifted out of himself into some transcendent space...that he calls "Paradise"... and there heard something that was said but can no longer be uttered. The confusions of the passage—displacement, contradiction, interrogation without resolution—correspond to the kind of extraordinary experience Paul claims to have had.

THE TRANSFORMED SELF: APOSTLESHIP

From such experiences of Jesus, not the physical Jesus who talked and ate and traveled with the first apostles, but the Jesus of religious ecstasy, emerges Paul's sense of adult identity. Here is how he comes to describe himself at the beginning of his Letter to the Romans: "Paul, a servant of Jesus Christ, called to be an apostle, set apart for the gospel of God..." (Rom 1:1).

This claim can only still seem audacious today. Peter and the rest of the Twelve were chosen directly by Jesus during his public life, and the Gospels offer ample instances of Jesus training these men to be the leaders of the church after his death. But Paul comes out of nowhere, an active enemy of Jesus' followers and a man obviously not chosen by Jesus during his life nor trained by Jesus. Unfazed by any of this, Paul asserts his own equality with the original disciples and indeed refuses to concede any particular authority to them over his own missionary work: "They saw that I had been entrusted with the gospel for the uncircumcised, just as Peter had been entrusted with the gospel for the circumcised (for he who worked through Peter making him an apostle to the circumcised also worked through me in sending me to the Gentiles)..." (Gal 2: 7–8). Paul's confidence in such assertions, the focus of his personal belief, and the basis of his subsequent theology is his certainty in his own individual election and redemption by Jesus. Which is to say that in Paul's autobiographical statements his intense sense of personal identity or selfhood becomes completely bound up with his sense of connection to Christ. The parallels noted in the preceding table of the paradigm of the kernel narrative emerge dramatically, emotionally, in Paul's claim to election, appointment, and divine love. "I have been crucified with Christ; and it is no longer I who live, but it is Christ who lives in me. And the life I now live in the flesh I live by faith in the Son of God, who loved me and gave himself for me" (Gal 2:20). One should probably take this highly paradoxical language to be an effort to write literally. Paul is sure that he has been crucified. That is to say, in some real sense he too was on the cross on Calvary. The same parallel holds at the moment he is writing. Christ is not dead but alive in Paul. The two lives are so intertwined that there is a kind of joint identity.

This necessarily leads to Paul's life as missionary, in which he replicates the public life of teaching and service that Jesus had led. "If I proclaim the gospel, this gives me no ground for boasting, for an obligation is laid on me, and woe betide me if I do not proclaim the gospel!" (1 Cor 9:16). Paul insistently repeats that he has chosen to follow Christ's wishes. Now, he simply does what he is told to do. Boasting and yet not proud (paradox being the stuff of Catholic utterance), Paul finds proof for the validity of his calling in the faith that now lives among those he has converted. "If I am not an apostle to others, at least I am to you; for you are the seal of my apostleship in the Lord" (1 Cor 9:2).

LOVE AND SELF-SACRIFICE

This proof is but one of many reasons for Paul's intense affection for his followers, Paul dealing with them "like a father with his children" (1 Thess 2:11). He proves the depth of his affection, just as Christ did, by facing up to opposition from God's enemies: "Though we had already suffered and been shamefully maltreated at Philippi, as you know, we had courage in our God to declare to you the gospel of God in spite of great opposition" (1 Thess 2:2). Anticipating that his fate will be just like that of Jesus—that the narrative kernel will continue to run true—Paul is sure of persecution and suffering—"We told you beforehand that we were to suffer persecution; so it turned out..." (1 Thess 3:4)—but he recognizes that his own suffering will only contribute to the vitality of the faith in his converts. "If we are being afflicted, it is for your consolation and salvation..." (2 Cor 1:6).

Indeed, if the conversion of the gentiles to Christianity is one validation of Paul's direct calling by Jesus, another proof is the opposition he constantly suffers. It makes him more like Jesus: "As servants of God we have commended ourselves in every way: through great endurance, in afflictions, hardships, calamities, beatings, imprisonments, riots, labours, sleepless nights, hunger..." (2 Cor 6:4–5). Paul's stress upon his own suffering and what he is sure will be his future martyrdom will simply help the growth of the church, as did Jesus' initiating redemptive death.

As the pattern of the life unfolds in these various autobiographical remarks from Paul's letters, the parallels with the life of Jesus become overwhelming. Those parallels, from the point of view of the emerging Catholic imagination, are the proof of the validity of everything Paul says and does. He is right, because his life is like the life of Jesus. The autobiography he is incidentally sketching in virtually every letter that survives is the narrative of the life of a Christlike man. The kernel narrative of redemption emerges vital and transformative in the life of the first converts.

FUTURE GLORY

Because this is so, Paul confidently looks forward to the eternal reward won for him by Christ's redemptive act: "I consider that the sufferings of this present time are not worth comparing with the glory about to be revealed to us" (Rom 8:18). There seem to be moments when Paul longs for death because in death he can be joined even more completely with the savior who chose him, the savior who had granted him moments of unutterable, ecstatic vision. This leads to a kind of intermittent otherworldliness in Paul's thinking, a longing to be rid of the body, of the earth, of all that holds him back from that which he completely yearns for: "But our citizenship is in heaven, and it is from there that we are expecting a Savior, the Lord Jesus Christ. He will transform the body of our humiliation so that it may be conformed to the body of his glory, by the power that also enables him to make all things subject to himself" (Phil 3:20–21). From sin and violence Paul moves to election, transformation, moments of visionary splendor, commitment, persecution, and suffering, and from there to a longing for death and the heavenly union with the Savior that he feels sure will be his.

The Tradition of Catholic Autobiography

This self-portrait of a man in a complex, highly emotional relationship with God and with other believers, whose whole life is transformed by faith and who takes on dangerous responsibilities despite criticism, doubt, and outright persecution, quickly became an imaginative model for what it means to be a follower of Christ. If the gospel narrative of the life of Christ has within it superhuman moments (walking on water, quelling a violent storm with a few words [for example, Matt 14:25 and 8:26]), the life that Paul describes can be taken to be entirely human, and therefore as a completely available paradigm for others to follow. In the centuries ahead, Christianity, following Paul's lead, would initiate and foster the act and the art of autobiography—the effort to discern and to find words to describe the evolution of the spiritual self—in classic works by people like Saint Augustine, Saint Teresa of Avila, Dorothy Day, and Thomas Merton. These writers, steeped as they were in the Christian scriptures, thought, felt, and wrote within the Pauline way of imagining. It might be interesting and useful also to read other celebrated autobiographies in these terms; for example, those of Jean-Jacques Rousseau, John Stuart Mill, C. G. Jung, and

Mary McCarthy, finding perhaps in them curious and useful parallels often through reversal: these writers replacing religious faith with skepticism and doubt, devotion to church with devotion to programs of secular change and improvement, hopes anchored not in heaven but in forms of reward available in this life.

What is clear is that Paul left early Christianity with his own story, the story of a man transformed, and the generations that followed read that story with joy and hope and made it their own.

CHAPTER SEVEN

The First Churches
Dura-Europos

The Earliest Christian Communities Emerge

The Acts of the Apostles describes the earliest Christian community as a fellowship of faith and love:

> All who believed were together and had all things in common; they would sell their possessions and goods and distribute the proceeds to all, as any had need. Day by day, as they spent much time together in the temple, they broke bread at home and ate their food with glad and generous hearts, praising God and having the goodwill of all the people. And day by day the Lord added to their number those who were being saved. (Acts 2:44–47)

Christians of the apostolic period were still figuring out the relationship between the traditional practices of their Jewish religious heritage and its temple worship and Christian rituals such as the eucharistic banquet, which had to be celebrated in some new setting. Paul's letters, emerging from a context perhaps twenty to thirty years later, address a mixed group of Jewish and gentile converts living in cities located in modern Turkey and Greece. These were people with a cultural background very different from the Christians of Jerusalem, and the differences among them are frequently the subject of Paul's pastoral writing. It has not been easy, even for modern archaeologists trying to determine the makeup of the post-Pauline church, to distinguish Christian from non-

Christian culture. Surveying "all known archaeological evidence of Christianity during the first three centuries," Graydon F. Snyder concluded that until the year 180 it was "impossible to distinguish Christian from non-Christian culture in 'funerary art, inscriptions, letters, symbols, and perhaps buildings...[because] it took over a century for the new community of faith to develop a distinctive mode of self-expression.'"[1] The church was just beginning to invent itself.

We can, however, say one or two things with some certainty about this very early church. It is likely that Christianity in the second century was largely urban in character and that it was located primarily in Asia Minor, Egypt, and North Africa,[2] though from the days of Peter and Paul there was also a Christian presence in the imperial capital, Rome. Thanks to the peace established by the Roman imperium throughout the Mediterranean basin it was easy at that time to travel in relative safety, and Christian missionaries followed well-established trade routes from city to city.

To an educated person of that era, early Christianity would have looked like one of many small, competing cults coming out of the East. The fact that some early Christian converts had been Jews meant—and here there is some archeological evidence—that Christian communities sometimes occupied the same neighborhoods as synagogues. Many early Christians were like Jesus' own chosen disciples, poor and from the working class, "ordinary people—Jewish and Syrian tradesmen grouped together in certain districts of Greek or Roman cities and a few pagan neighbors... [s]laves and artisans...and women."[3] Rodney Stark, in his remarkable study *The Rise of Christianity*, argues, however, that at the same time along with these relatively powerless people there must have been other Christian converts who "had a degree of [social] privilege...."[4] Stark is convinced these wealthier and more powerful members helped the church to grow more quickly through the influence of their financial resources and that they were even able at times to deflect state persecution because it was more difficult for local authorities to openly attack people with a certain degree of prestige. Historian Peter Brown also sees the earliest Christian communities as composed of people of quite different classes and economic backgrounds, "a variegated group."[5] This egalitarianism was a remarkable sociological innovation for imperial Rome, and it was the direct consequence of the Christian assumption, radical and even shocking for that time, that anyone could be a member of this religious group and that anyone, no matter how humble, no matter how scarred by an evil past, could be saved.[6] The defining trait of a community open and welcoming to everyone was already shaping the church.

Most of the time official Rome ignored Christianity, but now and then the government did switch to state persecution. Shifts in policy came with each new emperor and with the perception of those in power that the Christians were either a danger to the state or simply an innocuous cult, one of many equally irrelevant oddities in a complex and polyvalent society.[7] This meant that Christians could usually gather together and worship, but they had to be cautious and even to a degree secretive. They certainly could not build public places of assembly. "Only the state religion erected temples in the tradition of Greek and Roman architecture."[8]

The House-Church

All of this implies that early Christian communities faced an important choice. Jesus had been a wanderer. He lived without a home and without a physical place in which to meet with his followers. Even the Last Supper was held in a rented room. After his death his followers had to decide whether to continue to wander as he had or to settle. In the end they found a way to combine their evolving sense for the meaning of Jesus' teaching and the ordinary practices of their time and their culture through the creation both in Rome and in many provincial towns of the "house-church," in Latin *domus ecclesiae,* a direct evolutionary successor to the meeting places of the first Christians in Jerusalem.

Typically the house-church was located in an existing building within an urban center—a small cluster of rooms that might be modestly altered for community needs and particularly for such essential liturgical rituals as "the breaking of bread." Krautheimer points out the anonymity of these buildings, noting that "their resemblance to ordinary tenements would have made...[them] as hard to identify as the meeting rooms of contemporary sects installed in the tenements of New York's Harlem or London's East End."[9] The wealthier members of the community often owned the buildings in which these house-churches were located, and there is clear evidence that not only community worship but also charitable work such as feeding the hungry and educating new Christians took place there.

Krautheimer records a remarkably revealing bit of historical evidence taken from Roman police records. The authorities who broke into an illegal Christian house-church made a careful list of what they found inside. This was nothing less than

> the minutes of a confiscation of Christian property in a North African country town in 303 [and it] vividly reflect[s] the plan of such a *domus ecclesiae* and the function of its several rooms. Moving through the house, the police impound chalices, lamps, and chandeliers in the meeting room; wearing-apparel for the poor in a store room; bookcases and chests in the library; chests and large jugs in a dining-room.[10]

Each item in this tabulation tells us a great deal about what these early Christians were doing and about the way each room in the house-church functioned.

It's difficult to exaggerate the consequences that arose as the Christian community first began to locate itself within spaces set aside specifically for its own use. It is from this point in history that Christianity begins to fix itself into specific and hence limited contexts. While Jesus and his twelve disciples had been homeless and hence free to move anytime they chose, now Christians had a place to be and from which they could act but to which they were linked. With this of course came new responsibilities—financial obligations, the need to follow the laws and the practices of the local community, the dangers that emerge from exposure and position and so at times the need to defend that position, and so on.

It's not too much to say that this coupling of site, building, and community became at once a new version of incarnation. Just as Jesus the Son of God took on human form and thereby faced the physical limitations of body, time, and death, so his infant church located its spiritual life and action within a specific physical space and thus had to face the limitations and dangers as well as the possibilities that come with embodiment.[11]

The Only Surviving House-Church

By a series of fortuitous events, one of the most important archeological explorations of the twentieth century uncovered and made available for study the only known surviving remnants of an early Christian house-church. During the first World War a British soldier digging a trench accidentally came upon the remains of the buried and forgotten town Dura-Europos (modern-day Qualat es Salihiye). Dura had been built by one of the generals of Alexander the Great around 300 BC during the Greek occupation of eastern Syria,[12] and the names he gave it tell of the purposes this place was to serve, *Dura* meaning wall or fortress and *Europos* referring to the village in Macedonia where Alexander had been born; hence an Alexandrian fortified town, surrounded by a wall, on the banks of the Euphrates River. Excavations led by a team from Yale working under the supervision of Syrian authorities began in 1928. In 1932 Clark Hopkins and his colleagues uncovered in a modest building located next to the city wall the "sole archaeological representative for three centuries of houses dedicated to Christian use."[13] Thanks to a graffito scratched onto a wall by a "bored workman," we can be fairly sure that the rooms in this house were being modified "A.D. 231/2."[14] Thanks to another historical accident, which indeed is the reason that the building and its Christian rooms were preserved at all, we can be sure of when it was buried. In 257 the local Roman authorities were facing the probability of an attack by their Parthian enemies to the east, and in reinforcing the town wall they commandeered and filled with dirt, rubble, and sand this building as well as the building that contained a Jewish synagogue a block away.[15] Soon afterward the Parthians overwhelmed the local Romans, and Dura-Europos was abandoned. For this unusual reason the remains of both these buried religious community centers, which would have appeared to the casual observer to be simply piles of mud, survived until the twentieth century. Once the archeological excavation had been completed, the frescoes from the Jewish synagogue were transported to the Damascus Museum, while those from the Christian house-church were taken to New Haven, Connecticut, where they are now housed in the Yale University Museum.

The remains of the house-church at Dura, with its cycle of decorative wall frescoes, "sketchy and amateurish"[16] though they be, constitute for our purposes an extraordinarily significant example of the Catholic imagination at work just about two hundred years after the death of Christ. In this geographically remote place we can explore how among relatively simple people the Catholic imagination was at work.

Let us begin by considering the building: the earliest surviving Christian church. Then, we will take a look at how it is decorated: some of the earliest Christian pictures.

Dura-Europos: Community and Faith

The House-Church at Dura-Europos as Architectural Space

WHAT IT LOOKED LIKE

This house-church is across a narrow street from the town wall and adjacent to one of its defensive towers, in what was probably a quiet residential neighborhood, less crowded and less frequently used than the urban center. To reach the house-church one turned from the street that ran parallel to the town wall into a side street, and then came upon a door in the otherwise blind wall of the building.

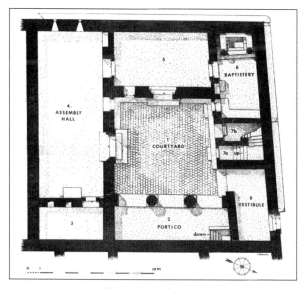

Figure 19. Floor plan of the house-church

Crossing the threshold, you entered a small reception room, probably dark and perhaps undecorated (nothing from this room has survived), and you had to turn right, then left to pass through the next doorway. Once beyond the reception room you found yourself in an open courtyard with the bright Syrian sky above, a row of decorative columns to your left, and doors on the other three sides leading to adjoining rooms. This kind of "peristyle" building with its enclosing exterior walls and open center space was typical of Mediterranean urban centers during the period.

The building had been the home of a relatively wealthy family and had only been slightly modified for Christian use. If you had gone on from the courtyard straight through the doorway to the south, you would have entered a fairly large room, its walls still decorated with a pagan "decorative moulded Bacchic frieze."[17] This room, some 16 1/2 by 43 feet, had a bench built into three of its walls; on the fourth there was a slightly raised platform. If instead you had turned to your right, you could have gone either into a modest-sized room on the west end or through the third door into an even smaller room in the northwest corner, where you would have seen walls decorated with crudely drawn frescoes and at its far end a modest stone canopy covering a stone "tub."[18]

THE USE AND MEANING OF THESE SPACES

What do these spaces tell us? Let us consider each in terms of the ideas that may animate them. Nothing is completely certain about this house-church, but archeologists and students of ancient architecture and of early Christian art have speculated for three-quarters of a century over what has survived at Dura-Europos. From their theories we may construct an interpretation that helps to advance our study of the emerging Catholic imagination.

The modest size of this house-church—the rooms could accommodate "a congregation of barely more than seventy," whereas the synagogue down the street had "seats for at least 120 worshippers"[19] —indicates the fact that here Christianity was still a very minor religious presence. The location at the edge of town tells us of the still peripheral character of Christian communities and also suggests a degree of caution. There is no effort to brazen forth the presence of a gathering place. The doorway with its blind reception room reinforces the impression that an effort has been made to conceal what is going on. Nonmembers would be unable to look in, and the general effect must have been of privacy on the verge of secrecy.[20]

The building is a family home transformed into a meeting place. In this it exactly replicates the earliest gathering places of Jesus' disciples and suggests perhaps a conscious effort to maintain a certain continuity with biblical Christianity. It also suggests the degree to which these early communities of faith may have felt like extended families, with one or two dominant male and female leaders (perhaps from the family of moderately wealthy donor-owners of the building) and a cluster of associated groupings: other families, friends, servants and slaves, people who came for help and stayed to become members—in a metaphorical way, children, nieces, nephews, cousins in faith—a living embodiment of Jesus' argument that his followers must leave their own fathers and mothers and join in a new and different kind of familial structure within the church (Matt 10:35). There is as well a simplicity in the dimensions, the layout, and the decoration of the whole interior of this building that suggests that Christ's way of imagining, its simplicity, material factuality, and its way of grounding the mind in ordinary things lived on in the imaginations of these early Syrian Christians. As we have seen, a central implication of the incarnation is that God can be found everywhere and in the humblest places—indeed is more likely to be found there than in the great and the expensive—and this simple place literally embodies that understanding of incarnation.

ENTRANCE

The doorway and the entrance room also help us recall how Christ imagined community, and his stern assertion of division. "I have not come to bring peace, but a sword" (Matt 10:34). This entry divides Christian from pagan and establishes the existence of a separate place. Passing through the doorway, the believer left ordinary space, the town with its noises, its business, its openness, its randomness, and entered into the enclosed, sacred space of another world, set off from daily life—hidden, yet still remarkably accessible.

The early Christian house-church constituted a sacred place dramatically different from the great temples in Athens, Jerusalem, or indeed the many temples for various gods located in Dura itself. Pagan temples and the Jewish Temple in Jerusalem featured enclosed central areas that only the priestly class could enter. Other people could go only so far, and then were required to turn over the necessary act of sacrifice or worship to a trained professional set aside by some form of particular consecration to perform regulated sacred ceremonies. These inner holy places were sites of great mystery. While the house-church was restricted to Christians—only the faithful were to enter, and only those who had been baptized could participate in the sacrament of the Eucharist—it was at the same time completely open to all who were members of the community. This made it a dramatically new kind of church.[21] In this aspect it carries forward the manner of Jesus' preaching and the way in which the Gospels picture him living. They show a Jesus ready to talk to anybody, pagan or Jew, sinner or saved, rich or poor. He is as comfortable with lepers as with Roman centurions, and he freely argues with his most inveterate enemies. This early Christian Church replicates the way in which Jesus met people. Though it does not boast of its presence, it is easy to enter. Anybody willing to join will find this door open.

INTERIOR SPACES

The largest room in the Dura house-church, the one with the benches around three walls and the slightly raised platform on the fourth wall, was clearly the gathering place for the eucharistic celebration. The platform was for the presider—a very modest elevation simply permitting the presider to be seen by everyone in the room; the benches offered the chance to some of the members to sit down. The pagan frieze with its allusions to Bacchus had not been obliterated when the room was remodeled because it was quite easy for early Christians to see in the pagan god of wine a symbolic anticipation of their Savior, who shared wine with his followers on their last night together and who transformed wine into his own saving blood.

The family gathering room of the former pagan owners was thus easily transformed into a room in which the Christian love-feast or *agape* took place. As du Bourguet points out, the design of the early Christian worship space "drew no inspiration from any pagan or Jewish model. Its origin lies in the...worship established by Christ in the institution of the Eucharist, the setting for which was the 'upper chamber' of a certain private house..." and ritual actions were "simply an extension of Christ's behavior in accepting the hospitality of one of his disciples...."[22] If a skeptical pagan had entered this room he might have asked, "Where is the secret, holy place?" The obvious answer is that for these early Christian communities incarnation implied a radical redefinition of the sacred. Their belief, manifested in the character of spaces such as this one, was that holiness or sacredness existed in the community of people themselves. They themselves had become "the Holy of Holies." The people constituted the point at which the divine transected the material world, in humble rooms like this one.

What of the other two rooms entered from the courtyard? The one to the northwest with the stone tub at one end surmounted by a small canopy can only have been the baptistery. (As we shall see shortly, its fresco decorations make this assumed purpose even more obvious.) For the people who shaped and used these spaces, the sacrament of baptism (initiation) was thus crucial, a ritual worthy of its own defined, independent place that is in symbolic relationship to the gathering place for the community. In the centuries to come, traditions of Christian worship were to continue this physical articulation of a spiritual idea, and particularly in Italy the custom emerged of devoting a separate building (a "baptistery"), frequently a large and elaborate one (in Pisa and Florence, for example) used for this sacrament.

And the room between this little baptistery and the larger assembly room for the liturgy, what was its purpose? Some think it may have been the place where catechumens were taught the elements of Christian belief. If it was an early form of assembly room, it may have been dedicated not only to education but to works of charity as well. It's important to recall that in the inventory of objects seized from another house-church cited earlier were included clothes to be given to those in need. This room at Dura-Europos may have been a place both for education and also for the charitable care of the needy.[23]

Taken as a whole, the house-church at Dura-Europos illustrates how early Christianity was discovering that ultimately the kind of building that matters is a building up of the people, of the body of Christ. The shaping of structure emerges from the inner life of the community. Shared belief, mutual caring, the *agape* worship of the sacred meal—these are the elements of Christian life and its foundation in incarnation, redemption, sacramentality, and community, and these basic traits of Catholic belief give form and meaning to this simple place.

The actual building at Dura on the eastern edge of the empire and of Christianity was soon forgotten. Certainly it was never a model for other places of gathering and worship. It survived into our own time because of a series of accidents. But the animating ideas exemplified in these ruins lived on and evolved and became the basis for the later churches and cathedrals of Christianity. The great achievements of later Catholic architecture are but further reembodiments in variant but similar forms.

The Frescoes from the House-Church at Dura-Europos as Iconographic Program

"The inspiration of the first Christian art is liturgical… utilitarian…[coming from] the faithful…."

Andre Grabar[24]

WHAT WE SEE

In the small room at the northwest corner of the house-church at Dura-Europos, the team of Yale archeologists found the building's only Christian pictorial decorations. These frescoes are simple, indeed amateurish in execution, and no one makes any claims for them in aesthetic terms. But these humble wall paintings do show us how a ceremonial room in a Christian house-church could be decorated in a provincial town early in the third century. They show us how the Catholic imagination was beginning the job of finding ways to picture the stories and beliefs of Christianity. As a cycle of pictures, they illustrate the shared faith of this early community.

There are two doors into this room, one from the courtyard and the second from the room that we have guessed to have functioned as classroom and storehouse for charitable goods. If we enter the baptistery through that door and look to the wall immediately on our left hand as we walk in, we see a woman standing at a well (Figure 20). "The wellhead is drawn with the illusion of modified depth and the woman holds the loose rope in both hands. Her body…is bent slightly forward."[25]

As we now begin to walk around the room, we continue to the left and on the far west wall we find just beneath the ceiling a small arch supported by two squat columns. Under the arch there is a curved ceiling painted blue and speckled with white stars. Beneath this rudimentary baldachin stands a stone tub raised from the floor by a small platform. On the far wall, under the arched ceiling and beyond the tub, there are figures clearly painted at two different points in time. The largest, dominating figure is a man carrying a

Figure 20. The woman at the well. Wall fresco

Figure 21. The good shepherd with Adam and Eve. Wall fresco

sheep on his shoulders. On the hill behind him there are more sheep. In the lower left-hand corner rendered in a different style are two much smaller figures, a naked man and woman covering themselves with aprons made of leaves, with a serpent nearby (Figure 21).

Figure 22. Women at the tomb. Wall fresco

Figure 23. The healing of the paralytic. Wall fresco

Now we turn to our right and look at the wall on the north side of the room, the wall facing the door we recently used to enter. On the lower part of this wall we see a single fairly large picture in which there is a very big, white, closed sarcophagus—it almost looks like a small house—and a row of women (three are prominently closer to the sarcophagus) walking toward it (Figure 22). Above this picture is a second strip of images, and here two different scenes flow one into the other. In the first of these pictures, the one nearest to the wall with the tub, we see a man carrying a cot on his back; next to him another man still lies on his cot, while a third man points to him in a gesture of command (Figure 23). Next to this picture we have a very different scene: there is a boat with men on board raising their arms in astonishment while in the foreground a man stands on the waves and reaches out to take the arm of a second man whose feet are disappearing into the water (Figure 24). All these figures are dressed in the simple clothes of the era.

Figure 22. The walking on the water. Wall fresco

If we go back to the two doors and look at the wall between them, we see a small niche set into the wall. Above it in Greek there

is an inscription reading "Jesus Christ is Yours. Remember Proclus."
Beneath the niche there is a picture of a young man raising a club
over a prostrate figure. Lettering on the picture tells us these are
David and Goliath.

WHAT IT MEANS

What can we learn about the emergence and evolution of the
Catholic imagination from these primitive images?

Perhaps the first thing that comes to mind is this: anyone ignorant of Christianity would find the whole room bewildering. What
possible, literal meaning could emerge from this peculiar collection
of figures? These images require decoding. That they are inscrutable
to the outsider may have been intentional—early Christians fear-
ing persecution may have wished to conceal their beliefs though
metaphor and allusion. But at the same time one must assume that
they picture episodes that had a particular importance for the community. To strangers they would be baffling. To local Christians
they would be illustrations of ideas and beliefs that were the basis
for how they thought and felt. It is indeed typical of most religious
art that it requires a knowledge of the stories, the articles of belief,
the worldview of the religion itself before it can be understood.
Sculptures of the Buddha, Indian manuscripts with pictures of
episodes from the life of Krishna, the wall decorations of ancient
Egyptian temples mean little or nothing to people unacquainted
with their respective religious sources. Much the same can be said
for the images at Dura.

Remembered textual sources would have been the key to the
people of this community, who would have used them to decode the
meaning of these images. Here we see already how crucial will be
the interplay between Christian texts and visual images in Catholic
art. These are pictures of moments that emerge from and exemplify
a narrative—illustrations of a story. They prompt the viewer to
recall the entire narrative and its analogical significance, and they
concern biblical texts in particular. The figure under the arch is the
good shepherd, the chief figure in a story told by Jesus, representing
God's tireless pursuit of the people he loves and his efforts to bring
them back to safety and happiness within the flock. The woman at
the well comes from the Gospel of John. Jesus promises her a saving water that will "become in [her] a spring of water gushing up to

eternal life" (John 4:14). Facing her are three other episodes from the life of Jesus. On the upper register he cures a paralyzed man (Matt 9:1–8). We see that man first on his cot unable to move as Jesus makes the commanding gesture to rise, and then we also see him on foot and now carrying the cot. Next to this picture we see the disciples on the Sea of Galilee, Jesus walking on the water and extending his hand to Peter, whose faith is not strong enough to buoy him up (Matt 14:25–33). Beneath these pictures, on the lower register, women who have been faithful followers of Jesus walk toward his tomb on Easter morning. They are about to learn the good news of the resurrection.

These scenes tell us of the lively knowledge of New Testament stories in this Dura community. With this knowledge these otherwise inscrutable pictures make simple, perfect sense. The other figures are similarly easy to decode if one knows the Hebrew Scriptures. The boy David slaying the giant Goliath, a story of virtue succeeding against impossible odds, and near to the good shepherd the smaller figures of Adam, Eve, and the serpent who has just tempted them into the first sin, emblematically indicated by the shame they feel at their nakedness and their clumsy efforts to hide their bodies in aprons of leaves.

ICONOGRAPHIC PROGRAM: THE INTERRELATIONSHIP OF IMAGES

But why did the community at Dura choose these figures, these specific episodes? What might be the inner logic behind the iconographic program of the room as a whole?

"Christianity is less a doctrine than a person, that of Christ," argues Pierre du Bourguet. "Christian dogma derives as much from His being as from His teaching. In Him the visible is the perfect expression of the invisible."[26] At the center of this room, beneath the arch with its sky of stars, looking over the tub in which new Christians were baptized, is a symbolic portrait[27] of Jesus[28] as good shepherd. The picture and its location do more than simply tell a story; they make a theological point. This is a baptistery, a room where people joining the Christian community undergo a ceremonial washing with water, symbolizing purgation from their past sins. The shepherd is a symbol of the Jesus who has brought them safely to this place. The little figures of Adam, Eve, and the serpent, probably added at a later time, are a reminder that the sins being purged began with this primal act of disobedience. The whole wall voices the theology of redemption: the fall, Jesus' life on earth as Savior, and the currently existing community of Christians who now see themselves as his flock. There can be little doubt that the images on this wall reflect the preaching that the Dura community heard regularly. It uses biblical stories from both Hebrew and Christian Scriptures in a synthesis that makes a theological point about a Christian sacramental ritual.

One of the messages of the good shepherd image is that first one must be carried. Salvation comes through Jesus. The figure metaphorically representing him dominates the whole room. The episodes from the life of Jesus that bracket this focal point on both the side walls extend the meaning of Jesus as Savior. The woman at the well—and in John's Gospel she is a Samaritan, an alien person who clearly symbolizes the gentiles who were already entering the church when John wrote and who conveniently represents the Syrian Christians of this community—this woman seizes upon Jesus' offer of a new kind of water that will bring eternal life. The use of the story in the baptistery clearly tells us that the Dura community was reading the Gospels analogically and understood this gospel story as being about baptism, the sacrament that is "a spring...welling up for eternal life."

First, one must be carried, and as Jesus brings the new water to this thirsting woman, so he enables those who wish to follow him to walk. The paralyzed man thus functions as a symbol of people crippled by sin. Jesus helps them get up...like the lost sheep first he must find them...but then he enables them to walk on their own morally and spiritually. Once redeemed the believer can do anything. Soon that mobility, that power to walk, becomes miraculous, and we see Jesus helping Peter to walk on water, saved now from the water that kills by the water of redemption.

As one thinks about image after image one sees thought patterns emerging. First, analogy is everywhere. The shepherd is Jesus, the sheep those he calls. The woman at the well, the paralyzed man, Peter, the women at the tomb all function as analogies to phases in the life of the Christian believer, moments of discovery, liberation, doubt, and joy. These individual scenes and specific stories are meant to be understood as interlinked with one another. They echo, amplify, and enrich the meaning of each specific story through symbolic parallels: using, as Jesus did, very simple, universal symbols such as water and walking. The series of pictures means more as an ensemble than any one picture could mean. Juxtaposition amplifies significance.

Paradoxes emerge. The two kinds of water—that which kills, that which saves. The two kinds of walking—on his own Peter sinks, but with Jesus' support he can do the impossible. The women walk too, processing toward the sepulcher of resurrection.[29] The place of death has become the place of new life.

Each one of these people functions as a witness: the woman at the well, the paralytic, Peter, the women of Easter dawn, all testify to the saving, redeeming achievements of Christ. In this sense Jesus is in each picture even when he is not literally depicted. Each and all voice aspects of his redemptive act. The later addition of Adam and Eve underscores the contrast between the lost Eden and the new Eden that is this very room in which newly baptized Christians enter into a new salvation. Ornamental decorations of stars and fruit painted on the archway suggest that the world viewed rightly reflects God's beauty and glory. Even the little picture of David and Goliath fits into the larger scheme: the story of a young boy slaying a giant suggests the power of goodness to defeat what appears to be overwhelming evil.

The House-Church at Dura-Europos and Jesus' Imagination

The way in which these images make meaning derives immediately from the way that Jesus taught, and the way his imagination worked. Just as he told simple stories often in a linked series, expecting his audience to discern the meaning and further implication of what he was saying, so these pictorial scenes show concrete, simple events full of implication. The way in which these figures and narrative episodes are depicted also emerges directly from Jesus' way of imagining. In Jesus' stories there is, for example, a striking absence of proper names, places, settings: rather, there is a simple universality about them. His characters are usually "a certain man," "a householder." The world in which they live is a countryside of farms and small towns. In these early pictures at Dura we have only bodies and the fewest possible symbolic elements: a boat, a cot, a snake. As in the stories of Jesus, what we see are people who are contemporaries of the Dura community—ordinary people dressed in ordinary clothes doing ordinary things. Or, when what they do is not ordinary, like walking on water, it is made to seem so by the plain, matter-of-fact way in which it is depicted. This resolute contemporaneity exemplifies a theological belief in the continuing incarnation: Jesus is still present, here, at this moment, looking just like his followers in the Dura community. He is not some remote figure out of a distant place and time; he is one with them, alive and present, and in fact he even looks like them. This too is a theological point, one we have already seen in our consideration of this house-church as architectural space. Incarnation means that Jesus is present in believing individuals, in the community as a whole, in the stories of his life, and in the sacraments of the church. All of that seems clearly implied by the suggestion that in the incarnation time and space collapse and Jesus is always and everywhere living and present.

There is an interesting and suggestive absence of hierarchical symbols in these pictures. No thrones, crowns, supporting cast of angelic throngs. Those were to come later. The Jesus in these pictures looks like an ordinary person except for his gestures of power. Pointing at the crippled man, he cures him. Reaching out a hand, he helps Peter walk on water.

In these images we see already emergent the double vision of the Catholic imagination discussed in chapter 3. A picture, no matter how ordinary and realistic, is never just a picture of some one or some thing; it is always latent with further meaning, a deeper meaning. A shepherd is never just a shepherd, a sheep just a sheep. Water always is more than just water. When we walk we are bound for destinations in this world and into the next. This doubleness is understood to be a property of existence itself, as it is simultaneously a way for works of art to express that doubleness. The insightful mind sees through the material surface to other and more important meanings. Each story speaks about other stories, and together they lead to a whole greater than the sum of the parts.

We have already noticed the inscription above the niche between the two entrance doors: "Jesus Christ is Yours. Remember Proclus." After so many centuries it is no longer certain who Proclus might have been. The owner of the building perhaps, or the man who commissioned the fresco paintings of the baptistery, the artist who made them, or simply a member of the community. But the inscription does tell us two things quite clearly. First, an individual person asks that the people using this room remember him by name. It matters to him that those who come after him think well of him as an individual. Second, the reason they should think well of him is not that he was wealthy, or skillful in painting, or enjoyed some kind of secular power, but that he has been one of the people who has given them the good news. He has helped make sure that Jesus Christ is theirs. In this sense the inscription in the Dura-Europos baptistery is addressed still to believing Christians everywhere, because it was thanks to communities such as this one that the Christian faith was passed down, the good news circulating ever further throughout the then-known world.

CHAPTER EIGHT

Death and Belief
The Roman Catacombs

Rome

We now move from the edge of the empire to its center, the capital city of Rome. Christianity has been present in this place since the time of the apostles, and traces of their presence can, with some certainty, still be found there. Beneath the enormous bulk of St. Peter's, indeed almost immediately beneath the central altar, below its foundations, below the foundations of the earlier church built by the Roman emperor Constantine, archeologists have found a small shrine erected as a cenotaph over what very early Christians thought to be the tomb of Saint Peter. This site, which was outside the walls of the ancient city, in a graveyard next to the Circus (horse-racing track) of Gaius and Nero, could well have been where the apostle was buried after being executed before the public in the year 64.

With time, despite such early persecutions, the Christian community in Rome grew. House-churches appeared in large tenement buildings. It was the Roman custom to affix to the side of a building a small marble tile naming its owner. This was a *titulus*, and buildings came to be known by the name of these owners. It is possible to identify the *tituli* that housed early Christian communities, and by the fourth century we know there were at least twenty-five of them in Rome. Pious custom sometimes declared, later, that these owners had become saints. When Christianity became legalized early in the fourth century, some of the major new churches in Rome were built directly upon the foundations of the old *tituli*, and scraps and bits of their original walls and foundations still lie beneath these churches today. The early fifth-century church of Saints Giovanni and Paolo is a good example of this process of evolution and adaptation.[1]

What the evidence at St. Peter's and at Saints Giovanni and Paolo indicates is (ironically for a religion founded by a wanderer with no place to rest his head) a profound rootedness on the part of Catholic Christianity. There seems to have been a conscious, persistent intent to preserve the memory of the original sites of Christian life and death in Rome. If a saint like Peter was martyred and buried in a specific place, then some kind of physical monument to that historical fact would be created and perpetuated. For the first centuries, such monuments had, necessarily, to be so modest that they would escape the periods of destructive persecution by the pagan authorities. When Christianity became legalized, after 313, ever larger and very public buildings grew up above the same places. Thus the locations of the earliest communities of the faithful and the sites of the earliest martyrs' deaths became permanently recorded in buildings that were the external, physical records of historical facts. In this we see, as earlier with the creation of the first house-churches, a further evolution in the understanding of incarnation. Christianity began with incarnation and its claim to historicity: that Jesus was a man who lived and died at specific moments in recorded time. It continued with historical narratives of the lives and actions of his apostles and of other believers. Christian architecture, which, as at Dura, began with liturgical and communal needs, soon took on as well this historical function, buildings standing as embodied records of the lives and deaths of Catholic believers.

Such monuments to the past had of course been popular throughout antiquity, and long before Christianity reached Rome there were arenas, temples, and triumphal arches scattered through the city center memorializing famous generals, civic and religious leaders, and important past events. Christian monuments continued this practice, but at the same time the underlying meaning of these buildings was radically different. To understand that difference we must consider how differently pagans and Christians looked at death.

The Presence of the Dead

Roman pagans reverenced their dead. They honored them, according to their means, with simple gravestones or enormous tombs. They celebrated them with rituals at the time of burial and in the following years ritually commemorated the day of their dying. But at the same time they felt a deep repulsion at the dead body itself. Roman law forbade burying anyone inside the city walls, and many Romans practiced cremation, the socially approved way of dealing with the body after death. While sanitation was certainly an important factor in these practices, traditional thinking about the afterlife was also significant. For pagans, if there was any life after death at all—and many believed that death ended existence entirely—the afterlife was in a vaguely imagined underworld where the good were taken to the Elysian Fields while the bad suffered in Hades. The departed drifted away from the living, and all that could remain was a regret at their absence.

From its very beginning, Christianity adopted a fundamentally different cluster of ideas about death and dying that were rooted in the incarnation and resurrection of Jesus. Both concepts "stressed the importance of the human body."[2] God had taken on human flesh and his physical body had returned after his death in a transformed, glorified, and eternal physical form. From the time of the earliest preaching of Peter and Paul, Christians believed that the same thing would happen to each one of the faithful. Further, they taught that Christians in a sense never really died. Yes, here on earth they left behind a corpse, but they continued to live spiritually with God in heaven, and when Jesus returned to the earth for the Second Coming at the end of the world, the final moment when his kingdom would reign supreme, all of the dead bodies of history would rise again and those who had been saved would enter in their bodily form into paradise.

These beliefs, which were so very different from pagan traditions, immediately effected important changes in the way Christians buried their dead. From the earliest days Catholic Christianity forbade the Roman practice of cremation, presumably at least in part out of respect for bodies destined for such glory. But there was another reason, captured in a story about Jesus. The president of a local synagogue named Jairus comes to Jesus, telling him that his daughter is sick and asking Jesus to come and cure her. When they reach Jairus's house the girl has died, and the neighbors criticize Jairus for bothering Jesus. The girl is dead and nothing more can be done. Everyone is "weeping and wailing loudly." Jesus turns to the crowd and says, "Why do you make a commotion and weep? The child is not dead but sleeping." He takes the hand of the child, tells her to get up, and she does so (Mark 5:38–49). Remembering this story, early Christians could readily conclude that, in a typical Christian paradox, their dead were not dead but really just asleep awaiting Christ's return.

And not simply asleep, lying there in the tomb. Jesus had risen at once and soon after had ascended into heaven, returning to his Father. Faithful Christians were assumed to do the same thing. As a consequence, while they had left their bodies behind, their spiritual selves were alive, aware, and now near to God. Pagan belief had imagined the dead journeying back to the gods. Egyptian and Etruscan tombs were filled with things from this world—food, weapons, even the bodies of dead slaves killed at the time of the burial of a wealthy person—under the assumption that the dead person would make use of these possessions in the afterlife. But for Christians the working assumption was that in the afterlife people didn't need things. They only needed to be remembered and respected. Indeed the power relationship worked in the opposite direction. The dead could actually help those they had left behind in the world of the living by interceding for them with the God who was now so accessible to them. Working with the analogy of the relationship between a faithful servant and a powerful master, Christians assumed that their dead would represent their needs to God. Peter Brown, in his important study *The Cult of the Saints: Its Rise and Function in Latin Christianity*, finds this concept a reflection of Mediterranean systems of "clean" power and patronage, a simple repetition in the spiritual world of the way things worked in the everyday business world Christians knew. Hence there developed the practice of praying not only to God but also to deceased human beings for counsel and help. Soon Christians concluded that certain dead people might be more influential than others—martyrs, for example, who had died heroically, or people of conspicuous virtue. Evidence of their influence with God could be found in events on earth that seemed beyond what one could normally expect: miracles. Stories about the life of Jesus collected in the Gospels had recounted his ability to cure illness, even raise the dead to life, and so it was reasonable to assume that such events could continue to occur, the holy dead asking Jesus to help the faithful living just as he had helped those who had believed in him during his life on earth.

What all of this meant was what we have already called in chapter 7 a collapsing of both time and space. While the body of a beloved one might appear to be dead, there were two different senses in which that person was not, in fact, dead. In terms of time, that person would in the future return to this very body and it would rise in a glorified form. In terms of space, that person was already in paradise, near to God but aware of the needs of those still alive on earth. The dead body became a point in both time and space where past and future, earthly and heavenly, joined.

The immediate and logical consequence was first that this body must be treated with the utmost respect. "The child is not dead, but asleep."

Additionally, it could only make sense that those still alive would wish to have access to the dead, a chance to be near them in order to pay respect and to communicate expressions of need by prayer and ritual gesture. The dead were powerful because of their closeness to God, and it made good sense to be near them. Since Roman law forbade burial in the city, Roman Christians from the earliest days began to bury their dead outside the walls. Since they were an outlaw community, they could not erect ostentatious monuments and indeed it must have seemed imprudent even to begin the extensive surface cemeteries that would be needed for this ever-growing community. Hence, catacombs.

Roman Catacomb: Bodies in Time

Roman Catacombs as Architectural Space

Outside the city walls of Rome, beneath the surface soil, lie layers of a kind of rock called *tufa,* which is relatively easy to dig out, but which, when exposed to the air, becomes harder and more brittle. Pagan Romans had already begun the practice of digging underground corridors through this *tufa* for burial sites. Christians, prizing the relative secrecy of this manner of burial, soon adopted their practice. They would dig "rectangular cavities"[3] called *loculi* into the walls of these corridors, one above the other, sometimes five high, like shelves to receive the bodies. It was easy enough to inter between one and four bodies into each *loculus*, and the importance of family unity frequently led to several people being buried in the same space. When it was full, the *loculus* would be closed up with brick or marble covered with a plaster facing on which would be inscribed the name of the family and the days of death and sometimes also painted decorations reflecting the faith of the people buried there.

**Figure 25. Burial niches with fresco of Christ Pantocrator.
Catacomb of S. Callisto, Rome**

Along these underground corridors, at certain points, the diggers would hollow out a larger space that looked exactly like a room or even a suite of two or three rooms called a *hypogeum*. Inside this space there would be pedestals to hold marble sarcophagi and arched niches called *arcosolii* where tombs could be located. The ceiling and walls of a *hypogeum* would be decorated with frescoes. These were vaults for more wealthy families, directly anticipating the family chapels later built into the side aisles of Catholic churches and the larger mausoleums one still finds in Catholic cemeteries.

With time Roman catacombs spread both horizontally and vertically deeper into the ground following the liberated logic of underground development in which the choice of direction was more or less determined by how hard it was to dig and by the whim of the diggers. In the end, the Roman Christian catacombs taken together came to include more than 350 miles of corridors. Even today they are still being explored.

From its earliest days, Catholic Christianity was a religion that stressed community, membership in community, and the interdependence of every member with every other member through God's love. The Roman catacombs as architectural space constitute a dramatic articulation of this aspect of the Catholic imagination. The interior of a given catacomb was a community center that, according to Christian belief, transcended time and space. Family members were buried together either in a more humble *loculus* or in a more opulent *hypogeum*. Walking along the corridors, one moved through a city of those who were, as we have seen, asleep in Christ and hence still in different ways present. Small oil lamps attached to the walls flickered dimly. Simply painted frescoes pictured scenes from the Bible, records of the faith. The poor and the rich lay near each other in a remarkable display of egalitarianism, those long gone linked to those recently departed by the labyrinth of old and new passages connecting them. The catacombs were places to visit in order to be close to the dead, who received visitors, honors, and gifts, and so, as was the custom in Roman society, the catacombs became gathering places for ritual meals and celebrations. The pagan custom of the *refrigeria* or ritual libations poured out at the tomb during the burial of the dead evolved into the Christian practice of "funeral or memorial banquets...held in cemeteries near sites hallowed by martyrs."[4] Soon the Catholic stress upon the sacramental life appeared as funeral rituals came to include the celebration of the Eucharist. And so, though "there is a continuity between pagan funeral practices and the Christian cult of the dead...[soon it was] no longer a familial ceremony, but involved the entire community and took place in the presence of the bishop." As time passed another element emerged in special devotion to the martyrs buried in a given catacomb. As we have seen already, the "martyrs had transcended the human condition....They were both near to God and here on earth. Their relics incorporated the sacred....The tombs and relics of the martyrs constituted a privileged and paradoxical place where Heaven communicated with earth."[5] Thus emerged the practice of laying out the space in a catacomb with a specific "orientation of the tombs of second- and third-century Christians toward the principal [or martyr's] tomb."[6] So too began the custom of strangers, pilgrims, coming to a particular catacomb in order to reverence the body of a martyr and to pray for the martyr's patronage in heaven.

When Christianity became a legalized religion in 313, every aspect of the catacomb became translated into the new, open-air churches that the Christian community began to erect: now the dead were buried inside the church, the wealthier with their family tomb sites, the more humble beneath the church floor. A community fortunate enough to have the remains of a famous martyr or two would place them in a conspicuous, central place and pilgrims would come from afar to pray there. The practice of decorating the walls and ceilings of the catacombs translated into the mosaics of fourth-century Roman churches. At the same time, the organization of space from the house-churches or *tituli* of Rome now reappeared as the places for congregation and priest to celebrate the sacraments of the Eucharist in the sanctuary of the church and baptism often in a separate building, the baptistery. In these ways the earliest Roman Christian practices evolved almost seamlessly into buildings that still exist and that have been in continuous use since the later centuries of the Roman Empire.

Roman Catacombs: Iconographic Programs

Moving through the catacombs today the contemporary visitor may be surprised at what is not on the walls. There are, for example, no pictures of Christ's crucifixion or of the events of the last days of his life, which, after all, constitute the kernel story or narrative that was the basis of Peter's and Paul's teaching and, one can presume, of much early Christian preaching. At the same time there are a large number—frequently a preponderance—of images from the Hebrew Bible. Noah, Jonah, Abraham, Moses, Daniel, and Susanna turn out to be favorite subjects. Additionally there are images from pagan myth: Orpheus, the phoenix, Apollo. And "[o]ften," Jean Lassus notes, "the

traditional [pagan decorative] motifs—cupids, the seasons, animals...
intermingled with the themes created by the Christians."[7]

These fresco images are not great works of art, by any measure. They are simple paintings done by local artists, or even perhaps
the digger-artisans who excavated the catacombs. In style they are
"strongly reminiscent of the paintings in private houses"[8] of the era.
This is an important point. The manner in which the images in the
Christian catacombs are painted uses the same pictorial techniques
one would find in the decoration of the homes of simple people, not
the brilliant exercises in color and perspective one finds in the
homes of the rich at Pompeii. Instead, this is how ordinary people
of the day imagined the world.

At times catacomb pictures in a given space may be surrounded by painted frames or garlanded with painted ornament so
as to define the limits of a pictorial space. So the good shepherd
painted on the ceiling of the cubical of the "Velatio" in the catacomb of Priscilla is surrounded by a bright red circle that defines its
outer limits (Figure 26). Within that circle the shepherd, dressed as
a working man with leggings and a shortened tunic, is framed on
either side by a pair of trees, each with a bird on top, each with a
sheep beneath. Here the artist has been at pains to create a symmetrical, ordered pictorial world, with Jesus at its center. At other
times, fresco images appear without framing and without any effort
to define pictorial space or to achieve any kind of pictorial balance.
Their hovering, unframed, spontaneous emergence from the wall
suggests that what mattered was not the presentation of a kind of
aesthetic order but rather simply the depiction of something with
important religious meaning to the painter or the person who commissioned the image.

As with the pictures at Dura, Roman catacomb painting
recalls Jesus' forms of imagining. The almost exclusive focus is on
a scene from a story, a moment taken from a narrative. The nature
of the episode is suggested by the bodies of people, not their facial
expressions—the faces are very simply pictured and lack individuality. These figures, as at Dura, are dressed in contemporary clothing
that is very simply rendered: the folds, for example, of a toga looped
over a forearm, or a woman's veil partly draped over her face. They
use things drawn from daily life: a stick, a knife, a loaf of bread.
Clearly we are in the imaginative world of Jesus' storytelling.

Figure 26. Romanized Christ as good shepherd.
Fresco, catacomb of Priscilla, Rome

Gesture communicates meaning, the relationships between characters and what they are thinking and feeling—the whole body thrown into symbolic, dancelike movement that expresses joy, fear, or reverence. Some of the postures used in these pictures are taken from religious rituals practiced by Roman Christians and were clearly to be read by the viewer as codified symbols. But the positions of these bodies are more than ritualistic—they suggest strong emotion. It is as if the moment depicted totally transforms the bodies of these people into living emblems of faith and courage, the external and visible expression of the divine present within the human. People in danger, people in prayer, people practicing religious ritual—these are manifestations of God's love, care, and intentions. God is embodied through them in space and time and lives in their lives.

Let's examine with some care a space from the catacomb of Priscilla,[9] located north and east of the center of Rome. It illustrates in interesting ways how the Catholic imagination worked in early Roman Christianity.

The "Greek Chapel"

Tradition has given this long, rectangular space the name "Greek Chapel" because there are two inscriptions in Greek on one of its walls: "Obrimo to his most charming cousin and fellow student Palladio, remembered with affection," and "Obrimo, to his sweetest wife Nestoriana, remembered with love."[10] Perhaps it was Obrimo who had this space created and then buried there both his wife and his cousin.[11]

The images here may be very early. Some modern experts date them at around AD 180, only a hundred and fifty years after the death of Christ, and thus perhaps fifty years before Dura-Europos.[12] The comparison with Dura is useful. We found there a complex of interrelated images dominated by the figure of Jesus symbolically represented as the good shepherd and literally pictured in scenes from the New Testament. In the Greek Chapel there is no isolated, individual depiction of Jesus at all. Instead there is a rather curious amalgam of scenes from the Hebrew and Christian Scriptures along with some images from pagan allegory. There are visual references to Abraham, Moses, Jonah, Susanna, the young Hebrews in the fiery furnace (from the Book of Daniel), as well as to Mary greeting the Magi, the raising of Lazarus, and the Last Supper. The high incidence of Old Testament scenes suggests that we need to learn to read the meanings that lie within these images, using as a key our understanding of how the Catholic imagination works. Indeed, if we do so, it turns out that the pictures from the Greek Chapel, no matter what their literal content, are actually full of references to Jesus and to what it meant to be a follower of Jesus in pagan Rome.

As with the murals at Dura, these frescoes begin with the assumption that the viewer will know the stories being pictured. Lassus points out[13] that they are so casually painted that only people familiar with the Bible will understand them. The full meaning of these images emerges not from the individual pictures but from juxtaposition. The more that one thinks of each image in relationship to the others, the more kinds of meaning it suggests. The choice of images and symbols used seems dictated by a theology presumably emerging from community discussion or from preaching. The linked images at Dura suggested the way Jesus linked stories together. Here in the Greek Chapel, the interconnections that create the whole iconographic program, the string or chain as it were of associated stories and episodes, suggests that the structural principle connecting one story to another to another may have emerged from the way in which both Jewish and later Christian prayers and hymns were constructed.

For the faithful Jew, it was difficult to evoke a God who was unutterable and unknowable in himself and who had forbidden his followers to make any visual images of him. How would one identify him? When God speaks to Moses on Mount Horeb, he identifies himself this way: "I am the God of your father, the God of Abraham, the God of Isaac, and the God of Jacob" (Exod 3:6). The string or list of human names evokes crucial events in the history of Israel. Thus arose the later practice of identifying God by listing and describing events from sacred history that exemplify God's love for his people and God's faithfulness in his promises to them—the promises to Abraham and to Isaac, the flight through the Red Sea, the years of wandering in the desert, the final coming to the promised land, and so on.[14] God's nature, intent, and wishes for people are reflected in these lists—in a way they constitute an oblique portrait of God. God is that consciousness and force which makes these things happen. The same structural principle can be seen to govern the iconographic program in the Greek Chapel. Taken all together, these frescoes constantly speak of a Jesus they only infrequently picture directly. They constitute a kind of visual poem or hymn that constantly, albeit obliquely, tells the viewer more and more about him as the eye scans the accumulating images.

Let's imagine walking into the Greek Chapel and consider what its frescoes might mean. Passing through the arched entryway, we see before us a long, rectangular space divided in two by an arch halfway down creating, in effect, two rooms. At the far end, a third arch frames a semicircular apse.

THE FIRST ROOM: THE ENTRANCE WALL

We are now standing in the first of the two rooms, and we turn around to look back at the wall behind us, the wall penetrated by the entrance we have just used. Above its arch we see "Moses striking the rock and water pouring forth" (Figure 27). The Jewish people wandering in the desert are dying of thirst. God commands Moses to do something utterly implausible: take his rod of authority and strike a nearby rock. He does what he is told and immediately water gushes forth (Exod 17:3–6). The fresco dramatically illustrates this moment: Moses, dressed as a Roman in a toga, stands to the viewer's right and, reaching his arm out, strikes his rod against a tall, rounded rock, from which water flows.

Figure 27. Moses striking the rock. Fresco (late third century), catacomb of Priscilla, Rome

Christians, beginning perhaps with the passage from Paul's Letter to the Corinthians cited in chapter 6, discerned in this episode an anticipation or a type of the sacrament of baptism. We have alluded already to this way of interpreting sacred texts in our discussion of Paul and of Dura-Europas, and by now the reader knows readily how to understand the meaning of such images. As God quenched the thirst of the Jewish people and brought them into the promised land, so now he brings each Christian the saving water of baptism. Moses becomes a type for Jesus. Hence over the entryway to this "Chapel" the ancient artist recalls and celebrates the baptism that prepares Christians to enter this sacred space. We might recall the image of the woman at the well situated at the door to the baptistery of Dura-Europas. The same kind of thinking is at work in both places.

Framing this scene from Exodus both to its left and right on the same wall are figures from another Old Testament story. To the right we see the silhouettes of three young men standing in the midst of flames (Figure 28). They are dressed in short tunics and oriental caps (Phrygian berets), and their open hands are raised above their heads, palms upward, in what we now call the "orant position." This is the stance used by the earliest Christians in Rome when they prayed. Roman pagans had stretched their arms directly over their heads as if reaching up to the gods to take down their help from the skies. The early Roman Christians did lift their hands above their heads, but with the arms more spread out and the palms extended upward, opening their bodies to whatever God wished to send to them. This is the dancelike pose taken by these men in the middle of the flames.

Figure 28. The three Hebrews in the furnace. Fresco (second half, third century), Cubiculum of the Velati, catacomb of Priscilla, Rome

The story comes from the Book of Daniel (Dan 3). The Jewish people have been conquered and now live in exile in Babylon. The tyrannical king Nebuchadnezzar tests them by setting up a golden statue and demanding that everyone worship it. Three young Jews refuse, declaring, "We will not serve your gods and we will not worship the golden statue that you have set up" (Dan 3:18). The king commands that they be thrust into a furnace so hot it kills the soldiers who push them in. But the young men walk in the heart of the flames praising God, and an angel of the Lord comes down and drives the flames outward so that they remain cool and without pain. They call on nature to bless and glorify God in an ecstatic song.[15] The stunned Nebuchadnezzar thinks this angel looks like "a god" (3:25). He releases the three young men and blesses the God of the Jews, forbidding his people to speak badly of him.

Early Roman Christians could recognize in this story a typological anticipation of their own situation. We have already seen that from time to time the authorities would demand that Christians offer reverence to Roman gods, and when the Christians refused they were martyred, sometimes in remarkably cruel ways. The story of the faithfulness of the three young Hebrews constitutes a biblical type of this situation, and its happy conclusion can immediately be understood as a consolation, suggesting that Christians too, even if they are martyred, can expect God to redeem them from the fire in the afterlife. The descending, saving angel was readily seen as an anticipation of God's Holy Spirit—a figure even greater than "a child of the gods"—which had descended upon the apostles in Jerusalem on the day of Pentecost.

The three young men are to the right of the entrance. Opposite them on the left a figure dressed in a "tunic and pallium"[16] looks their way—perhaps the prophet Daniel witnessing this triumph of faith. These sketchy frescoes are "the oldest representation of this episode"[17] in Christian art.

Near to the three young men is a very different image: the mythic bird known as the phoenix. It rises from a burst of flames, its head glorified by a halo. Usually the phoenix is shown atop a palm tree. This version of the phoenix on the flaming pyre is "unique in ancient painting."[18] What is this pagan image doing in the Greek Chapel? The fable of the phoenix tells of a bird that lives to a great age. As it dies it bursts into flame, but from its ashes a new phoenix arises. Christian typological thinking is already adopting and adapting not only Jewish but pagan precedents here. The phoenix becomes a symbol or a type of Jesus, killed on the cross but after three days resurrected, his body now glorified. The artists who painted this wall clearly wished to make the connection between the Jewish story of the three young men in the furnace and the pagan story of the phoenix and to read in both of them the typological anticipation of Jesus' resurrection.

The flames in both images and in both stories create an interesting symbolic parallel, which in turn points to an ancient way of thinking about fire as a kind of cleansing or purgation. Just as the water of baptism is anticipated in the story of Moses and the rock in the desert, so the purgative flames of testing and death by martyrdom purify the Christian believer, burning away all that is evil and false and leaving only the purged soul ready to enter into a new life in paradise. These pictures connect traditional story, symbol, and theological meaning into a new and interlinked pattern, a pattern dominated by Christian paradox in which natural opposites reflect and mutually reinforce each other. Salvation by water—baptism. Salvation by fire—martyrdom. Contradictory images joined by paradox and celebrating being a Christian in an era of persecution.

THE FIRST ROOM: THE SIDE WALLS

Now we turn around and look at the walls between the entry and the first interior arch. To our right and to our left on the side walls we see frescoes depicting episodes from another part of the Book of Daniel, the story of Susanna (Figure 29). This too is about Jews living in exile in Babylon, but unlike the story about the fiery furnace, this narrative is exclusively set in the Jewish community. Susanna, a woman trained in the Mosaic Law and highly virtuous, is the beautiful and faithful wife of the Jewish leader Joakim. She walks every day in her garden with her servants. It is a kind of Eden of innocence and beauty. However, two old men, lascivious voyeurs "inflamed by passion," spy on her from two different hiding places. When they learn that they are both after the same thing they decide to force her to yield to their desire. One day when Susanna's maids have withdrawn and their mistress prepares to undress and bathe, the two old men burst out of the bushes and demand that she give herself to them. If she doesn't they threaten to accuse her falsely of meeting a lover here in the midday heat. Her response is, "I will fall into your hands, rather than sin in the sight of the Lord" (Dan 13:23). In a fury the frustrated old men accuse her before her husband and the rest of the community of adultery. These men enjoy both honor and authority because they are judges. Confronted by them, Susanna is forced to lower her veil and suffer the shame of revealing her face to everyone. The men put their hands on her head, the symbolic gesture of accusation. Susanna knows what comes next: stoning is the penalty for adultery (13:34). However, at this crisis moment God inspires the prophet Daniel. He demands the right to interrogate each accuser separately. He asks them where they saw this illicit meeting. Each old man describes the encounter as taking place under a tree—but each specifies a different kind of tree. The discrepancy in their accounts proves they are liars. Now Daniel as prophet speaks for God: "You shall not put an innocent and righteous person to death" (13:53). And to the second accuser he adds, "A daughter of Judah would not tolerate your wickedness" (13:57).

Figure 29. Susanna accused. Fresco, catacomb of Priscilla, Rome

On the right-hand wall of the Greek Chapel there is a depiction of Susanna going to bathe, her head partly covered by her mantle, her arms raised, her hands open palms upward in the orant position. To her left we see the two old men in togas pointing at her threateningly, while to her right another a man—probably Daniel the Prophet as witness—stands watching. On the facing wall we see two further moments from this story: Susanna being accused by the old men, who put their hands upon her head; then a tree serves as a division, and beyond it we see Susanna and another figure, perhaps Daniel again, with their arms lifted in the orant position, praying in gratitude for her vindication.

For early Roman Christians, this story of false accusation and unwavering faith in the face of persecution and the threat of death must have seemed a direct reflection of their own experience. Daniel's ringing cry, "You shall not put an innocent and righteous person to death," must have consoled them when they were anticipating future official suppression. Susanna can easily be interpreted as a type for the individual faithful Christian forced to defend his or her belief in the middle of a hostile world, and, additionally, as a figure representing the church as a whole, falsely criticized and persecuted for its loyalty to God.

The Greek noun *ekklesia*, which originally meant "a duly summoned assembly of people," is used in the New Testament as the word for "church." In Greek grammar it is a feminine noun. Christian artists beginning with pictures such as these adopted the custom of picturing the church as a woman, perhaps at first simply because the word is feminine, but soon people began reading into this practice all those virtues of nurturing, sympathy, vulnerability, and kindness traditionally associated with women and particularly with mothers. So from *ekklesia* to "Holy Mother Church" was a simple step, and Susanna, the beautiful, highly educated, faithful wife beset from without by rapacious enemies easily became a symbol of the church.

THE FIRST ROOM: THE FAR WALL

There is another image of church, faith, and indeed, finally, of Jesus, on the fourth wall of this first room, the wall formed by the archway that divides the two sections of the Greek Chapel. Above the arch against a pale ochre background we see three cloaked men stepping briskly forward, their arms extended. Each is holding something. At the right side of the image a seated woman holds a child on her lap (Figure 30). This is the Adoration of Magi and one of the "oldest of all known illustrations of the Virgin with Child."[19] It acts as a kind of keystone to the images on all four walls. With Moses we found faith rewarded with salvation. With the young Hebrews in the fiery furnace and the story of Susanna we found that same faith tested by persecution and rewarded by God's ultimate protection. In the picture of the Magi we find yet another image of the faith of Roman Christians and the Roman Church as a community: like the Romans, the Magi were gentiles, pagan wise men in search of God. Their study led them to expect "the child who has been born king of the Jews" (Matt 2:2), and their courage and persistence helped them in their long journey to Bethlehem where they finally found what they were seeking. They readily symbolize the

Roman faithful, and their reverent postures, the gifts they bring, reflect the giving of self active in the church.

Figure 30. Adoration of the Magi. Fresco, catacomb of Priscilla, Rome

THE SECOND ROOM

Now we step through the arch that divides the two rooms of the Greek Chapel, passing under the Adoration of the Magi. Entering the second room, we turn around to look back at this side of the wall penetrated by the arched entrance. Above us we see the resurrection of Lazarus from John's Gospel. Here is Carletti's description: "At the door of the burial vault, which is without stairs, appears a mummy, and the Savior is reaching out to him; nearby are two women, presumably Martha and Mary, the sisters of the dead man restored to life."[20]

If we turn around and look in the other direction at the final arch in the room, the arch in front of a shallow, semicircular apse set in the far wall, we see over that arch and against a dark red background a picture of the sacrament of the Eucharist (Figure 31). The ritual moment is pictured entirely in Roman terms. At the typical Roman semicircular dinner table or *stibadium* sit seven people in white togas, including a woman with a veiled head. The person sitting to their far right (our left) is a bearded man whose arms are extended. He is breaking the eucharistic bread in a gesture that came to be known as the *fractio panis* or breaking of the bread, a moment in the eucharistic celebration that symbolizes simultaneously (1) the

Figure 31. Breaking of the bread. Fresco, catacomb of Priscilla, Rome

breaking of Christ's body in death, which redeems all believers, and (2) the dividing up of the Eucharist so every member can take some—this latter becoming a symbol of both unity and multiplicity. In front of this figure is a Roman drinking cup with two handles, a plate with two fish, and another plate with five pieces of bread. At the ends of the table are baskets of bread: four to our left, three to our right, making seven in all. Every detail echoes gospel scenes in which Jesus feeds his followers, and two, five, seven, which are all primary numbers, lend themselves to various interpretations. This scene can easily be understood both as an illustration of the gospel story of the Last Supper, in which case the bearded figure is Jesus himself, or as a depiction of the early Christian Church ritually remembering that moment in the Mass. Indeed, it is probably wisest to see it as representing both simultaneously. The picture imagines Jesus and his disciples as looking exactly like contemporary Roman Christians, and it stresses that through the enactment of the ritual of the mass the two moments become one.

The story of the raising of Lazarus from the dead (Figure 32) is "the scene found most frequently in Roman cemeterial paintings"[21] and for good reason, since it is a story of Jesus bringing back to life one of his dearest friends. The promise in that story is the central motivating concept of the whole practice of catacomb entombment. The fresco that faces it, the picture of the Last Supper/Eucharist, depicts the sacrament that gave these early Christians that hope for

Figure 32. The resurrection of Lazarus. Fresco, Cubiculum of the Annunciation, catacomb of Priscilla, Rome

resurrection, as well as the sacramental ritual they themselves practiced in or near the catacombs when they memorialized their dead loved ones. If the first room of the Greek Chapel is about faith under duress and the rewards of church membership, then this second room takes us deeper into Christian belief, with one of its crucial miracles and its most frequently repeated sacrament.

But here too we find scenes from the history of the people of Israel. On the same wall as the Lazarus story we see Noah and the ark (Gen 8:18). Near to the picture of the Eucharist, on its left side, we see Abraham on the mountain raising the knife in his right hand, preparing to sacrifice his son Isaac because of God's command. To the right of the Eucharist is Daniel in the lions' den (Dan 14:31).

ICONOGRAPHIC PROGRAM OF THE SECOND ROOM

By now we are ready to find in such stories typological anticipations of Christianity. Just as Jesus raises Lazarus from death, so God with the ark saved Noah and all living things from death by drowning. Jesus intervenes in the later story, God in the earlier. In both cases hope is in new life.

Already in the New Testament the story of Abraham prepared to kill his son at God's command had been read as a type for God the

Father and Jesus—in Jesus' death God's generosity goes beyond that of the Jewish patriarch in sacrificing his own Son for the sake of humanity. There are two kinds of salvation in this parallel. God stays Abraham's hand and the boy Isaac lives. God permits Jesus to die, but as a paradoxical consequence all believers have hope of eternal life.

Daniel is yet another figure of faithfulness to God. The pagan king Nebuchadnezzar demands that everyone worship him. Daniel refuses and is thrown into the lion pit. God protects him and he is untouched, proving to the king and everyone else the power of the God of the Jewish people.

God saves Noah, Isaac, Daniel, and Lazarus from the threat or the reality of death and permits them to enter into new lives. Again and again the threat of death is overwhelmed by divine love. These are the stories the early Roman Christians chose to console the survivors of the dead people buried in this place. The eucharistic celebration, again the key image of the room, represents the sacrament that re-presents the event that is the basis for this faith and this hope.

If now we go back and stand at the entrance to the entire "chapel," we see two kinds of gift giving. On the first arch, which is nearer to us, we see the Magi bringing their gifts to Mary and Jesus—offering themselves and their faith. On the second and slightly more distant arch we see the *fractio panis*: the gift of Jesus, who, in response to the offering of faith in him, feeds his people communion broken for each one of them.

The Greek Chapel and Catholic Imagining

What we find in the Greek Chapel is a remarkable degree of sophistication, not in the execution of these simple, almost primitive images, but in the ideas they illustrate, reflecting perhaps the preaching, the prayers, or even the hymns of this early Christian community. They suggest how deeply read in scripture, both the Hebrew Bible and the New Testament, this community must have been. Further, they show us how these people thought about sacred history and their own place within it.

INCARNATION
Because the concept of incarnation was so important for them, these early Christians came to the understanding that God, and

God's Son Jesus, were both inside and outside of time—time being that limiting dimension applicable to created things but not to the divine. God acts in time and through history, and history reflects or voices God's will. God can be found everywhere in history but is never constrained by it. As God's people, Roman Christians understood themselves to be participating in a sacred history that is simultaneously within and outside of time. They were themselves both bound within a specific moment and yet part of something ahistorical, perennial, and constant. We see this exemplified in the figure of Susanna. Her story is a part of the past, but the people who depicted her on the wall of the Greek Chapel imagined her dressing just as they did and praying just as they did. The same thing is true for Moses, the Hebrews in the fiery furnace, and so on. These figures are in a way contemporaries of the people who painted them because they are all participating in the sacred history that is the incarnation of God's will within time. This is why typological thinking became so important a part of the early Catholic imagination. To the criticism of their pagan and Jewish rivals that Christianity was a brand new religion and lacked historical richness and depth, these Christians responded by saying, "Our history goes back to the beginning of Creation; our Christ has cast his glowing shadow in a thousand archetypal forms." They discerned the

> indissoluble unity of the story of salvation, of the Old and the New Testaments. For them, the Old Testament in its entirety was a "prophetic word."...Each word of the Scriptures, they believed, spoke of The Word—that is, of the Logos, Christ. But at the same time they conscientiously maintained the historical nature of all that had been enacted in the story of salvation.[22]

From the viewpoint of Christian typology, every story from Jewish tradition can be understood as in some way anticipating or prophesying the coming of Jesus. Further, what they knew about the people of Israel and about the good news of Jesus and his followers could be seen as anticipating or indeed prophesying things about their own day and their own lives. Since God rescued the faithful Jewish young men from the fiery furnace, he will do the same, somehow, for present faithful Roman Christians. The story from the Book of Daniel anticipates Jesus, but it also anticipates their present moment.

SACRAMENT

From the point of view of the incarnation, then, time is both linear and simultaneous. God and Jesus the Logos link present with past and, as the Greek Chapel constantly suggests, the past and the present speak to each other and speak about each other. Further, because the sacraments of the church are both the reenactment of historical events such as the Last Supper and the constant reincarnation of those events in the present moment with the priest at the Eucharist handing out the body of Christ, "history...was made ever-present for them by its sacramental re-enactment...."[23] The sacraments do not repeat history; they make the events of sacred history constantly alive and present within the community. For the Catholic imagination the Mass is not a bit of theater in which a scene from the life of Jesus is played out for an audience to watch; it is rather a moment when Jesus is again actually present among them and in which the miracle of the Last Supper actually takes place again right before their eyes and, more than that, they are invited to join in just as Jesus' disciples were, and to partake in the sacred meal.

The consequence of this line of thought is an important instance of the double vision of the Catholic imagination: as van der Meer puts it, "This constant double-image—Prefiguration and Fulfillment, shadow and reality, past and present—is the distinctive, basic feature of Early Christian thought."[24] And he recounts a delightful example of this in the way in which Saint Augustine preached to his community in the North African city of Hippo. After the reading of texts from scripture he would take his seat and begin by saying, "We have...heard the fact, now let us search for the mystery that lies hidden behind it."[25]

TYPOLOGY AND MEANING

Thinking in terms of typology has already expanded in the practice of the Greek Chapel to include not only Jewish but pagan motifs. The phoenix in flames crowned with its radiant halo illustrates how Christians were already drawing out of earlier traditions forms of meaning that they took to be analogous to and prophetic of their own Christian beliefs. One of the great intellectual projects that absorbed Christianity during its first centuries was the process of determining how much of the richness of Greco-Roman culture might be adopted and adapted to Christian use, and one of the strategies used in this process was the argument that, like the Hebrew people, the pagans too had anticipated, unconsciously, the Christian truths to come. So they told the story of the phoenix, but it was only when Christianity appeared that the inner meaning, what Augustine calls "the mystery that lies hidden," could be discerned. By the time of Dante's *Divine Comedy*, that climactic work of the later Middle Ages, it was possible to write of hell, purgatory, and heaven using as many figures from pagan as from Christian history. The Roman epic poet Virgil leads the Christian poet Dante through two-thirds of his adventures because Dante, writing with the double vision of the Catholic imagination, saw typological anticipations of Christianity in almost every aspect of pagan culture.

Typological thinking is everywhere throughout the myriad catacombs of Rome, and if we consider how many ways Jesus is pictured there, in images coming from the first to the fourth century after Christ, we can see how freely Roman Christians adopted both Jewish and pagan precedents, finding in all of them anticipatory prefigurations of their Savior: Jesus, for example, as the Greek god Apollo (St. Peter's; Mausoleum of the Julii, mid-third century),[26] or as the reed-playing Greek mythic figure Orpheus (catacomb of Domitilla).[27] As the shepherd—a figure as popular in classical as in Christian art (in the catacomb of Calixtus we find the earliest instance painted above the remains of Pope Cornelius in Crypt of Lucina),[28] or as Samson, the Jewish hero of great strength (in the late, elaborate cycle of the catacombs in Via Latina). As Jonah (in the Mausoleum of the Julii), or as Isaac (in the catacomb of Priscilla, hypogeum of the Velatio).[29] Jesus is also frequently pictured in the allegorical figures of the Teacher (catacomb of Domitilla, mid-fourth century; sarcophagus of Via Salaria, early third century)[30] and the Fisherman (Mausoleum of Julii; catacomb of Callixtus, second half of the third century).[31] Christians readily understood Jesus in his life and work to be analogous to all of these figures, from the god of the sun to the teacher of a new wisdom to the worker for the salvation of others who "catches" people not fish. Like Isaac he was destined to be a sacrificial victim, and like Samson his courageous strength pulled down the temple of idolatry. Like Orpheus the music of his teaching leads the dead back to life, and like the shepherd he cares lovingly for each of his flock. Just as each example in this wide range of parallels tells us something different about Jesus, so seeing that there is something of Jesus in these various types suggests that he can still be found today in the lives and the work of the fisherman, the teacher, the shepherd, even as he was once anticipated in the pagan myths of the sun and of rebirth.

Standing at the entrance to the Greek Chapel, one sees first the Magi approaching the Virgin and Child, then the eucharistic banquet and the mutual sharing of the bread of life. Both images remind the visitor of the importance of community for these Roman Catholics. The sacrament of the Eucharist celebrates the unity in diversity of the members of the church, all joined by the body of Christ, just as the earlier journey of the Magi celebrates the journey each person takes in seeking and ultimately finding the Savior. In all of these ways the Greek Chapel, as we have now seen, is filled with a synthesis of pagan, Jewish, and Christian images:

1. Images of Jesus: his incarnation both as a man and in history

2. Images of the salvation Jesus won for all: represented in the heroes and heroines of faith who endure shame and danger fearlessly

3. Images of the sacramental life of the church: baptism, Eucharist

4. Images of the importance of unity to the community of Christian faithful: a unity that is not interrupted even by death, as these frescoes decorating a place of burial constantly proclaim

The heterogeneity of materials being employed by the Catholic imagination in such catacomb decorations become a unified whole thanks to the unifying ideas of early Christianity. Everything speaks of Jesus, and in the way that Jesus was accustomed to speak.

CHAPTER NINE

Beginning
Catholic Poetry
Prudentius

The World of Prudentius

Despite its illegal status, the Christianity of Dura-Europos and of the Roman catacombs continued to grow and to spread throughout the empire during the third century, though not without intermittent state opposition. This climaxed in the "Great Persecution," which began in the year 303. The ruling emperor Diocletian had some years earlier declared, "The ancient religion ought not to be censured by a new one. For it is the height of criminality to reverse that which the ancestors had defined...." Now once and for all he tried to eliminate Christianity, his state apparatus focusing on "Christian bishops, priests, and deacons" in an effort to root out the power structure of the new church. This continued "in parts of Asia Minor, Syria, and Egypt, for eleven years."[1] This is the last, heroic period of the early Christian martyrs.

The rise to power of Diocletian's successor Constantine, however, brought with it an abrupt reversal in the history of Rome and of Christianity (Figure 33). After defeating his rival Maxentius at the Milvian Bridge in 312, Constantine announced that during the battle he had been blessed with a vision in which he was told to conquer his enemies under the emblem of Jesus, the cross. He fully believed that Jesus had helped him win not only the battle but also the title of emperor. Months later, with the Edict of Milan (313), "Constantine recognized Christianity with open favour and granted

Figure 33. Bust of Constantine
The Emperor Constantine (ca. 274–337) made Christianity a legal religion within the Roman Empire and gave impetus to the building of Christian worship spaces, including the basilica in Rome that served as the central church of Western Catholic Christianity until it was replaced by St. Peter's during the Renaissance.

it official standing."[2] Not only did Christianity become legal, but soon it began to crowd out its religious rivals, including traditional Roman paganism. Constantine and his successors "progressively forbade public sacrifices, closed temples and colluded in frequent acts of local violence against major cult sites...."[3] By 438 the revised Theodosian Code of Roman law proclaimed that "there was to be little place, in the new Roman order, for heresy, schism, or Judaism, and no place at all for the 'error of stupid paganism.'"[4] From being a persecuted minority, Christianity had become the dominant, indeed the official, religion of the empire.

Early in his reign, Constantine initiated an impressive building program. At his command large Christian basilicas were erected not only in Rome (Figure 34)—the first St. Peter's is a Constantinian church—but also on what were presumed to be the sites of sacred history in Jerusalem: "the grotto of the Nativity...the site of the Resurrection and Crucifixion..." and so on.[5] The now-public and legal hierarchy of church officials soon took on important roles as

leaders in secular as well as sacred matters, and the liturgy celebrated in the huge new structures evolved into highly formalized rituals. In some places the intimacies of the house-church were
replaced by long processions through city streets, the ample use of
incense, costly attire for bishops and priests, and stiff protocol in the
regulation of prayer and the sacramental life. Devotion to Christian
martyrs led to the construction of pilgrimage churches and the practice of making long journeys to reach the resting place of a particularly holy person. It was an era of immense intellectual ferment,
with Christian theologians, philosophers, and mystics studying
Jewish and pagan traditions and drawing from both whatever elements they might synthesize with Christian orthodoxy.

Figure 34. Old St. Peter's. Fresco, S. Martino ai Monti
This fresco depicts the interior of the first St. Peter's Basilica in Rome. A com-
parison with the drawing of the basilica at Pompeii illustrates how this typical
Christian building developed from early Roman architecture.

This is the world of the poet Prudentius. "It was," as T. R.
Glover writes, "the age of the victorious church, mistress of the
Roman world, and not yet seriously dreading the heathenism and
savagery of the German. Prudentius writes with the consciousness
of victory."[6]

Prudentius: Life and Works

Aurelius Clemens Prudentius was born in 348 in what we now call Spain, perhaps near to Zaragoza, then a provincial town named Caesaraugusta. This area had been a part of the Roman Empire for centuries, and certainly Prudentius thought of himself as a Roman. He received a typical classical education and worked as a lawyer and later as a government official, receiving honors from the emperor. He was a "fervent Christian...."[7]

In his mid-forties Prudentius began writing poetry. Between 392 and 405, when his poetical works were published, he proved himself remarkably prolific and innovative. He wrote long didactic poems on theological topics such as the incarnation and the origin of sin. He initiated the tradition of Christian allegory with his *Psychomachia*, which uses personifications of conceptual abstractions to picture the struggle between vice and virtue. His *Peristephanon* is a cycle of poetic narratives describing in often gruesome detail the heroic deaths of Christian martyrs, most of them from the era of Diocletian. His cycle of twelve odes called the *Cathemerinon* or *The Daily Round* voices the spirit of Christian religious celebration through the cycles of the day and the religious year. All in all, in a brief span of years, Prudentius became "a pioneer in the creation of a Christian literature, and had the credit of originating new types of Christian poetry...."[8]

While Prudentius was relatively unknown outside of Spain during his life, "towards the end of the fifth century he became 'a living factor' in the spiritual life of Christendom...."[9] By the Middle Ages he had become one of Europe's "most popular authors. No one was more universally read and imitated, and no books, with the exception of the Bible, were so abundantly provided with Old High German glosses as *The Daily Round* and the *Peristephanon*."[10] Assessments of specialized scholars in our own day echo the high esteem of Prudentius's medieval readers. Macklin Smith argues that Prudentius "is the best Latin poet between the Augustan Age and the twelfth century...the only poet of Late Antiquity...who could successfully imitate Virgil and Horace...."[11]

Prudentius and Roman Poetic Tradition

Smith's reference to Prudentius's revered Roman predecessors is important both to any assessment of his achievement as a poet and to our study of the Catholic imagination, because it was Prudentius's conscious choice to adopt the style and manner of Augustan Roman poetry and to use that medium for the expression of Christian belief and feeling. He

> has not cut himself off from the old culture....[Rather,] steeped in the work of classical Latin poets [he]...regards...pagan literature and art not as things to be rejected but as part of the inheritance into which Christian Rome enters...appropriating Latin poetic forms, lyric, epic, didactic...to show the world that the subject-matter of the new faith can fill ancient moulds.[12]

In doing this Prudentius repeated in poetry the achievement of the anonymous artists who decorated the catacombs. Just as they had translated the rhetoric of decoration from ordinary Roman homes into a way of ornamenting Christian tombs, so Prudentius adapted the manner of the great poets of the Roman past for his Christian beliefs. He works, however, in a way far different from his earlier Christian predecessors. Theirs had been the humble effort to decorate spaces used by ordinary Christians in reverencing their dead. Prudentius aspires to fit his work into the tradition of the greatest Latin poets. While there may well have been fine writers of Christian poetry before Prudentius, it is with his work that we see an important, very early example of the Catholic imagination aiming at the highest levels of artistic achievement.

Prudentius's writing embraces a number of different genres, and there is a lot of it: the standard edition of his works fills two good-sized volumes. For the sake of practicality, let us look at a single book, the collection of "hymns" as he called them, *The Cathemerinon*. Here we find twelve poems emerging from the tradition of the Latin ode, which had for centuries been dominated by the four books of odes written by Horace.

It is always difficult to study poetry in translation—invariably so much is lost. In the discussion that follows we get a few glimpses of the words and phrases of Prudentius's actual work in his own Latin, but for the most part we are looking at three different translations into English. One, by H. J. Thomson,[13] is in prose and it is quite strictly literal, giving a rather flat-footed but extremely accurate account of everything Prudentius has put down. The other, by

David R. Slavitt,[14] is by a poet. It has the excitement of actual poetry, but this translator has worked very freely, not only adapting Prudentius's language to modern idioms but at times compressing several lines or more of Prudentius into a word or a phrase. The third, by the present author, is an English language version of one entire poem from *The Cathemerinon* in order to provide the reader with a sense of what a whole Prudentius poem looks like. We use Thomson for the particulars, Slavitt for the poetic surge, Pfordresher to get a glimpse of Prudentius at full flight, and we will remain regretful that it is not possible to examine Prudentius solely in his own Latin.

In his Hymn IX, "A Hymn for All the Hours" (Figure 35, pp. 170–75), we will see many of the characteristic elements of Prudentius's art that we can then, in subsequent pages, consider individually, in terms not only of Hymn IX but of the other hymns as well. The poem begins with the Speaker calling for his servant boy to bring him his lyre. He is prepared to celebrate Christ's great deeds (lines 1–7). He will sing in the traditions initiated by the Hebrew king and prophet David, the poet who created the Book of Psalms, who had already foretold the wonders that Jesus, the creator of the world, the Alpha and the Omega, the beginning and the end of all, would achieve (8–20). The poem then begins a catalog of Christ's miraculous works: the creation of the world (22–27), his own incarnation as a man (28–47), his miracles such as turning water into wine (lines 48–53), the healing of lepers (54–58), making the blind see (59–62), calming a storm at sea (63–66), curing a woman afflicted with a hemorrhage (67–70), raising the dead (71–82), walking on water (83–88), casting out devils (89–96), feeding thousands from five loaves and two fish–an anticipation of the sacrament of the Eucharist (97–105), making the deaf hear (106–11). He then turns to the legend of Jesus after his death on the cross descending into hell to liberate those imprisoned there (118–37) and celebrates the victory of the crucifixion (138–47). Joyously he derides Satan in his defeat (148–54) and then returns to the wonders of creation and redemption from sin and death achieved by a Jesus now enthroned at God's right hand (155–78). The poem ends with a vision of all creation celebrating Christ through the ages to come (179–87).

Figure 35
Hymn IX: *Hymnus Omnis Horae* ("A Hymn for All the Hours")
By Aurelius Prudentius Clemens
Translated by John Pfordresher

Hand me my lyre, my boy,
for I mean to sing out
in traditional rhythms
and in rich and sweet melody
the celebrated deeds of Christ.   5
For him alone I compose this song,
for him alone my lyre rings with praise.

Christ is the one whose coming
David, king and priest, foresaw,
celebrating with song, the plucked harp, and the   10
    ringing drum
as the heavenly spirit inspired him,
filling him to the very marrow of his bones.

We sing now of marvels which are real,
proven. The world around us verifies
them and will not deny the wonders   15
God fashioned to teach us through his own, human self.

Born from his Father's heart before the world emerged,
named the Alpha and Omega,
Christ is the fountain from which all wells
and the final statement which closes all things,   20
all things which are, once were, or someday will be.

He gave the command and created all;
He spoke and made the earth, the sky,
and hollowed out the seas,
the three different aspects of this created world,   25
and whatever lives there
under the celestial spheres of sun and moon.

A body shaped to perish, limbs fated for death,
He put them on so that humanity, the seed of Adam,
cursed to die, would not stay mired, damned by the Law,   30
in the depths of Tartarus.

O blessed beginning! a virgin in childbirth
brought forth our salvation
fashioned by the Holy Spirit,
and the boy redeemer of the world   35
revealed his sacred face.

Cry out heavenly heights, cry out all you angels,
all places and things which are good cry out
in praise of God;
let no tongue be still   40
when every voice sings in harmony.

See! He is the one
the ancient seers foretold,
the one promised
in the faithful pages of the prophets;   45
now he springs out, shining,
let everything, together, praise him.

Amphorae filled with clear spring water
now flow with the finest Falerian wine.
The wine steward tries to explain   50
how this wine came from the water jug
and the master of the feast is astonished
at its rare savor.

"Limbs with deadly sores, putrefying flesh,
I command you wash them," He says;   55
they do as He bids;
and the swollen skin is purged
the wounds purified.

You, Christ, anoint eyes
darkened, buried in what seemed eternal darkness,   60
using the healing mud and nectar of Your own mouth,
opening them, healing, letting in the light.

You rebuke the mad winds with which the
    gloomy storms
stir the oceans from their very depths
vexing the wandering ship;   65
they obey, and over mild waves spreads the calm.

The very hem of Your sacred robe a modest woman
furtively touches and immediately is cured;
now the pallor leaves her cheek—
healed is the once constant flow of blood.   70

He saw the young man
snatched from his own sweet youth,
He saw the mother taking him to the grave
with her last tears;
"Get up," He said, and the youth gets up   75
and stands, returned to his mother's side.

Lazarus, now four days shut out from the
    sun's light
hidden in the darkness of the tomb
He orders back to vigor.
He returns to the breath of life,   80
and the fetid flesh freshened
Lazarus breathes once again.

He walks upon the level of the sea,
He treads upon the surface of the waves,
and the shifting waters of the deep   85
offer his feet a pathway,
they do not yield
under the pressure of his holy step.

A man, long used to living in a graveyard,
chained, grinding his teeth in a mad, animal rage,   90
flings himself down and kneels
when he senses Christ is near.
Driven out by Christ's exorcism,
the plague of demons in a thousand forms
attacks a herd of filthy pigs   95
and plunges them into the waves of black water.

Bring the baskets of uneaten fragments,
twelve in all, leftover after five thousand
ate their fill from five loaves and two fish.
You are our meat and bread,   100
You our perennial sweet savor.
I do not know who could be hungry

at your eternal, sacred feast;
Not filling an empty belly
but fostering life itself.   105

The closed pathway of the deaf man's ears,
once ignorant of all sound,
at Christ's command
empties clean of its thick obstructions—
Now able to enjoy the sound of voices   110
and open even to whispers.

Every affliction yields,
every weakness driven out,
the tongue speaks
long fettered by silence,   115
the happy cripple
now carries his pallet through the town.

Yes, lest even those living in Hell
should miss salvation,
He generously descends into Tartarus;   120
the shattered door yields to Him,
torn bolts fall, the hinge destroyed.
That door so ready to let in the fallen,
so tenacious in keeping back those who
      would return,
its bolt he throws back,   125
liberating those who have died;
the law reversed, the dark threshold now is open
to the people returning.

But while God's tawny new light
illuminated the cave of the dead,   130
while his bright day filled the astounded darkness
      of Hell,
above the earth the sad stars faded in the dirtied
      heavens
and the sun took refuge in filthy, rust-colored
      mourning clothes,
giving up his chariot of light
and in sorrow hiding himself.   135

And it is said earth shuddered
glimpsing the chaos of an eternal night.

Now free my voice, the music of my imagination,
free my quick tongue,
to tell his passion's victory,   140
tell of the triumphant cross,
sing of the sign, marked on our foreheads,
which shines out so brightly.
Oh, what a new miracle, that wound of his
    astonishing death!
From his heart flowed waves here of blood, there   145
    of water;
The water, certainly, washing us clean of sin,
while blood wins the crown of victory.

The Serpent saw the holy body become an
    accepted sacrifice;
saw, and lost at once its burning poisonous venom;
wounded now, in terrible pain, the hissing   150
    throat shattered.
What good, groveling Serpent, did you gain
in that new world by striking down,
through your devious lies,
the first human creation?
That human form has been washed free from guilt   155
by receiving God.

To a brief experience of death our Saving Leader yielded,
that he might teach the buried dead a future rising,
dissolving the shackles of their sinful past.
Then a multitude of patriarchs and saints,   160
now finally returning on the third day
with the Savior who first created them,
put on again their mortal flesh
and marched forth from their tombs.
From the slime living limbs came together   165
from dry, glowing ashes,
the cold dust becoming veins and arteries, warming,
bones, nerves, and marrow
wrapped around with a covering of skin.

Later, with human calamity at an end   170
and life brought back to all,
to the high and lofty throne of the Father
as a conqueror he ascended,
to tell all of heaven of the fame and glory of
     his passion.
Hail, Judge of the Dead! Hail, King of the Living!   175
Stay on guard at the right hand of the Father,
You who are known for Your virtue,
issuing forth from there as the just avenger of
     all wrongs.

Now it's You the elders and the youths,
You the chorus of infants,   180
You the crowd of mothers and virgins, and
     innocent girls
acclaim in one resounding, pure, harmonious song.
Let the flowing waters and the waves, the shores
     of the seas,
rain showers, seething fires, snow, hoar-frost,
the woods and the winds, night, day,   185
gather to celebrate together You
through all the coming ages.

Prudentius: Song from the Earth

The Predecessor: Horace

The Roman poet Quintus Horatius Flaccus (65–8 BC), like our poet Aurelius Prudentius Clemens, began life as a public man, serving in the army of the rebel Brutus and later, having accepted the victory of Caesar Augustus, as a clerk in the treasury office. Thanks to the aid of the wealthy patron Maecenas, who gave him a farm in the Sabine Valley northeast of Rome, Horace was able to turn in the middle of his life to writing poetry. His *Odes,* the self-evident model for Prudentius's *Hymns,* use traditions of Greek poetic form and meter. In them Horace sometimes addresses friends, his patron Maecenas, and even the emperor, offering advice or praising admirable conduct.

Horace is an Epicurean, and some of his odes urge the reader to make the most of the pleasures of brief life. "Even while we speak, envious Time has sped. Reap the harvest of to-day, putting as little trust as may be in the morrow!"[15] He has the pagan's rueful vision of death: "a common night awaiteth every man, and Death's path must be trodden once for all....Without distinction the deaths of old and young follow close on each other's heels; cruel Proserpine [goddess of the land of the dead] spares no head."[16] He writes frequently of sexual love and usually with the bitter sense of its brevity and the disloyalty of lovers. For example, he warns Lydia what will happen with the fading of her beauty: "Thy turn shall come, and thou, a hag forlorn in deserted alley, shalt weep o'er thy lovers' disdain, when on moonless night the Thracian north-wind rises in its fury, while burning love and passion...shall rage about thy wounded heart."[17]

Horace is a highly self-conscious artist and from time to time he takes a moment to write about his reasons for choosing to be a poet. In the very first ode of his first book he surveys many different sorts of human enterprise and the kinds of glory and reward that accompany military life, wealth, and other endeavors. "Many delight in the camp," he notes, "in the sound of the trumpet...and in the wars that mothers hate. Out beneath the cold sky, forgetful of his tender wife, stays the hunter ..." and so on. But, "Me the ivy, the reward of poets' brows, link with the gods above... if you rank me among lyric bards, I shall touch the stars with my exalted head."[18] What he craves is the public awards given to famous poets symbolized in the wreath of ivy leaves. There is more than a touch of egoism at moments such as this, a kind of Roman pagan egoism in which the achievement of the artist is thought to make him akin to the gods themselves.

Prudentius's Transformations of Horatian Traditions

In a telling gesture four centuries later, the Christian poet Prudentius in his second hymn echoes Horace's First Ode from the First Book in reproducing the list of occupations and their expected rewards, but then reversing Horace's conclusion.

> This is the hour that profits all for carrying on their several businesses, be it soldier or citizen, sailor, workman, husbandman or huckster. One is carried away by desire for fame in the courts,

another by the grim war-trump; and here are the trader and the countryman sighing for their greedy gains. But we, who know naught of paltry gain or usury or eloquence, nor show our prowess in the art of war, know Thee, O Christ, alone. Of Thee with pure and single heart, with devout voice and song, on bended knees with tears and singing we learn to make request.
>   (From Hymn II, "A Morning Hymn,"
>   lines 37–52; trans. Thomson)[19]

Prudentius means the reader to remember Horace and his hope that his poet's head will graze the very stars themselves, and he then goes on to insist upon a Christian modesty in which the self is nothing, the praise of Christ everything. Here are his words:

> te mente pura et simplici,
> te voce, te cantu pio
> rogare curvato genu
> flendo et canendo discimus.
>   (Hymn II, lines 49–52)[20]

Pura mente and *simplici,* the pure and simple mind, or heart, is what he seeks, in trying to create a *cantu pio* or reverent song. The "me" of Horace's line 29 with its egoism is replaced with *te,* the word "you" referring to Christ in line 49 and repeated twice in line 50, each time in the dramatic initial position, to drive home the point that for Prudentius the aim of poetic achievement is worship of Christ and putting him first, and not self-aggrandizement.

In the third hymn, Prudentius returns again to the distinction between the old and new poetry invoking the classical spirit of inspiration: "Put away, my Muse, the paltry ivy-leaves wherewith thou hast been wont to encircle thy brows; learn to weave mystic garlands...and wear thy hair wreathed with the praise of God" (Hymn III, "A Hymn before a Meal," lines 21–25; trans. Thomson).[21] This new, Christian muse will create a new kind of music. Here is the beginning of Hymn IX:

> Hand me my lyre, my boy,
> for I mean to sing out
> in traditional rhythms
> and in rich and sweet melody

the celebrated deeds of Christ.
For Him alone I compose this song,
for Him alone my lyre rings with praise.

Christ is the one whose coming
David, king and priest, foresaw,
celebrating with song, the plucked harp, and the ringing drum
as the heavenly spirit inspired him,
filling him to the very marrow of his bones.
　　　(From Hymn IX, lines 1–6; trans. Pfordresher)

In this characteristic Christian mingling of the Jewish and the Roman, Prudentius will use "traditional rhythms" (found in the works of Latin poets such as Horace) while looking to the same source of inspiration as the Jewish poet-king David—he who, as Prudentius says, "Spiritum caelo influentem per medullas hauriens,"[22] that is, "The heavenly spirit inspired…filling him to the very marrow of his bones" (Hymn IX line 5). This is an invocation not to the classical muse but to that *spiritum caelo* or *Creator Spiritus* of the Catholic imagination, the subject of this study, asked to flood the "medullas," the marrow or innermost center of the poet's mind and heart.

The themes of the various hymns in Prudentius's collection wittily reverse favorite Horatian themes. For poems of bitter love lost, poems of divine love gained. For Epicurean reveries on seizing pleasure before it disappears, a forecast of the endless pleasures of paradise. For the praise of secular men of wealth like Maecenas and of power like Caesar Augustus, the praise instead of God, Father, Son, and Holy Spirit, seen as the source in the end of all joy and all power. Prudentius indicates again and again that his poetry begins with the traditions of the great poets of the Latin tradition, but at the same time it is something altogether new.

A New Heaven and a New Earth

There is a terrific surge of high spirits in Prudentius's poetry that comes from his sense that here he is making something fresh and transformative. The very first poem in the collection, Hymn I (Figure 36), is a celebration of this new dawn.

Figure 36
From **Hymn I:** *Hymnus ad Galli Cantum*
("A Hymn for Cockcrow")

'Coco rico,' the rooster crows.
The dawn is come, and he sings to those
who lie abed. So Christ does, too,
rousing our sluggish souls to the new
    dawn of His being.
Beds are for bodily sickness or sloth,
but the sun is up, and now God's truth
shines in the skies, as birds declare
from rooftops into the morning air
    the glory of seeing.

Let every daybreak symbolize
the falling away of scales from eyes
hungry for light...

The dawn air breathes a promise we
delight to hear—that misery
and sin may vanish as some bad dream.
Miraculous, morning may yet redeem
    our grievous sins.
The phantoms that roam the world at night
know this and therefore abhor the light
of God's creation that purifies.
They flee to the murk and hide their eyes
    when the day begins.
    (From Hymn I, lines 1–44; trans. Slavitt)[23]

Perhaps what strikes one first about the opening lines of Hymn I is the simplicity of the moment described: we are in the plain, everyday world typical of Jesus' imagination. It is dawn and everyone is still in bed. As the poem says later, "Under the blankets, the body's heat is cozy."[24] At the same time, a brilliant light fills the sky. The central analogy is clear. Christ is the rooster of the new dawn, the herald waking the sluggish world to the light of a new faith, a new era in history. The rising sun, another analogy for Christ, drives away not only the groggy confusion in the head of the sluggard but also the dark phantoms of ignorance and sin that roam in the night and linger deep inside of each of us.[25] With his advent comes a clarity of seeing full of the promise of understanding, action, and goodness now arriving. The double vision of the Catholic imagination finds meaning in this simple, concrete scene, which, because it now implies so much more, is full of delight and promise. The poetry of the *Cathemerinon* is frequently nature poetry, and as in this case it finds God in the songs the earth is singing. Here we see a fulfillment of Catholic belief in incarnation broadly understood. The poet finds God in the beauty of nature and in the robust energy of his own body. The dawn tells him of divine love and of a hope for human redemption. The nature Prudentius writes about is the humble, ordinary, everyday nature of the parables of Jesus, a barnyard world that, nevertheless, can sing the glory of God.

The ode had been at times a vehicle for Horace's praise of his friends and of official Rome. Prudentius's hymns too are frequently poems of celebration, but always of the divine, at times achieving an ecstatic vision in which the whole created world joins together in praise of God, as in the conclusion of Hymn IX.

> Now it's You the elders and the youths,
> You the chorus of infants,
> You the crowd of mothers and virgins, and innocent girls
> acclaim in one resounding, pure, harmonious song.
> Let the flowing waters and the waves, the shores of the seas,
> rain showers, seething fires, snow, hoar-frost,
> the woods and the winds, night, day,
> gather to celebrate together You
> through all the coming ages.
> (Hymn IX, lines 179–87; trans. Pfordresher)

Passages such as this indicate that Prudentius remembers the Judeo-Christian conviction that God uttered the word of creation:

> He gave the command and created all;
> He spoke and made the earth, the sky,
> and hollowed out the seas,
> the three different aspects of this created world,
> and whatever lives there
> under the celestial spheres of sun and moon.
> (Hymn IX, lines 22–27; trans. Pfordresher)

Now all of creation, the most ordinary and universal elements of creation, respond, the movements of water, light, heat, and cold dancing to the rhythm of its praise. Prudentius was almost certainly recalling the extended song celebrating God that, in the Book of Daniel, the three young Hebrews (whom we saw in the "Greek Chapel" in the catacomb of Priscilla) sing in the midst of the fiery furnace. Here is only a part of it:

> Bless the Lord, sun and moon,
> praise and glorify him for ever!
> Bless the Lord, stars of heaven,
> praise and glorify him for ever!
> Bless the Lord, all rain and dew,
> praise and glorify him for ever!
>
> Bless the Lord, every wind,
> praise and glorify him for ever!
> Bless the Lord, fire and heat,
> praise and glorify him for ever!
> Bless the Lord, cold and warmth,
> praise and glorify him for ever!
> (Dan 3:62–67 NJB)

In writing about the birth of Jesus in Hymn XI, Prudentius again imagines the whole of nature, animals, flowers, even sand and rock, filled with joy at the coming of the Savior.

> The earth, I ween, thickly besprinkled all the countryside with flowers, and the very sands of the desert were scented with nard and nectar. All things rough and rude were conscious of Thy birth, O Child; even the hardness of stone was overcome and clothed the rocks with grass. Now honey flows from the crags, now the oak sweats drops of perfume from its dry trunk, and the tamarisks bear balsam. How holy Thy manger-cradle, King eternal! The nations through all time, even the dumb beasts, hold it sacred. The brute cattle adore it, a mere herd without knowledge; the senseless tribe adores it, whose only vigour is feeding.
> (From Hymn XI, "A Hymn for the 25th of December,"
> lines 65–84; trans. Thomson)[26]

In chapter 2 we considered the implications of the incarnation, and there we noted how one can imagine the world, which is God's creation, as somehow speaking of its Maker. In Daniel and in Prudentius we find this notion. Everything in creation voices an awareness of its source. If one listens properly, one hears a song of praise in every thing. Playing with that notion, Hymn XI imagines that upon the birth of Jesus there is a moment of particular joy that fills even the animals and the rocks.

Jesus as Hero

The guarded caution with which the catacomb frescoes alluded to the events in the life of Jesus is now a thing of the past. As we have seen, in Hymn IX, Prudentius in praising Christ exults in one episode after another from the Gospels: Jesus cures illnesses, calms the sea, walks on water, exorcises devils, feeds the multitudes. The cross, earlier an emblem passed over by Christians perhaps as too painful or too shameful to be rendered, now becomes a source of joy and of pride. "Tell His passion's victory," he proclaims,

> tell of the triumphant cross,
> sing of the sign, marked on our foreheads,
> which shines out so brightly.
> Oh, what a new miracle, that wound of his astonishing death!
> From his heart flowed waves here of blood, there of water;
> The water, certainly, washing us clean of sin,
> while blood wins the crown of victory.
> (Hymn IX, lines 140–47; trans. Pfordresher).

Christian paradox finds in the bloody death of the Savior only triumph over sin and death. The "sign...which shines out so brightly" is that sign that Constantine suddenly witnessed through a vision given him in the midst of battle and that now in baptism and later in confirmation is signed upon the brow of each Catholic in sacramental oil. The blood and water that sprang from the pierced side of the dead Jesus now appear as the water of baptism, the wine of the Eucharist, the sacrifice that wins the martyr's crown of victory. These intensely carnal and almost gruesome paradoxes were to become central to Christian sacramental thinking and imagining, mainstays of Catholic poetry, preaching, and picturing for the next fifteen hundred years.

Reimagining

Prudentius is always a poet both of the spirit and of the concrete, physical world. Because he is a Catholic poet he insists upon the conjunction of the two. His is an emphatically material world but always infused with a divine presence. He recognizes as both Christian and poet that individual things are simultaneously themselves and analogical figures—"hae...imagines"[27] as he calls them—for divine truths. On the one hand, this means that when he imagines episodes from the Gospels such as Jesus' parable of the good shepherd, he does so in a complexly physical way. On the other hand, he is always aware of their theological content.

> When a sheep lags behind because it is sick, and is lost from the healthy flock, wasting its wool by catching on thorny bushes along unfrequented ways in the rough woodland, He as a tireless Shepherd calls it again, and driving off the wolves, takes the load on His shoulders and carries it, and so brings it home cleansed and restores it to the sunny fold; restores it to the meadows too, and the green field, where no rough, prickly burs quiver and no bristling thistle arms its shoots with spikes, but the grove is filled with palms, the bending leaves of grass flourish, and the glassy stream of running water is shaded with evergreen bay.
>
> (From Hymn VIII, "A Hymn after Fasting,"
> lines 33–48; trans. Thomson)[28]

In considering Jesus' teaching we noticed his frequent demand that people imagine themselves into the story he is telling, essentially taking it over and making it theirs, as in the example from chapter 1 of the neighbor asking for a loaf of bread. "Suppose...," Jesus asks, and the listeners must carry the story forward in their own minds. This passage from Prudentius's Hymn VIII is typical of what was to become the fondness in Catholic art for doing just this kind of further imagining, or reimagining, returning to the gospel stories and elaborating them through the building up of further physical details, the artist's imagination dwelling on the simple story first told by Jesus and intensifying it by making every material element of it real. This is one way in which an empathetic imagination gets into Jesus' story, making it more and more "real" and reacting emotionally to

each "real" detail as it emerges. In Jesus' telling of the original parable, the sheep is simply lost. As Prudentius's imagination works on
the story, he sees the sheep as not only lost but "sick" and torn by
thorny bushes that catch at its wool and pursued by wolves who get
so near that the Savior must drive them off. What emerges is a
heightening not only of the picturing of the scene but of emotion:
the sheep is sick, hurt, terrified by pursuing wolves, and since the
sheep is after all a metaphor for you and me we readers feel its
anguish as our own and we feel too the rush of gratitude as the
Savior picks us up to carry us back to safety. At the same time,
Prudentius in his typical exultation cannot keep from transforming
these earthly scenes into a new paradise. The good shepherd brings
the sheep back to a meadow that is heaven but on earth, full of
growing things but all of them tender and nourishing. In this sense
he is both a nature poet and a religious poet, and he initiates what
was to be for both Catholic and Protestant poetry after the
Reformation a tradition envisioning God's love in terms of the
earthly paradise, as in this example from Hymn V.

> He calls the weary over the sea of the world and guides His
> people, cleaving the storms; souls that have been tossed by a
> thousand distresses He bids go up into the country of the
> righteous. There all the ground is covered and scented with
> beds of red roses; watered by running streamlets it pours forth
> rich marigolds and soft violets and tender crocuses. There balsam,
> too, exudes in a stream from its slender shoot, the rare cinnamon
> breathes its scent, and the leaf that the river by whose stream it
> grows carries from its hidden source to its mouth. The blessed
> souls over the grassy meads sing their sweet song in harmo-
> nious concert, and pleasantly sound the melody of their hymns,
> as with white feet they tread the lilies.
>   (From Hymn V, "A Hymn for the Lighting of the Lamp,"
>   lines 108–24; trans. Thomson)[29]

Passages like this are intensely sensual: smell, touch, taste, hearing,
sight, all are provoked by the vision of an earthly heaven of bliss.
Characteristically this Catholic poetry reveling in its incarnational
vision has no wish to damn the pleasures of the senses, the joys of
the life of this world, but at the same time it insists that they reach
their greatest intensity when they are suffused with the divine.

See how through the waters the encircling nets draw the shoals that roam in the wave: and fish fall to the rod too, caught by the sharp, piercing hook, their too trustful mouth wounded by the bait. The land pours forth its native wealth in all the riches of its corn-crop, while here too the vine's branches luxuriate with leafy shoots and the berry that is the nursling of peace flourishes. All this abundance is in the service of Christ's followers and supplies their every need.

(From Hymn III, lines 46–55; trans. Thomson)[30]

A second look at a passage such as this indicates how the analogical imagination is at work. Certainly Prudentius means to celebrate the earth's abundance and the fact that God provides for his people. At the same time there is an undercurrent of suggestion that this divine provision is sacramental in character. We have noted how pictures of a fisherman in the Roman catacombs echoed Jesus' invitation to his first followers to come and be fishers of people. And we have had occasion many times to note that whenever one runs into a reference to wine we must consider the possibility that there is a double reference not only to wine itself but to the sacrament of the Eucharist. The "berry that is the nursling of peace" is the olive, the source of the oil used in Catholic sacraments for anointing. What emerges is the clear and repeated suggestion that the beauty, the abundance, the worth of the world come from the God who made it, and that the world is itself a form of sacrament, which the formal sacraments parallel and echo each in its own way.

At times Prudentius presses his tendency to reimagine biblical scenes and to celebrate ecstatically the divine in everything, to extreme lengths. His Hymn XII, "Hymn for Epiphany," presents an intentionally shocking reimagining of the story from Matthew's Gospel in which Herod, the reigning Jewish king at the time of Jesus' birth, fearful of Jesus as a future rival for power, decrees that every firstborn son under the age of two be killed (Figure 37).

As in his cycle of poems on the Christian martyrs, Prudentius here revels in gruesome, realistic detail in what can strike some readers as a cruel fascination with wounding and pain. But in fact he has a very distinct point to make, rooted, as so characteristically for him, in Christian paradox emerging from his confidence in redemption. Certainly the deaths of these children were horrific. But at the same time each death led immediately to the martyr's crown, and these first flowers of the new church bloom at once in the garden of paradise, playing their children's games for eternity beneath the blissful eyes of their God. Every horror becomes a joy, and joy is thus discerned in the midst of horror, Christian double vision taken to an extreme.

Figure 37
From **Hymn XII:** *Hymnus Epiphaniae*
("Hymn for Epiphany")

...Herod decrees the death
of every infant boy. His mood
is black. His soldiers hear and obey:
 red rivers of blood

pour from Judea's cradles. They snatch
suckling babes from their mothers' breasts,
hack at their helpless bodies, slash,
 and stab at their chests

in a barbarous frenzy. Herod's men
smash tiny heads on stone walls,
splashing blood and milky brains.
 It truly appalls,

and we look away but with no relief,
for on all sides are outrageous troubles.
A soldier is drowning a child in a barrel.
 He watches the bubbles.
The gurgling stops at last, and he smiles—
as we must, too, for these infant boys,
first martyrs in Christ, those earliest flowers
 cold wind destroys.

They are blooming still in the field of the Lord.
At the sacred altar forever they play
with God's own crown and with palm fronds frolic.
 (Lines 97–132; trans. David R. Slavitt)[31]

The new poetic tradition that Prudentius helps initiate thus turns from the pagan search for worldly fame to the selfless praise of the Christian God. Emerging from the Catholic imagination it uses imagery from ordinary life: nature, human occupations, simple things. It returns again and again to light and its cyclic struggle with darkness. Every image functions analogically. Nothing remains simply itself. Everything has the complex multiple meaning discerned by the double vision of Catholic imagination. Thus the things of this world are seen as essentially sacramental: gifts from God that the sacramental rituals of the church emblematize. This new poetry proclaims the life and the death of Jesus, and it revels in the paradoxes of a redeemer God who dies, of martyrs slain but victorious.

Structure and Meaning: Within a Poem

Just as meaning emerges from the spatial relationships between the rooms of the house-church at Dura-Europos and from the peculiar layout of the galleries and larger open spaces within the Roman Christian catacombs, so meaningful implications emerge from the way in which Prudentius shapes the unfolding word by word and line by line of the images, allusions, and ideas in his individual poems and in the way he collects his individual poems into the form of a highly organized whole, his book *The Daily Round*.

The Horatian tradition of the ode prizes an irregular, wandering logic. The poet muses, dreams, remembers, exclaims—but feels no obligation to present the stages of a reasoned argument. So, for example, in Ode 12 of the First Book, Horace ends with praise of Augustus Caesar as victorious in battle and an emperor who "with justice rule[s] the broad earth...."[32] But before he reaches this conclusion Horace makes reference to Clio the muse of history, to the singer Orpheus, to the gods Jupiter, Athena, Bacchus, and Apollo, as well as to a fairly long list of Greek and Roman mythic and historical heroes. This goes on for more than fifty lines before he gets to what seems his actual topic, praise of the current emperor. But that's the point of the Horatian ode as a form and the source of one of its chief delights: the poet gracefully and knowledgeably plays with myth, legend, history, and so on, weaving them together into a new pattern of meaning that then illuminates his ultimate topic.

Prudentius's hymns are built on the Horatian model. Within an individual poem he freely touches on stories from Hebrew and Christian tradition and at times makes an allusion even to pagan mythology, all in the context of nature, the seasons, and episodes from daily life—but the actual subject of all the hymns is one thing: the praise of God. Each hymn develops this subject in a different way, but all ultimately effect the same celebration. In considering the structure of Prudentius's hymns we are immediately reminded of the linked or chain structure of images in the Greek Chapel and of the tendency of Roman catacomb decoration generally to connect stories together into patterns that articulate ideas about God and the Christian faith. Reading Horace, Prudentius must have noticed with delight how readily the Augustan poet's tendency to make references to Greco-Roman myth could be adapted to his Christian subject matter. And, just as with the Roman catacombs, Prudentius makes extensive use of typological references to Jewish history and scriptural traditions. It is perhaps not surprising that one encounters what have become by this time favorite typological analogies. Prudentius makes reference to Jacob wrestling the angel (II), Daniel in the lion's den (IV), Moses with the burning bush, leading the people of Israel through the Red Sea, striking the rock for water (V), Joseph interpreting dreams (VI), and Jonah and the whale (VII). These allusions constantly serve as illustrations of a Christian theme, because for Prudentius and for the Christian tradition in general there is a real continuity between Jewish leaders and prophets and the later story of Christianity. All participate in the unbroken line of sacred history. Hymn VII is about fasting, and so Prudentius recalls a series of biblical heroes who fasted: Elijah, Moses, Jonah, John the Baptist, and Jesus. For Prudentius these figures are *patriarcha noster*,[33] our patriarchal fathers, and their significance lies in the fact that "cum facta priscorum ducum / Christi figuram pinxerint." That is, "the deeds of old-time leaders pictured the figure of Christ":[34] typology as an anticipation of what comes to fulfillment in the incarnation.

Structure and Meaning: Within The Daily Round

Each of the hymns in Prudentius's collection has a title, and together the titles serve as a guide to the logic of the book as a whole. Here we see quite conscious ordering and structuring taking place, and certain kinds of meaning emerge from number and sequence. There are twelve hymns in all, just as there were twelve tribes of

Israel and twelve apostles. The number means fullness as well as combinatorial richness: two sixes, three fours, four threes, six twos.

A Christian Day: Hymns I through VI

The first six of the hymns form a cycle following the hours of the day and the movement of the sun's light through the sky. The titles are

I. "Hymn for Cockcrow"

II. "Morning Hymn"

III. "Hymn before Meals"

IV. "Hymn after Meals"

V. "Hymn at Lamp Lighting"

VI. "Hymn before Sleep"

They can be considered as meditations on kinds of time—early and late, social and private, light and dark. God, the God whose incarnate presence emerges at all times and in all situations, is present in each kind of time, but the implications of that presence and of divine love vary depending upon human need. As the skies darken, for example, people have need of the comfort of the divine presence as they face the night of evil and death.

> ...You are our lamp with whom we fear
> no evil. With You we have steel
> and flint, and oil and wicks. We'd feel
>
> our way in menacing darkness, grope
> in apprehension, but for the hope
>
> we have of You.
> (From Hymn V, lines 4–9; trans. Slavitt)[35]

Slightly different is the joy at a shared meal when another form of God's generosity is the subject of thanksgiving.

> ...You are nourishment, our sweet
> and salt, our spice. Unless the Lord

leaven our bread and flavor our meat,
we take no pleasure at His board
whereon is spread our feast.
(From Hymn III, lines 6–10;
trans. Slavitt)[36]

In this particularly Catholic moment, Prudentius writes in a way
that many other religious traditions would find blasphemous. God
is within the sugar and salt, the leaven and the juice.

This structuring of the day in these six poems raises interesting
questions about the structuring of life itself, an issue Prudentius was
surely considering—it was a topic very much of the moment in the
early fifth century.

We are all perhaps familiar with the traditions of Christian
monastic life: people live in community, separated in some way or
another from the other people in their society. They live according
to a schedule that devotes specific activities to the various hours of
the day: prayer, work, charity, and the sharing of meals and of the
sacraments. Christian monasticism began in the Egyptian desert.

> In the fourth century, the change from persecution to imperial
> recognition of the church brought a sense of security and creep-
> ing worldliness in its train; in this situation those who hankered
> for a more intense religious commitment were increasingly
> attracted by the idea of total withdrawal from the community.[37]

There were different forms of this "withdrawal." Saint Pachomius
(ca. 292–346) initiated the development of monasteries in the desert
wilderness beyond Thebes (known as the Thebiad). "The distinctive
things about the life of the Monastery were its fellowship—the daily
round of collective worship in the oratory and the common meals—
and the insistence upon total obedience to the commands of the
superior."[38] By the end of the fourth century, that is to say, just before
Prudentius began writing his poetry, Saint Martin of Tours (d. 397),
one of a number of people adapting Egyptian monastic practices for
western Europe, "organized [in 372] his disciples as a colony of her-
mits at Marmoutier, outside Tours."[39] With the start "of the fifth century the monastic movement was still widely regarded as a fringe
phenomenon. It had not yet won acceptance by the secular world or
even the general approval of the ecclesiastical hierarchy."[40] At the

same time, the fervent devotion of the monks drew the admiration of some Christians for its dedication and focus.

Prudentius's six poems about the cycle of the day are not conspicuously poems for monks or poems that emerge directly from the monastic life. But they seem to adopt a new, monastic way of thinking about the day as a cycle of prayer and activity being adapted to the lives of every ordinary Christian. Their movement from darkness into light, their celebration of the joy of the communal meal, their anxious consolation in the face of the oncoming night fits the common experience of most people, and they imagine a way in which the formulated and consistent devotion of the monk might be a part of the ordinary person's daily life.

SACRAMENTAL TIME

These six poems demonstrate a sacramental consciousness in which the shared meal at the center of the cycle—Hymns III and IV within the set of three pairs—is a moment of both physical and spiritual nourishment, the food at table seen as analogous to the divine bread and wine of the Eucharist. They also exemplify the kind of temporal simultaneity or sacramental time so central to the Catholic imagination. In these poems the great figures of sacred history are all contemporaries. As the daylight dawns in Hymn I, for instance, the poet recalls the disciple Peter, who had betrayed Jesus in the night and who now longs for the new day in which he can "retract, undo his grave mistake...,"[41] and he also recalls that it was

> At cockcrow Christ returned from the dead.
> It was, therefore at just this hour
> that death in its all but limitless power
> was overthrown.
> (From Hymn I, lines 65–73; trans. Slavitt).[42]

In this form of consciousness, the specific moment or point in the cycle of the day is a moment when Peter stands there yearning for a second chance and Jesus "at just this hour" emerges victorious from the tomb—the very same moment when the poet throws back the warm blanket and steps into the new light. All participate in the moment.

The monastic day, with its cycle of waking, prayer, work, refreshment, and return to sleep, encapsulates the year (from winter

to summer to winter again), the life of the individual (from child-
hood to maturity to old age), and all of history (from creation to the
moment of redemption to the end of time), each hour seen as link-
ing together different kinds of time through a sacramental temporal
simultaneity. Perhaps Horace thought this way too when he wove
together his allusions to the gods, mythological heroes, and his
Caesar, but certainly for Prudentius sacred time gives a particular
kind of meaning, indeed a powerful logic, to his use of allusion—his
Peter, or Moses, or Jonah still live within the moment; they are his
contemporaries, and references to them are not references to those
long dead but instead to living brothers and sisters within continuous, simultaneous divine time.

REPETITION AND VARIATION: THE SACRED DANCE

While the poetic cycle illustrates and works through simultaneity it is also deeply concerned with difference. Recall the ecstatic
close of Hymn IX we have already briefly considered:

> Let the flowing waters and the waves, the shores of the seas,
> rain showers, seething fires, snow, hoar-frost,
> the woods and the winds, night, day,
> gather to celebrate together You
> through all the coming ages.
> (From Hymn IX, lines 183–87; trans. Pfordresher)

Here all of natural creation celebrates God but each element in its
own way.

Repetition and variation are two central aspects of both dance
and music. If in dancing one consciously performed a sequence of
movements, all of them different from each other and all of them
unrelated to each other, the "dance" would appear chaotic. Dance
traditions emerge from a repetition of gesture and movement, much
like Prudentius's analogy to the celebration seen in the very waves
of the ocean. The waves rise and fall but never quite in the same
way, and so dancers repeat the movement of feet, arms, bodies but
with variation. In exactly the same way, music consists in certain
repeated tones that constitute melodies or, in songs, refrains, and
musical development emerges from varying a melody, adding new
melodies, and so on, but with the periodic repetition of the origi-

nating melody. The structure of Prudentius's cycle of daily hymns is, as we have noted, exactly this: each hymn voices praise for God, but the kind of praise voiced changes with each hymn. Sameness coupled with difference, repetition coupled with variation. In this way what these hymns say, their cognitive content, is harmoniously parallel to the very nature of music and dance, and so their structure is the structure of the dance of the ocean wave, the rhythms of the day, the cycle of the seasons.

Hymns VII through XII: Cycles of the Year, of Life

The second half of *The Cathemerinon* is made up of three pairs of poems:

VII. "Hymn before Fasting"

VIII. "Hymn after Fasting"

IX. "Hymn for All the Hours"

 X. "Hymn for the Burial of the Dead"

XI. "Hymn for Christmas"

XII. "Hymn for Epiphany"

The two poems on fasting constitute models for preparing for a period of purgation and self-discipline and completing that exercise. They balance the need for the faithful Christian to step back from the pleasures of ordinary life and the corresponding need to return to that life, grateful because it is God's gift.

The "Hymn for All the Hours" is, in fact, a celebration of Jesus' incarnation and our redemption. The following poem, Hymn X, "for the Burial of the Dead," carries on the argument a step further by imagining the resurrection all Christians will someday share.

> Bodies that lay dead and still and mouldering in their tombs will be carried into the flying breezes in company with their former souls. This is why we spend such great care on graves, this is why the last honour awaits the lifeless frame and the funeral procession graces it, why it is our custom to spread over it linen cloths of gleaming whiteness, and sprinkled myrrh with its

Sabaean drug preserves the body. What mean the chambered rocks, the noble monuments, but that something is entrusted to them, which is not dead but given up to sleep? This earnest care the provident piety of Christ's followers takes because they believe that all that are now sunk in cold slumber will presently be alive.

(From Hymn X, lines 41–60; trans. Thomson)[43]

Here we see the beliefs that animated the people who dug out and decorated the Roman catacombs given full and explicit voice.

The final pair of poems deals with two festival days already popular in the Christian devotion of the fourth century, Christmas and Epiphany, celebrations of the incarnation and of the revelation of that incarnation to all nations, emblematically embodied in the Magi who come to worship the child Jesus.

Whereas the first six poems of the cycle structure the day, the latter six suggest some of the different ways by which the year and indeed one's whole life might be structured: the annual cycle of festival days, the private cycle for periods of penance and self-renewal, the celebration of life as redeemed and of death as the doorway to an eternal life. It's not unreasonable to think of these poems as Prudentius's own experiments in a literature of the seasons of the year and of life that he has not worked out as fully as he has done with the single day. They are samples of how one might begin much larger poetic projects of a similar nature. The Christians who read his poems in the ensuing centuries understood this, and sections of Prudentius's hymns were actually adapted for music and entered the Christian hymnal.

Voice

The Horatian *Odes* are highly personal. The voice speaking in them is always identifiably that of the author—urbane, knowledgeable, witty, a bit melancholy, taking his chances where he finds them. He makes reference to his Sabine farm, his friends, the Rome of his day. In the odes he directly addresses a fairly long list of imagined readers: his patron Maecenas, people he has known, such as the soon-to-be-sad Lydia, even the emperor Augustus. The rhetoric of address in Horace's poetry creates the picture of an imagined community of individuals to whom he writes.

Prudentius also has moments where he speaks as an individual. We have seen him in Hymn IX calling to a servant: "Hand me my lyre, my boy…" (line 1). And we have seen him rejecting the laurel wreath of poetic fame for the sake of a humbler art. Elsewhere he acknowledges the fact that he shares in the common human condition: "spes eadem mea membra manet, / …ignea Christus ad astra vocat" (from Hymn III, lines 201 and 205).[44] "The same hope awaits my limbs…Christ calls [them] to the glowing stars." But much of the time the voice in these poems speaks in the first person plural: *nos* or "us."[45] He voices what he presumes all (*omnes*) think and feel,[46] and he frequently exhorts everyone to do something as in the first hymn and its call *vigilemus*[47]—"stay awake." While allusions to himself in the first-person singular are appropriate for Prudentius the Roman poet, the use of the first-person plural, the "us" and the "we," is far more apt for the maker of hymns, simply because hymns are to be sung by and for the community. It is in this communal voice that Prudentius usually writes, and his poetry voices the feelings and needs of the collective.

The Jesus of the Gospels teaches his followers to pray, telling them they should directly ask God for what they need. In the Lord's Prayer he directs them to say, "Give us this day our daily bread." There is a certain audacity in this form of address, which commands the divinity to do something for ordinary people, but Jesus says this is how you should address God his Father. Prudentius's poetry creates a complex picture of the implied relationship between the voice of the poet and his God. At times he follows Jesus' direction and makes requests in the form of commands: "Tu, Christe, somnum dissice,"[48] he says in the first hymn: "You, Christ, scatter our sleepiness." This is coupled with a sense of love—Christ as *dux bone*, the "kindly guide" whom Prudentius asks to "give light again, O Christ, to thy faithful ones": "Lucem redde tuis, Christe, fidelibus."[49] At other times Prudentius tells his reader about Christ, and then he writes as witness looking from a distance. So in the second hymn Jesus is described as "hic testis, hic est arbiter" or "he is witness, he is judge."[50] Now we recognize his power.

Taken altogether, the poet of the *Cathemerinon* acts as a voice for the collective Christian community, and in so doing stresses one of the four characteristic traits of Catholic belief. He speaks for "we" and "us"—for the experiences all share. And he speaks to

God, sometimes in the mode of a highly personal direct address, working under the assumption that an incarnate God listens and cares. His is a loving, fostering God, not, as in Horace, a remote and punishing divinity. This, we have come to see, helps constitute a distinct form of Catholic consciousness of self: the self in relationship to God and to the community. It stems directly from Saint Paul's letters, among other sources. The self thinks, talks, feels in relationship to the other both divine and communal, and the self exists and has meaning and worth in terms of these relationships. This is a very different stance from the egoistic pride (perhaps well justified) of Horace's ambitions and helps define Prudentius's contribution to the development of a specifically Catholic imagination.

CHAPTER TEN

The Celtic North and
The Book of Kells

The Foundation of Iona and the *Peregrinatio*

Off the northwest coast of Scotland lie the Hebrides, a scattering of islands floating in the gray waters of the Atlantic. One of the smallest, Iona, lies at the western tip of the large island of Mull. This remote, tiny place might seem at first glance to be as far away in location, climate, and culture from the sunny world of Prudentius and from the Mediterranean sources of Christianity as one could reach in Europe. And yet in the seventh and eight centuries, Iona became a vital center for the spread of Irish Catholic faith and the source of some remarkable artistic achievements, achievements in which the encounter with the pagan Celtic culture of northern Europe and the British Isles led to some very new and distinctly different forms of Catholic imagining.

The Romans never invaded Ireland. Outside the limits of the power and culture of the empire, the Irish, during the first centuries after Christ, maintained a strong cultural independence. And yet there was contact. Though land travel through a Europe with few roads and many warring peoples was always difficult and often dangerous, ancient peoples found it relatively easy to travel long distances by sea, by which relatively heavy cargoes could be readily transported from one place to the next. And so bits and pieces of the Mediterranean made their way to Irish shores. Modern archeology has found "large amounts of pottery at...sites in southern Ireland...much of which originated in the eastern Mediterranean and North Africa."¹

By the beginning of the fifth century, shortly after Prudentius's poems were published, Christianity was spreading along these trade routes, and soon the Roman church took an active hand in directing that development. In 431 Pope Celestine is said to have sent Palladius to the Irish, and in the next year, 432, the man traditionally credited with the conversion of Ireland, Saint Patrick, arrived. However, Ireland's remoteness encouraged a good deal of independence from the authority of Rome. The Irish church went its own way much of the time and developed surprisingly "strong connections" not with Rome, but "with the Coptic church of Egypt"² and particularly the traditions of Egyptian monasticism (which we glimpsed briefly in chapter 9). As a consequence, the administration of the Irish church became "primarily monastic rather than episcopal."³

Columba

The most famous and most influential Irish monk of these early centuries was undoubtedly the man named in Irish Colum Cille, or, to use the Latin form of his name, Columba. As a prince of a warrior tribe, the Ui Néill, Columba found himself, even after his ordination, involved in a particularly bloody battle at Cul Drebene in 561. Later that year—or perhaps after an interval of two years (that is, in 563)—Columba left Ireland for the island of Iona, where he and his companions, twelve in number, founded a new monastery (Figure 38). Legend has it that he was forced into exile because of his participation in Cul Drebene. In one particularly affecting version of the story, it is said that as a part of the peace negotiations Columba was told he had to sail until he could no longer see Ireland or hear the ringing of its church bells, and Iona was the closest he could come to his native land.

Perhaps Columba did have to leave Ireland for political reasons, but it is very clear that he then chose to make his new institution at Iona the jumping-off place for an ambitious campaign to bring Christianity to the British mainland, and he must have known that this tiny island was an excellent point from which to begin such a

Figure 38. Iona
The island of Iona became the center from which Saint Columba (521–597) and his monks set out to Christianize Scotland and the north of England.

campaign. While today it is inconvenient and laborious to reach Iona by car, by the frequently traveled sea routes of Columba's time it lay "at the very heart of [a] multi-cultural northern Britain."[4] From Iona, Columba and his men traveled into what is now Scotland, converting the pagan Picts and rapidly establishing a chain of monasteries throughout Scotland and later the north of England. After his death, Columba's followers continued this process, moving south into France, Germany, Switzerland, even into northern Italy. Iona turned out to be an excellent starting point for the spread of Christianity into what had been remote and even hostile locales.

This tiny island had another meaning, less practical and more deeply spiritual. Crucially important for Irish Christianity was "the phenomenon of *peregrinatio*, of endless pilgrimage for God undertaken in foreign lands." For a man like Columba, separated from his clan, "all places are equally strange, equally 'heathen' lands....All places [are] equally empty of human meaning and, so, could be filled with the vast, invisible presence of God."[5] Iona lies low in the water. On three sides one sees only the ocean. It presents the religious contemplative with an excellent place for silence and prayer. Its vast expanses of sea and sky may have suggested to a man steeped in the traditions of Irish Celtic monasticism that this place so seemingly empty was just the place in which to find an infinite God. Irish monks were said to be particularly given to standing all night long up to their shoulders in icy sea water, their arms thrust skyward in prayer chanting the Psalms from memory. Iona is a perfect place for that kind of devotion.

Figure 39. Celtic cross
The Celtic cross combines the figure of a cross with a circle and is thought to have had pre-Christian origins. The example in this photograph stands in Donegal, birthplace of Saint Columba.

Accounts of Columba picture him as very much a prince, a strong-willed administrator, sure of his judgments and demanding of his men. They describe him as chronically restless. One of his most constant activities was transcribing manuscripts, and far into the night he could be seen in his little hut on the hill above the Iona monastic settlement, pen in hand, copying one of the books of the Bible. In the centuries before Gutenberg invented the printing press, this was a very practical way to spread the word of God. With time the Columban monasteries became renowned throughout Europe for their manuscripts. He was also a dreamer, given to visions of angels. And he wrote poetry.

"By the end of his life, Columba's achievement was monumental: he had founded Iona and a number of connected monasteries in the west of Britain and in Ireland, and the influence of this network of churches extended into kingdoms..." in modern Scotland, England, and Ireland. "But he and his followers would have considered these achievements minor in comparison to what he was seeking to attain: wisdom, learning and holiness....By the time of his death [in 597] he already had an incomparable reputation for just these virtues."[6]

The *Altus Prosator*

Tradition attributes to Columba a series of poems that have survived into our own time. The one most likely to have actually come from his pen is the Latin *Altus Prosator* or song of the "High Creator." It is highly important for our current investigation because it offers a glimpse into the imaginative world of the Iona community, and perhaps more particularly a brief but revelatory example of how Columba—the man whose powerful and creative leadership had such a significant and transformative influence upon European Christianity in the seventh century—thought and felt. Indeed, it represents a new moment in the evolution of Catholic imagination.

Altus Prosator, like Prudentius's hymns, is a poem praising God, but it is almost completely uninterested in telling the story of the life of Jesus. Instead, it is primarily devoted to a celebration of the power of God implied by a long account of the creation of the world and a slightly shorter description of how the world will end. Power and the implications of power lie at its center.

Looking at a specific passage, we can begin to get an idea of how this poet imagines his world. Describing the first sin of Adam and Eve and the subsequent expulsion of Satan into hell,[7] he begins to brood over how everything passes. This suggests the "momentary glory of the kings of the present world...."[8] Satan becomes the first example of a constant cycle of pride, rebellion, and divine punishment with the overreacher "cast down at God's whim."[9]

The passing of all vain ambition then suggests images of the endless change going on in nature. Suddenly we are on Iona, an island world where "clouds bear wintry floods from the fountains of the Ocean...in azure whirlwinds, / to do good to the corn-fields..."[10] and where "the Lord often sifts down the waters bound in the clouds...slowly flowing across the tracts of this earth, freezing and warming at different times, the rivers flow everywhere, never failing."[11] The natural world is important for this Celtic poet, and here there is a concrete awareness of the world of the Hebridean Islands and of how the ecosystems of a maritime climate operate. At the same time it is surprising and important to note that these lines also reflect, as Clancy and Marcus point out in their edition of Columban poetry, not just careful observation but also a good deal of scholarly reading. The poet here includes allusions to biblical texts, to the Spanish encyclopedia writer Isidore of Seville, and to the philosopher and theologian Saint Augustine.[12] The *Altus Prosator* comes from a writer who has read extensively and who understands the world in terms of the advanced learning of his era.

Synthesizing Literary Traditions

Then the *Altus Prosator* considers the humbling of vain pride and ambition through allusion to mythic traditions from both Greco-Roman and Irish sources. The stanza following the lines just quoted continues using imagery of ocean waters this way:

> ecce gigantes gemere sub aquis magno ulcere
> comprobantur incendio aduri ac supplicio
> Cocytique Charybdibus strangulati turgentibus
> Scyllis obtecti fluctibus eliduntur et scrupibus.[13]

Clancy and Marcus translate:

> See, giants are shown to groan in great affliction beneath
>   the waters,
> to be scorched by fire and in torment,
> and stifled by the swelling whirlpools of Cocytus,
> covered with rocks, they are destroyed by billows and
>   sharp stones.[14]

Sharp-eyed readers will notice that the translation, while using the term *Cocytus*, the name of one of the rivers described in classical mythological accounts about the underworld, passes over two other terms in the Latin—*Scylla* and *Charybdis*—that also come from Greco-Roman myth and refer to one of the challenges that faced Odysseus. He found himself forced to sail between the monster Scylla, who leaned out from her cave to snatch up and devour mariners from passing ships, and the whirlpool Charybdis just offshore, which was equally rapacious. The poem is in the process of alluding to yet another episode from Greco-Roman myth, and this returns us to the theme of the whole passage, which is the punishment of excessive ambition. The new gods, led by Zeus, having defeated the Titans, imprison them under the earth, or, as in this case, beneath the sea—the agonized thrashing about of the victims thus accounting for earthquakes and sea storms. This acts as an analogy for the punishment God has imposed upon Satan for his rebelliousness.

Analogies of this kind illustrate the sophisticated level of classical scholarship current at Iona during Columba's time and the ease with which an Iona poet could weave allusions to classical pagan myth into a description of the sea. Like the artists of the catacombs (as, for example, in the depiction of a phoenix of the Greek Chapel), this writer feels no anxiety in adopting pagan stories and his lines take on a greater degree of horror with his references to the monsters of antiquity. Clancy and Marcus suggest that the curious confusing of punishments described in these lines—the poor giants suffer simultaneously, it would seem, from fire, water, and sharp stones—may be in fact "an echo of a common feature of Irish myths and sagas, in which someone dies a 'triple death.'"[15] This free, creative mingling of a wide and somewhat eclectic variety of sources was to become typical of Iona culture.

Columba and the Monstrous

There is a darkness, a grotesquerie, a fascination with the demonic in this poem that is absent from the sunnier, more optimistic writing of Prudentius's *Daily Round*. Early in the poem we get a narrative of the first rebellion of Lucifer and his expulsion from heaven.

> The great Dragon, most loathsome, terrible, and ancient,
> which was the slippery serpent, more cunning than all
> the beasts

and than all the fiercer living things of the earth,
dragged down with him a third of the stars into the pit
of infernal places and sundry prisons,
fugitives from the true light, hurled down by the Parasite.[16]

The *Draco magnus...terribilis et antiquus*[17] seems to come from north European myth, such as the Germanic Nibelung tales, and it illustrates this poem's absorption in the terrible and the monstrous. Later, surveying the world God has made and ordered, the poet continues:

It seems doubtful to no one that there is a hell down below
where there are held to be darkness, worms and dreadful
    animals;
where there is sulphurous fire burning with voracious flames;
where there is the screaming of men, weeping and gnashing
    of teeth;
where there is the groaning of Gehenna, terrible and ancient;
where there is the horrible fiery burning of thirst and hunger.[18]

Several of the details here come directly from the teaching of Jesus, who also occasionally issued threats and warnings about the terror and suffering awaiting those who did not join in his kingdom. Doubtless, dwelling upon such scenes served Columba the aggressive missionary as a means to persuade people to embrace Christianity and to remain faithful to its precepts. But further, there is a fascination here with terror and suffering that goes beyond the words of Jesus and beyond the rhetoric of preaching, a relish in all that is the opposite of God's love and tender goodness. This darkness, too, is a vital part of the Catholic imagination.

The concept of incarnation is about the ways the divine transforms the material, but never in Christianity has this meant that all things are consequently good and safe. We saw in chapter 2 that the initial premise of redemption is that we begin with a fallen world full of evil and suffering, and in this poem we find a vigorous assertion through what a modern reader might call "fantasy" that all is not yet well and that people need to seize the opportunity to be redeemed. Dragons lurk beneath the earth, as Titans thrash beneath the sea, and legions of devils are now tied up somewhere down in Hell, lest "by the horror of whose faces and the sound of whose flying / frail men might be dismayed, stricken with fear...."[19] One may perhaps conclude that the poet, despite his hopes, remains fearful of these invisible presences, which are very real to him and which constitute an important and perhaps even necessary element in the world as he imagines it.

Biblical "Realism" and Celtic Dragons

To readers skeptical of Christianity's claims to veracity, perhaps everything about Christian belief seems to be an aspect of "the fantastic," and it might be asked what kind of distinction is being made here in my efforts to define the specific imaginative characteristics of the *Altus Prosator* and Columban Christianity. One can make a useful distinction between New Testament events such as the execution of Jesus by Roman authorities—what appears to be manifestly something that could readily happen in historical terms—and far more miraculous (and hence difficult to validate) episodes such as Jesus walking over the waters of the Sea of Galilee. But the characteristics of the "more miraculous" events of the New Testament are quite limiting. They all occur at known places and within the frame of historical time, and virtually all of them consist of echoes from earlier Hebrew sacred texts. God the creator quelled the waters with a word, and his power to do so is celebrated in the Psalms. The Messiah will come with healing for the lame, the halt, and the blind, and so Jesus too heals. There is a clear correspondence between the marvelous in the Gospels and traditions of Judeo-Christian belief about God's power and God's plan. Some readers accept these events as literal, others as figurative emblems indicating the meaning and importance of Jesus' life. But to even the most unusual gospel events the evangelists give a kind of ordinary practicality in their descriptions. Here is a crippled man. Jesus tells him to get up. He does.

While in the Gospels there are devils that tempt Jesus personally and possess human victims, rendering them bestial, there are no dragons, no talking animals, no helmets of invisibility, no magic gems or genii springing out of lamps. There are no other gods in the skies or predatory monsters in the sea. In this sense, the gospel narratives are far more historical and realistic than are the cycles of Greco-Roman or Germanic myth. There, more evidently and dramatically, one sees the products of a kind of extravagant, fantastic imagining, which is fabricated out of bits and pieces of the observed world but put together by the mind in forms never seen upon the earth, the consequences of processes of exaggeration and distortion familiar to us from the dream and the nightmare. The introduction of that kind of material into Catholic imagining gives a peculiar, vivid, and somewhat alarming quality to the vision of works like the *Altus Prosator*, and constitutes a significant and innovative adaptation of Celtic and Germanic materials for Catholic purposes. Admitting the dimensions of the dream expands the radius of the imagination into the realms of the unconscious.

This, it should be stressed, is a modern way of reacting to the poem's "great Dragon." Almost certainly for Columba and his followers, dragons were real and had to be combated. In the first full biography of Columba, written in Latin by Adomnan (679–704), one of Columba's successors in the role of abbot at Iona, we read of Columba and his men trying to cross Loch Ness in Scotland on their way to convert the Picts and halted by a monster lurking in those depthless waters who had been devouring the local people. Columba tells one of his men to swim across to the other side to get a boat moored there, and as he does the monster appears pursuing the poor man. Columba makes the sign of the cross in the air and the beast stops just short of his prey, thwarted by the power of Christ. This, it turns out, is the first recorded instance of a sighting of "the Loch Ness monster," and it illustrates the fact that for Columba, Adomnan, and probably many of the other monks of the Iona community dragons were a part of their thought-world. They constituted an element of reality as they imagined it and when they imagined the world, it was a world with dragons.

The *Altus Prosator* closes with the end of time, a vision of the "brightest sign and standard of the Cross" shining in the heavens. Then the poem concludes, stressing the fascination with sharp divisions so typical of Jesus' imagination, "we shall surely fly off to meet him straight away, and thus we shall be with him...according to the eternal merits of our rewards..." sharing in a paradise where one hears "the singing of hymns eagerly ringing out" and sees "thousands of angels rejoicing in holy dances..." while the "raging anger of fire will devour the adversaries / who did not believe...."[20]

Prudentius records in grim detail the suffering of the final Roman Christian martyrs in his cycle the *Peristephanon*, but he is dealing with what for him were already events of the distant past. There is a peculiar kind of triumph, almost of comfort, in his gory details, which, as in his description of the slaughter of the innocents cited in chapter 9, are understood to be the proud emblems of martyrs now in paradise. By contrast, the horrors of the *Altus Prosator* seem to be very real and quite immediate. Columba and his fellow monks lived perilous lives. They had to travel through alien lands still governed by pagan tribes and they had to face dangers both from the rugged landscape of northern Britain and the strange, hostile peoples they sought to convert. There must have been many times when it seemed to them, as when they crossed Loch Ness, that the monstrous and the terrible were very near. Their imaginative world was shaped not only by the books they had received from a distant Mediterranean culture but also by the myths and legends of the Celtic and Germanic peoples who were their immediate neighbors, and that latter world is full of a darkness and menace that make Scylla and Charybdis seem rather meek by comparison: the world of the ancient dragon, the worms of the darkness, and the invisible devils hovering in the air nearby.

The Book of Kells

A First Glance

By far the most famous creation of the Columban monastic system is a manuscript copy of the four Gospels now called *The Book of Kells*. Almost everything about it is mysterious, starting with its history. Let's trace it backward in time. At present, it is the most prized possession of the Trinity College Library in Dublin. A long line of dutiful tourists passes by each day seeking to glimpse a page or two, and their admiration for it is well justified. Around the year 1653, the governor of the Irish county of Kells had sent this thick, oversize manuscript book to Trinity College for safekeeping—the countryside was in chaos, the Irish people fighting a civil war against the Protestant reformer and English ruler Oliver Cromwell, and the ancient monastery at Kells was in ruins. Back in 1007, when Kells was a prosperous monastic community, records show that the manuscript was already there, because in that year it was stolen and was not recovered for more than two months. But, where did it come from originally? And when was it made? Now we enter the realm of speculation. There are many theories. The most widely accepted today is that the manuscript was made at a Columban monastery, most likely Iona, in the first years of the ninth century. At that very time Viking raiders who were annually harrying coastal towns in Britain started periodic attacks on the Iona establishment. Prudently, some of the monks left the island for the relative safety of Kells within the interior of the Irish mainland, and it's reasonable to assume that they transported the treasures of their monastery—including this manuscript—there for safekeeping.[21]

The Book of Kells is "a large-format manuscript codex of the Latin text of the gospels,...the most lavishly decorated of a series of gospel manuscripts produced between the seventh and ninth centuries...."[22] What does it look like? First comes what publishers today call "front matter": etymological lists of Hebrew names, "canon tables" that help the reader to compare parallel passages, and short summaries of the events in the Gospels. Then, the Gospels themselves. Prefacing each Gospel are initial pages decorated with complex, abstract patterns—including a page on which the first letters of the gospel text are elaborately embellished and distorted. Within the ensuing text body there are a number of full-page figural illustrations that show the influence of remote, archaic Byzantine and Egyptian Coptic painting. "Having on their native ground no tradition of representational art and no background of iconology," the artists who made the manuscript "depended for the illustrational side of their work on Byzantine or other Mediterranean book paintings or on ivory or wood reliefs."[23] The text is "written in a bold and expert script of a type best described as 'insular majuscule.'"[24] Virtually every text page is, moreover, decorated with abstract designs and interlinear drawings all in color. More than any other aspect, it is the richness and complexity of these designs that have made the *Book of Kells* world famous. These decorations are so consistent in style and execution and also so numerous that they are presumed to have been made by a team of artists, but artists who had learned to work to a pre-agreed formula in such a way that there is a single stylistic manner throughout. As we shall see in some detail in a moment, these decorations, unlike the full-page pictures, echo Celtic and Anglo Saxon sources. Gospel books as large as *Kells* were almost certainly intended for use in ceremonies, and at other times would have been left on the altar of a monastery church as a display item. Such books were "highly prized" by their culture and "the finest artistic craftsmanship of the time was lavished on them."[25]

These are some of the material facts that help to describe the book as an object. It is also useful to quote the description written in 1185 by the Welsh traveler Giraldus Cambrensis of a book he saw in Kildare—perhaps not the *Book of Kells* but another manuscript in the same tradition. Giraldus's point of view is that of a medieval clergyman, and his description of such books captures something beyond their material character:

> There are almost innumerable...drawings. If you look at them carelessly and casually and not too closely, you may judge them to be mere daubs rather than careful compositions. You will see nothing subtle where everything is subtle. But if you take the trouble to look very closely, and penetrate with your eyes to the secrets of the artistry, you will notice such intricacies, so delicate and subtle, so close together, and well-knitted, so involved and bound together, and so fresh still in their colourings that you will not hesitate to declare that all these things must have been the result of the work, not of men, but of angels.[26]

It is important to consider the significance of what Giraldus points out. In manuscripts like *Kells* there is a complexity one can miss unless one looks and studies carefully; this is an artistry of secrecy that leads only the careful viewer to intricacies that seem possible only for angels. Why are study and mystery so important here?

The Cult of the Manuscript

A consistent logic governs what we might call "the cult of the manuscript." As we learned in chapter 2, rooted deep in Jewish and Christian belief is the conviction that God himself is a poet, and that through words God created and ordered all that exists. John's Gospel elaborated upon this theme, describing Jesus as being himself the Logos or divine Word incarnate who uttered all of creation, who became a man to explain to people through language what God wills for them, and who continues to live within language itself.

We can connect these Christian ideas with a very old Jewish interpretive tradition that finds every word, every syllable, even every letter of the Bible full with God's being and God's meaning. Reading the Bible according to this tradition means puzzling over the hidden implications that may lie behind each element of the sacred text. There have been any number of Christian mystics and theologians who have also subscribed to this way of scrutinizing. Why the choice of this word and not that one? Why is this word the first in a sentence and why does that one only come later? Is there a reason to begin a sentence with a word beginning with this syllable, or this initial letter? Do mysterious implications divinely intended lie beneath the obvious, primary meaning, revealing themselves only to careful, diligent, closely attentive reading? Seen from this perspective, the Bible as a tangible, physical object becomes a locus of secret power, a site where a hidden divinity abides.

Irish monasticism clearly locates itself within these intellectual and spiritual traditions. They provide a sophisticated justification for the making and the decorating of manuscripts. To copy a manuscript is to preserve, multiply, and disperse God as Word. Objects as sacred and as mysterious and as powerful as these merit the most lavish of decoration and ornament because they are the most valuable things upon the earth. The artists who made the *Kells* manuscript used precious materials like gold and powdered lapis lazuli, ignoring, or perhaps we should say delighting in the costliness of these materials.

There was a kind of "magical cunning," as Peter Brown argues, in this activity that connects

> the scribes of the Book of Kells and the craftsmen who produced the great votive crowns, the Crosses and the relic-cases of Gaul and Spain....Their task was to take "dead" matter, associated with the profane wealth and power of great donors—precious pigments, the skins of vast herds [the source of vellum manuscript pages], gold and jewels—and make them come alive, by creating from them objects whose refulgent, intricate surfaces declared that they had moved, beyond their human source, into the realm of the sacred.[27]

Sacred, precious, and also quite literally powerful. It was a custom for Irish warriors to go into battle with someone carrying a copy of the Gospels before them, in hopes that divine might would radiate from the book and win them the victory.

The Book of Kells, far more than even the *Altus Prosator,* illustrates certain crucial transformations that took place as the Catholic imagination moved into new cultural contexts. In order to understand and to weigh the significance of those transformations, let us look first at its full-page pictorial illustrations. Then we can turn to the far more significant decorations that ornament virtually every one of its pages.

Pictorial Illustrations

As we have seen, Roman Christian catacomb frescoes place events from the Bible within the known contexts of their creators' daily world. They stress the meaning of physical gesture and, given the limited skill of the people who made them, seek a simple naturalism in representation. Prudentius, reimagining gospel scenes in his hymns, works hard at taking this even further, building up material detail in an effort to make the moment as imaginatively "real" as possible. In both cases, Catholic incarnational thinking is at work. While *Kells* continues the tradition of pictorial illustration of sacred persons and events—indeed its "narrative scenes [are] the earliest to survive in Gospel manuscripts"[28]—another very different spirit animates them.

JESUS ARRESTED

Folio 114r, a full-page depiction of Christ being arrested on the night before his death (Figure 40), is a helpful example.[29] At the center of the page we see Christ. Following what we recognize as a Catholic tradition, he is imagined as looking just like the people who made this picture, in fact as one of their contemporaries, so he is a man of northern Europe, blue-eyed, with a full head of curly blond hair and a red beard. The two officers apprehending him are red-haired but have sharp, jutting chins and dark black beards and moustaches that not only differentiate them from Jesus but make them look sinister.

This picture, however, is anything but a realist's effort to imagine a moment in the life of Jesus. The bodies of the figures have unnatural, indeed anatomically impossible positions. Jesus' arms extend out from his waist, jutting up at a 45-degree angle, while his legs appear to break at the knee, also turning out at the same 45-degree angle. The two arresting soldiers twist sideways in profile to look directly at Jesus, and the arm of the man on our right has to be unnaturally long in order to hold back Jesus' forward movement. The artist who made this image had no interest in anatomy or in three-dimensional rendering. There are reasons for these stiff and unnatural gestures. Jesus' extended arms suggest the posture that he will be forced to take when he is crucified, at the same time also alluding to the open arms of the Savior who welcomes his people. The artist who made this page was far more interested in these two symbolic possibilities than in verisimilitude. He wanted this image of Jesus to speak of what would ultimately be won from this moment of indignity and pain. He is picturing not so much a man as ideas about that man.

Figure 40. The arrest of Christ (Folio 114r)

He was also interested in creating symmetry, to the point where every aspect of the left side of Jesus' body, his arms and legs, the folds of his garments, exactly parallels every aspect of the right side of his body. They are mirror images of each other. The lines that define this figure take on a life of their own, creating symmetrical forms, and the bold curves of Jesus' red cloak emerge as a virtually abstract pattern—pattern and abstraction mattering more, perhaps, in this way of imagining than the realistic picturing of concrete things. But why would symmetry matter? What meaning emerges from having each half of the picture mirror its other half? In this respect the *Kells* illustration of Jesus arrested exemplifies a much larger tendency in early medieval art, as described by C. R. Dodwell in his *Painting in Europe 800–1200*.

> The artist saw outward appearances as something superficial, if not actually misleading, and so he was unconcerned with mere verisimilitude. His interest was rather to express what he knew lay behind the appearance. The resultant art is an abstract art in the sense that the artist's interest was not physical reality but his conceptions of the spiritual and emotional forces beyond reality. It is also abstract in a more physical sense, for the figure itself is more and more seen in terms of abstract shapes and forms.[30]

One of the implications of the symmetry in this picture is that a moment in Christ's life that may seem painful and desperate is actually a part of a much larger plan, and if understood in terms of the whole history of salvation and redemption its momentary shame and panic resolve themselves into a larger serenity and order.

The three figures of this picture do not appear in a natural setting—there is no effort to suggest that the scene is at night, or that it takes place in a garden. Instead, they are surrounded by a heavy arch decorated with two Greek crosses. This is not so much a narrative moment as it is the hieratic memory of such a scene translated into its symbolic elements. Behind the figures strangely sinuous plants sprawl out of blue pots. They look like grape vines, or perhaps they are fantastic olive trees. Both interpretations have been suggested. Here too it is not nature but a theological point that is being illustrated: Christ is "the anointed one." The plants are symbols of an idea, and the artist is quite indifferent to botanical accuracy.[31]

VIRGIN AND CHILD WITH ANGELS

The full-page illustration of the Virgin and Child with Angels [folio 7v] is much the same (Figure 41). Mary sits upon a fantastically unnatural throne, its deeply curved seat perfectly matching her own posterior. Though her head and shoulders directly face the viewer, somehow she is able to twist her body at the waist so that the lower half of her body is in profile. Her pouting mouth and wide-open, staring eyes seem immobile, sepulchral. There is no life in her look. A golden veil, thick and heavy as lead, swaths her head, and beyond that a halo, a broad disk ornamented with crosses, sets her apart even from her son, who has none. This blond Jesus, a boy around three years old, sits on her lap looking up at her. They are both flat against the surface of the picture, surrounded by angels swinging incense censors and *flabella,* disks on long poles used in Eastern Christianity to suggest that these are sacred persons and to keep away the flies. All of this against a white backdrop, with no effort to picture a time and a place. As with the arrest of Jesus, these figures from the Bible have been borrowed from sacred history and made permanent, rigid, iconic representations of theological ideas. People in these pictures are imagined in terms of what has become a highly artificial tradition, quite remote from the imagination of Jesus, who loved to tell stories about "a certain man...."

Figure 41. Virgin and Child with Angels (Folio 7v)

JESUS ENTHRONED

What clearly matters to the makers of this book are not the actual bodies of the people depicted but rather manifestations of their power, and the power of pictorial symbols. This is dramatically apparent in a full-length portrait of Jesus on 32v (Figure 42). The man depicted as the Savior is the same as in the arrest scene: same hair, same clothes. Here he is seated on a throne, and he holds up for us to see a closed book and points at it to indicate the centrality of Bible texts for the world of Irish Christianity. Surrounding this figure on all sides are symbols: the cross, the peacock, two evangelists, angels with their wings folded, the sacred communion host, grapevines and olive trees, snakes. The peacocks here stand upon blue vases in which grapes and olives are growing, and the sacred host is fixed to their wings as if it were a badge embellishing their bodies. These various symbols are symmetrically ordered, an angel on each side of Jesus, a peacock on each side, and so on. Everything is then surrounded with a border, a heavy rectangular shape that is itself in turn defined by a thick, black line. The overall effect is of enormous stillness: the border enclosing the entire picture and keeping it fixed; and within, the profusion of symbols all balanced and themselves in a kind of orderly pattern; and at the center, Jesus, staring at the viewer, pointing at the closed book, as still and immobile as all the other elements. Clearly the men who made this image liked the immobility, the stillness, the balance, the powerful sense of unity— all concentered in the mournful, direct stare of Jesus' blue eyes.

Figure 42. Christ (Folio 32v)

The symbols speak pictorially of theological aspects of Jesus. The communion hosts, the grapes, and the olives suggest the sacraments. The angels and evangelists represent those he sends as bearers of his good news. But the peacock? The artists who made the *Book of Kells* were fascinated by animal and bird symbolism. A widely dispersed legend held that the peacock had flesh so dense that after its death it would not rot. For this reason it became a useful symbol for the Jesus of the resurrection, the gorgeous beauty of the male bird adding a further dimension in suggesting the beauty of Jesus in his power and goodness.

The peacock had already been a christological symbol for a long time when the *Book of Kells* was made. In the catacomb of Priscilla in the so-called Arcosolium of the Peacock we find a rendering taken from Roman pictorial traditions. There we see the bird in profile, neck and chest erect and looking forward, elegantly thin legs walking ahead, the long stiff sweep of tail feathers extended. It's a skilful bit of painting, far more confident and anatomically correct than most of the fresco work in the catacombs. By contrast, when we turn to the peacocks depicted in folio 32v of *Kells* we see a transformation of the original appearance of the bird into a stylized image. Here the peacock has a long, sinuous neck, a pouting, hooked beak, and large, wide-open eyes. The heavy dark blue body of the bird is flecked with gold, and its tail feathers are ornamented with diversely colored triangles. The catacomb peacock comes from a tradition of naturalism, the peacock in *Kells* comes from a tradition of the fantastic.

Images of the Fantastic

We have noted the stylistic consistency of the decorations in *Kells*. Throughout the manuscript the depiction of the peacock never varies in the way in which it reproduces the head, the body, the feathers. But, as is always the case in the realm of fantasy, each of these elements can undergo dreamlike distortion. Meehan's fine book illustrates how the artists who made the *Book of Kells* delighted in taking the stylized form of their peacock and stretching the neck until it was as long and as flexible as a snake, and transforming the body into a simple lobe of color. As the distortion increases, in many instances what began as the neck of a peacock becomes almost pure line: a curving, twisting line that defies the rules of anatomy and laces itself into knots. There is still a hint—perhaps a stylized head and beak—to tell us this is a christological symbol, but essentially the symbol has become an element in a pattern, a pattern bred in nightmare.

Symbolic depictions of the four evangelists also appear again and again in *Kells*, their repetition "like a primitive litany or spell that evokes their four names, over and over."[32] While in *Kells* there are stiff, hieratic portraits of the four writers, much more common is the use of the four visual symbols that had come to represent the evangelists in Christian tradition. Those symbols emerge from two sources, both dream-books: the Book of the Hebrew prophet Ezekiel and the Book of Revelation. God announces himself to Ezekiel through a prodigious revelation. In the sky the prophet sees a whirlwind of cloud and bright fire and in the middle of the fire "four living creatures." Each has wings, "they sparkled like burnished bronze" and each one has a head with four faces. The faces are of a man, a lion, an ox, and an eagle (Ezek 1:4–10). Images such as this provoke endless interpretive debates.

What did the writer wish to infer with such a description? Without trying to enter that debate one can make this simple observation: a passage like this seems to carry on the traditional Jewish prohibition against making images, since it is virtually impossible to depict visually what these words seem to describe. One of the points of the description then becomes this: it is impossible to make pictures of God's messengers. They are beyond picturing.

Another way to consider the vision is to say that insofar as it does defy ordinary visual experience it comes from the illogic of a dream world. The author of the Book of Revelation adopts many elements of Ezekiel's prophecies for his own writing, including the "four beasts," which he too sees in his vision of heaven. This time each of the four faces has become an entire creature: "the first living creature like a lion, the second living creature like an ox, the third living creature with a face like a human face, and the fourth living creature like a flying eagle" (Rev 4:7).

But what do these beasts symbolize? Later fanciful Christian exegetes argued that in them we find prophetic anticipations of the four evangelists, and they created rather implausible identifications: John's Gospel soars to new heights of visionary wisdom so he is an eagle, while Mark's Gospel begins with John the Baptist in the desert—certainly a lion of the Lord. Luke exemplifies the tranquility of the ox with his initial nativity narrative, and Matthew's Gospel, which opens with the list of Jesus' human ancestors, is symbolized by the figure of a man. Later still, "St. Gregory's homilies on Ezekiel explain[ed] the symbols as the four stages of Christ's life...a man in his birth, a calf in his death, a lion in his resurrection, and an eagle in ascending to heaven...."[33]

The symbolic images of the evangelists do not appear in the Roman catacombs, where indeed we find a very limited repertoire of symbolic pictures and instead a typically realistic stress upon human bodies in symbolic postures. But in *Kells,* as with the peacock, they are everywhere. And just as with the peacock, the artists who made the *Book of Kells* invented stylized versions of all four figures that they could reproduce easily and then scattered them through their decorative schemes, sometimes in distorted forms. The peacock and the "four beasts" of the evangelists are favored in *Kells* precisely because they are fantastic, the stuff of legends, emerging from the visions. They suggest that there is in Irish Celtic culture an eagerness for the marvelous that sought out these elements of Catholic visual tradition and expanded on their possibilities. Here the unnatural beasts of nightmare are at home.

Abstract Decoration

Abstract line and pattern emerge in the *Book of Kells* from the artist's analysis and progressive distortion of actual things: birds, animals, vegetation. In many, many instances what appears to be a passage of completely free linear invention turns out to have on closer scrutiny a bit of a head at one end and perhaps a foot or tailfeather at the other. Pure, absolute abstract pattern is somewhat rare, but pattern is everywhere.

What kinds of pattern? Everywhere there is curvilinear interlace in which lines weave in and out of each other in mazes that the eye can only sometimes follow; there are roundels in which one finds figures or lines interlaced; spirals, multiple spirals, and horn shapes; crosses single and at times multiple.

Folio 183r (Figure 43) is a helpful but also problematic example. The text in large letters comes from the middle of Mark's narration of the crucifixion and reads "Erat autem hora tercia," or "It was now the third hour" (Mark 15:25). Christ has been nailed to the cross. He looks down now on the Roman soldiers as they throw dice for his clothes. From their point of view he's already a dead man. This is as painful and tragic a moment as Christ ever experienced.

Figure 43. "Erat autem hora tercia" (Folio 183r)

On the page of the *Kells* manuscript the letter *E* of the first word *Erat* is filled in with golden linear interlace; the other letters are elaborated with jagged lines, and one is looped through by a curving line with a snake's head. Framing the words are twin fanciful borders decorated with interlace (some of it composed of peacock necks, some of snakes) and checkerboard patterns. In the middle of the page an angel holds out an open book. Perhaps one's first reaction is surprise bordering on dismay. There isn't a single emblem on this page that might seem to suggest the tragedy of the moment being described. There isn't even a cruciform pattern. The page is colored in gold, a dark blue-grey, rusty reds, and tans. The skeptical conclusion one might draw is that the men making this page were not even thinking about its contents or its meaning for their lives. Instead they simply seem to be playing visual games.

Abstract Decoration and Meaning

We might begin to understand what is going on, not only with this baffling example but with the decorative schemes of the *Book of Kells* generally, by recalling our discussion of the Judeo-Christian traditions of biblical interpretation that stress the complexity and the mystery of the Bible. For the Iona community, God's book was mysterious, never to be fully comprehended. Rather than seeking one, single meaning for a word or a sentence, this tradition prized multiplicity, layers of meaning, expecting a complexity and richness beyond the limits of any one reading. Indeed, "the tradition of exegesis not only allows but encourages a considerable degree of ambiguity, so that a single narrative sequence might carry several thematic threads...."[34] The imaginative response to this in the *Book of Kells* is the analogous complexity of its ornamentation, functioning as a visual metaphor for the value presumed inherent in text. If the meaning of this moment during Christ's crucifixion is full of a mystery that can only be penetrated through meditation, prayer, and vision, and if this mystery contains contradictions within itself—paradoxical joy emerging from grief and triumph from shame—then the way to ornament the text is to use precisely these kinds of complex, ambiguous decorative patterns that enrich and suggest but never seek to definitively explain.

Where do these patterns come from? The patterns found in the *Book of Kells* are by no means unique. Many were derived from or are at least the same as the ornament found on secular objects made in contemporary pagan and Christian communities: on weapons, armor, dishes, and jewelry—everyday things from Celtic and Anglo-Saxon cultures. Their adaptation for sacred purposes reflects a persistent characteristic of the Catholic imagination, which is to find the divine within the ordinary and to read everyday life with that double vision that discerns the inner, transcendent meaning in things. We can carry this argument further still. The traditional ornamental patterns in *Kells* were ultimately derived from the bodies of animals, birds, people, but their forms were then artificially colored and exaggerated through unnatural distention so that progressively the natural structure of the body was lost, transformed into line. These lines, however, remain the dynamic, vital lines of growing things: roots, brambles, weeds—tangle, but not confusion.

Carefully studied, the seeming tangle becomes a lace or a knot, a planned interweaving of lines.

This is clearly a visual metaphor that represents a reality that at first seems chaotic but turns out to have structure, interdependence, and plan. Or, to be more precise, various structures and plans simultaneously. This is what Giraldus Cambrensis saw when he wrote, "If you take the trouble to look very closely, and penetrate with your eyes to the secrets of the artistry, you will notice such intricacies, so delicate and subtle, so close together, and well-knitted, so involved and bound together...."[35]

Penetrating to the Secret: Incarnation and the Limits of Human Understanding

One perceives in such decorative patterns levels of organization that emerge sequentially. First there is simply the ordering of things on the page. At this level, one sees "the overall sweep of the designs...[that were] visible at a distance to a congregation sitting in the body of a church."[36] Then, a little closer, one sees the larger ornaments: enlarged letters, human and animal heads, decorative symbolic figures such as the evangelists. Then, looking even more closely, the smaller ornaments within the larger ones, interlace inside the body of letters, ornaments within ornaments, visible only to someone who is very close to the manuscript and hence is privileged with the right to study it minutely. Meehan's research shows that many of the most minute interlace patterns are made up of symbolic animals (snake, peacock, lion) and symbolic objects (the Eucharistic host, grapes, the sacramental chalice)—which, as we have seen, are elements of a long-standing Christian iconographic tradition (Figure 44). The implication clearly emerges that the closer we look and the more carefully we study this book, the more complex it becomes. But if we keep scrutinizing and analyzing, what we ultimately find, symbolized in endlessly varying ways, is Christ, Christ the lion and peacock, chalice and host, which is to say a Christ of complexity, ambiguity, and multiple signification.

The decorative scheme of the entire *Book of Kells* is thus a single, repeating visual metaphor for a theological reality that has ever subtler, ever deeper levels of organization and meaning. If the eye

Figure 44. "In principio erat verbum" (Folio 292r)

fails in its efforts to trace the knot of an interlace or fails in the effort to determine whether a form is animal or vegetal, if the relationship of one symbol or image to another continues to baffle, well, so too does the Christ whose incarnation remains a mystery even to those who love him. Defying any simple, univocal interpretations, evading explanation and easily shifting from one sort of signification to another, the *Book of Kells* is uncannily correspondent to our modern concept of the physical world, with its levels of organization: molecular, atomic, subatomic. The further we go, the more random and logic defying the theory of modern physics becomes. That the ornamentation in *Kells* is meant to say much the same thing about the Gospel is clear from its use on the first pages of gospel texts. Here, as we have seen, the initial letter(s) of the book itself are almost lost in the richness of the ornament, clearly suggesting the radiance, multiplicity, and complexity of their meaning—that is to say, the meaning of sacred scripture is infinite. From this exalted perspective it would have been a mistake to fill folio 183r with grim images of the crucifixion, because the meanings of that event are so multiple and complicated that to give any one of them priority would be somehow to falsify the richness of the moment. Better the abstract pattern and its analogical implications.

This way of imagining the world and its divine creator—as a complex series of interwoven patterns that only time, sensitivity, insight, and perhaps divine aid can even partially and fitfully reveal—may account for the frequent picturing in *Kells* of the evangelists, both in their human forms as men and in the symbolic forms given them in the Book of Revelation (man, lion, ox, and eagle), and its similarly frequent depiction of angels. The angels were the first messengers sent from God with his new and mysterious message. The evangelists, later in history, were to write down the narrative of his mysterious plan and its fulfillment. Together they constitute a central source for illumination. Thanks to what they came to say, people can begin to see. And so we find them in the midst of *Kells'* Celtic interlace, promising as it were that all that baffles us is, at least, from God and of God.

Incarnation then, that first trait of Catholic vision, appears in *Kells* paradoxically not so much in the full-page illustrations with their stiff and unnatural human figures as in its use of decorative pattern, pattern derived from everyday objects, pattern evolved from natural forms, plants and living creatures, but woven together into elaborate visual conundrums that first defy the eye to comprehend them and later resolve themselves into knots, lace, labyrinths, the eye following them in and out seeing where they lead, how they interconnect. Pattern is an analogy to God's creation, hence to God's will, finally to God's voice incarnate in the words on the page.

But this is not by any means the only implication of the ornament in the *Book of Kells.* Indeed given the analysis we have been developing we might expect that if we find the interlace pattern and its complexities we might also find its opposite.

Order and Power

To begin that inquiry, let us first turn back to the *Altus Prosator,* where we find the Columban poem picturing the world this way:

> By the divine power of the great God is hung
> The globe of the earth, and the circle of the great deep
>   placed about it,
> held up by the strong hand of almighty God,
> with columns like bars supporting it,
> promontories and rocks as their solid foundations,
> fixed firm, as if on certain immovable bases.[37]

The order, the massiveness, the fixity that this passage attributes to God stands in striking contradiction to the endlessly nervous movement of the interlace. And yet this aspect of God is also in the *Kells* decorative scheme.

Typically both the full-page portrait and narrative illustrations in *Kells*, and also the full-page decorations, are surrounded, or framed, with heavy rectangular borders that echo the rectilinear shape of the page itself. In planning these borders the Iona artists "borrowed from architectural forms for their layout," designing "heavy frames with something of the character of carved wooden structures to give weight and emphasis...."[38] Within these borders, space is frequently subdivided into squares and rectangles. Arch forms are sometimes used to surround sacred figures and lists of parallel passages in the "cannon tables," but the arches too appear within a rectilinear frame. Within these massive boundary rectangles, circles, and disks appear in the ornament but always subordinated to what is the straight line of the page. This recurrent need to establish boundary lines and a firmly defined geometric order is clearly a visual analogy for the God of order, who centers the world on "solid foundations." And we might speculate that this straight line of divine truth imaged by these borders, which in *Kells* is easily seen from a distance by the ordinary worshiper to be massive and obvious, up close becomes composed of endlessly shifting complexities of interlace. One sees this clearly exemplified in folio 292r (Figure 45), a decorative first page for the beginning of Saint John's Gospel, displaying the Latin phrase, *In principio erat verbum,* "In the beginning was the word." The *Kells* artists chose to decorate this phrase with massive dark blue vertical forms that weigh down the left and right sides of the page. A melancholy Jesus sits above the ornamented letters with his hand across a book page. Facing this page to its left in folio 291v we have another massive page border, again dominantly outlined in dark blue. At its edges, four huge crosses formed of interlace create a boundary within which we find Saint John the Evangelist seated upon a Byzantine throne, his head surrounded by a double halo, holding up his pen in one hand, and a book in the other. The two pages, viewed facing each other, evoke an aggressive, almost menacing divine authority that seems to provoke the rueful expression of the Jesus on 292r.

Figure 45. Animal interlace (Folio 250v)

We have noticed the fascination with divine control, authority, and punishment, and with a corresponding terror provoked by the contrary, negative power of evil in devils and dragons that one finds in the *Altus Prosator*. That same fascination reappears in the *Book of Kells*, in the delicate interlace so frequently dominated by the menace of heavy borders, for example, and also in the narrative illustrations of subjects such as Jesus being tempted by the devil from Luke chapter 4, and Jesus being arrested by his enemies in Luke chapter 22.

The Devouring

But there is a different form of dark vision in *Kells*' use within decorative schemes of images of biting and devouring. Nothing is shown more frequently throughout the designs than the jaw of one beast clamped onto a part of the body of another beast: birds, snakes, lions biting other birds, snakes, and lions, and also biting people's heads. These images seem to capture the blank-eyed, mindless voraciousness of creation and the equally empty shocked stare of those being devoured. It's difficult to know whether such images were received by the first audience for *Kells* with amusement or grim assent. The use of the image of the lion roaring and devouring may indeed, as some argue, represent Christ and his eagerness to devour those he cares for with love, but in examples such as folio 124r, where flames seem roaring from the beast's mouth one recalls instead Jesus' warning that the "devil like a roaring lion seeks whom he may devour."[39] It would be comforting perhaps to conclude that the motif of devouring is nothing but a bit of Irish Celtic whimsy, but it is far more likely that instead it carries out in a very literal way the manuscript's vision of a world still full of evil, sorrow, and pain, a world still in desperate need of the redemption that can only come from the Savior whose life is told four times over on these very pages.

CHAPTER ELEVEN

Warrior Christianity I
The Franks and the Utrecht Psalter

The Franks and the Saxons

The earliest Christian art emerged from the Mediterranean world that Jesus himself knew, and from small communities of believers who were periodically in danger of public torture and execution. The caution, the modesty, the dependence upon God's mercy and power that we observed in the house-church at Dura-Europas and in the Greek Chapel from the catacomb of Priscilla reflect the public status of the earliest Christians. Prudentius, by contrast, coming from an era when Christianity had become the official religion of the Roman Empire, reflects the exuberant sense of security of his era. This, it turns out, was a delusion, and with the collapse of imperial power the church entered a new period of testing. Columba and his monks, traveling through the mountainous regions of Scotland, represent one aspect of this new period, and their synthesis of indigenous Celtic and Germanic cultures with a Christian vision rooted in Rome, Egypt, and Byzantium (indicated, for example, by the illustration pages for the *Book of Kells*) exemplifies the new worlds into which the Catholic imagination was moving. The darkness and menace in the decorative patterns for that book—its fascination, for example, with biting, its bizarre, distorted fantasy creatures—reflect the anxieties and fears felt by Celtic Catholics at the beginning of the ninth century.

We turn now to two works that were probably created about thirty years after the *Book of Kells* but that come not from a remote monastery in the Hebridean Islands but rather, in all likelihood,

227

from Benedictine libraries sponsored by what was at the time the most powerful dynasty in Europe. In doing this we enter necessarily into the issues arising from the complex historical interrelationship between Christianity and secular power. In one way or another the church had been involved with and had aided governments and their armies ever since 312, when the Roman emperor Constantine adopted the sign of Jesus as his battle standard. The eastern Roman Empire, centered in Constantinople, the city he built, for centuries warred against its neighbors and rivals and later acted as a bulwark of Christianity against the rising power of Islam. Even groups as small as the Irish clans had carried gospel manuscripts into battle. But in order really to understand developments in the Catholic imagination we must, for the first time in this study, consider the historical emergence of what was to become one of the central nations of Europe. The story we trace is about gaining power by violence and then imposing one's will upon others, and it is about the relationship of Christianity to the processes of winning and losing. We will find in the celebrated *Utrecht Psalter,* an illustrated book of Psalms, a work of art reflecting the attitudes and the feelings of the Franks—Catholics who, through power and violence, "won"—while in chapter 12 we consider the Saxon epic *The Heliand,* a poetic narrative emerging from the Saxons, a people who had "lost" to the Franks and been forced to convert to Christianity and who were now not only defeated but oppressed. In both cases we trace the ways in which paradox, that recurrent, profoundly Catholic way of thinking, leads at least to a relativizing if not a reversal of what one might mean by winning and losing.

The Dynastic History of the Franks

A Germanic tribe living on the lower reaches of the Rhine, the Franks first made contact with Roman imperial power in 253. In 358, Julian,[1] the Roman commander in Gaul, conquered the Salian clan of the Franks and formed an alliance with them. But in the early fifth century, Rome was withdrawing its troops from northern Europe, and the Franks, like many other tribal groups, were left to fend for themselves. Their forces united together, at least for a while, under Clovis (ca. 466–511), who in 486 overthrew the last Roman governor in Gaul and went on to progressively subject neighboring tribes to his authority. At first a staunch believer in the gods of his ancestors, in 496 Clovis converted to Catholic Christianity under the influence of his wife, the Burgundian princess Clothilde.[2] He was baptized at Reims (Figure 46). This marks the beginning of what was to be a long-lasting alliance between Frankish monarchs and the Catholic Church. At the death of Clovis in 511, the Frankish kingdom was divided among four heirs, and a period of struggle ensued. Gregory of Tours, in his very early (ca. 592) *History of the Franks*, captures the peculiar quality of this era.

> There were many deeds being done both good and evil: the hea-then were raging fiercely; kings were growing more cruel; the church, attacked by heretics, was defended by Catholics; while the Christian faith was in general devoutly cherished among some it was growing cold; the churches also were enriched by the faithful or plundered by traitors....[3]

After more than two centuries of this kind of confusion, in 751 the unromantically named Pepin the Short was anointed king of France by Saint Boniface, the Anglo-Saxon missionary to the Germans, an event that marks the beginning of the Carolingian dynasty. Pepin's son Charlemagne became king of the Franks in 768.

Figure 46. The Baptism of Clovis
The baptism of Clovis (466–511), king of the Franks, was notable in that the Franks under Clovis were the first barbarian nation to convert directly to Catholic Christianity and not to Arianism.

Charlemagne

From the beginning of his reign, Charlemagne was nothing if not ambitious. He soon launched upon a series of aggressive attacks against his neighbors, which led in time to a Frankish Empire that stretched south to the borders of modern Spain, included all of modern-day France and Germany, and took in as well a substantial piece of northern Italy. Perhaps Charlemagne's most recalcitrant foes were the Saxons, a Germanic people living to the north of Frankish territories. For thirty-two years (from 772 to 804), these independent tribes resisted Charlemagne's efforts to convert them to Christianity and to make their lands a part of his imperium. Charlemagne's forces fought them implacably, slaughtering as many as 4,500 Saxon warriors on a single day (in 782) because they refused baptism. His final victory, in 804, included the massive deportation of troops of this defeated enemy to other parts of his empire.

Like his predecessors, Charlemagne worked closely with the church. In 781 he went to Rome for Easter and the baptism of his son Pepin by the pope—thus ensuring church sanction for his son's succession to his throne. On Christmas Day in 800, Pope Leo III crowned Charlemagne as the emperor of the West, and in the ensuing centuries this event came to mark the beginning of what was later to be called the Holy Roman Empire, "the nucleus of medieval and modern Europe."[4]

THE CAROLINGIAN "RENASCENCE"

Thirty years of warfare led to Charlemagne's coronation as emperor. It also contributed to the wealth of his court, financed as it was by "the booty captured by his armies during the rapid expansion of his Empire, especially in the last quarter of the eight century...."[5] Charlemagne aimed not just at power and wealth, however, but also at the creation of a new cultural center in the north, nothing less than a "renascence of the arts and literature...an attempt to recreate what was believed to have been the golden age of early Christian Rome. Contemporaries called it a renovatio: a renewal...."[6] To this end, in 782 Charlemagne invited the celebrated English scholar Alcuin of York (735–804), whom he had met in Rome in 780, to create a school for educating members of the royal court and their children. Alcuin soon attracted other scholars,[7] creating what Charlemagne himself, remembering the history of Greek philosophy, called an "academy." In the town of Aachen, in what is now Germany, Charlemagne began in 786 to build a complex of royal buildings modeled on imperial Byzantine precedents and from 794 he took up permanent residence there. This was consciously intended "to become Roma Secunda,"[8] and "it had all the components necessary for an imperial center: an audience hall, porticoes that led to a large courtyard at the entrance to a round, domed chapel. Aachen was a stage-set, in which the ceremonies that surrounded a ruler of 'imperial' pretensions could be played out."[9]

Charlemagne's court now began to patronize the arts. This was no simple accomplishment. As with the court school, invitations went out to the best-known artists of the day to come and work for the emperor. Much of what they achieved has been lost through time. Of the celebrated buildings of the palace complex only the royal chapel remains. Today, "the particular contribution of the Carolingian period to European civilization rests on the evidence of literature and so-called minor arts of manuscript illumination, ivory carving, and goldsmith's work."[10]

For Carolingian culture, the making of manuscripts assumed the same importance that it had at the Columban monasteries during the same period. There was a great concern for accuracy. Charlemagne commissioned Alcuin to create a "correct" text of the Bible, free from the errors that had crept in with successive transmission. Emissaries were sent to Rome seeking the most reliable sources. Indeed, "this cult for the 'authentic' is one of the chief characteristics of the Carolingian renewal."[11] Using these "authentic" texts, artists from Italy, Byzantium, and Anglo-Saxon England now began to make luxurious manuscript copies, some lavishly decorated, some even lettered in gold. Images from these books were to live on in the imaginations of European artists throughout the next century, influencing the picturing of sacred events.

Charlemagne died in 814, and his son and successor Louis I the Pious (814–840) in a curiously generous mood gave away much of the artistic treasure his father had heaped up—to his siblings, to Pope Leo III, and to the poor. But his genuine love for learning led to continuing support for manuscript production.[12] Under his rule the making of manuscripts was transferred from Aachen to the ancient city of Reims, where Clovis had once, centuries before, been anointed. There under Ebbo, archbishop from 816 to 835,[13] the Benedictine monastery of Hautvillers created some of the most celebrated manuscripts of the early medieval period. This work was very much a product of the Carolingian court. Ebbo had been librarian to Louis the Pious, and his commissions clearly reflected royal policy. It was almost certainly from this source and within this context that the book now called the *Utrecht Psalter* was created, sometime between 820 and 835.[14]

The *Utrecht Psalter:* God and the Warrior

A First Glance

First, the manuscript's name. As our discussion has already made clear, this is, if anything, the "Hautvillers" Psalter. But with the passing of time the manuscript came to the University Library in Utrecht in the Netherlands, where it has been beautifully cared for. In recent years the university has sponsored a major research conference on the Psalter and has issued a highly useful CD-ROM version of the entire manuscript.[15]

A *Psalter* is typically a copy of the Hebrew Psalms, the one hundred and fifty religious poems preserved in the biblical Book of Psalms and traditionally attributed to the Israelite king David and other specially trained Hebrew poets. The term *psalter* comes from the Greek word *psalterion*, a lyre used to accompany a singer. The Psalms had been, and still are, the center of Jewish prayer. From its earliest days Christianity also adopted the Book of Psalms as its book of prayer, and for two millennia Christians have prayed and sung these ancient poems.

In the last decades of the fourth century, Saint Jerome (347?–419 or 420) translated the Psalms into Latin three times. The first of the three, the "Gallican" version, translated from the Septuagint (a Greek translation of the original Hebrew), was incorporated into the Vulgate version of the Bible, the Bible text used in the Catholic Church until the twentieth century. The *Utrecht Psalter* reproduces and illustrates Jerome's Latin, with all of its peculiarities and particulars in play.

Unlike the *Book of Kells*, where color and ornament are on every page, this manuscript is instead illustrated by sketches, one for each of the hundred and fifty Psalms, executed, it would appear, very quickly, full of movement and energy, done in a red-brown ink. Strictly speaking, the whole book should not be called an "illuminated manuscript" at all, but rather the Psalms with illustrations.

The script used for the Psalms is rustic capitals, a form of lettering already outdated in the ninth century. Uncial, a more quickly written script, had been in use for "some centuries."[16] This suggests that the scribes and artists who created the manuscript wished it to look "old" or "authentic." And this is certainly also true for some of the aspects of the drawings, which frequently quote or echo late antique images and which depend upon a style of picturing that had been adopted from Hellenic sources in Byzantium, but now adapted by north European artists.[17] It is difficult to exaggerate the importance of this blending of Hellenic and north European. As Peter Lasko puts it in his *Ars Sacra*, "In this style, North Western Europe seems to have found the really satisfactory synthesis of classical art and northern expressive intention, sought ever since the first works of art in the Mediterranean classical tradition reached the north during the seventh century."[18]

Every page of this manuscript is, as is frequently the case with medieval manuscripts, full. Starting after folio 1, there is a rectangular illustration about 4 inches high and covering the whole span of the page left to right, then the psalm text. If one psalm ends at the top of the page, then the illustration for the next one will be in the middle. In some cases the page ends with an illustration referring to a psalm that begins on the following page.

While these drawings may "ultimately derive from the illusionistic style of Late Antiquity," that "same illusionism is keyed up into a style that transcends it. The artist is anxious to capture the inner dynamism and not the outward show."[19] They are

> drawings in...a style of tremendous exhilaration....The landscapes themselves are imbued with an inner excitement....The figures rush from one side of the page to the other, their turbulent draperies awhirl with dynamic movement....Everything is intoxicated with animation....The whole world is galvanized by an inner ecstasy.[20]

They are, as Pietro Toesca has observed, "almost beyond comparison with any other illuminated MS of western art."[21] Beckwith indeed argues that this is nothing less than "one of the most extraordinary sequences of drawings in the whole history of art.... The total effect is a bewildering richness of imagery drawn...with a dynamic force which transcends any late antique models which may have been used."[22]

Picturing the Psalms: Literalism

The artists who illustrated the *Utrecht Psalter* faced unusual problems when they began working. We have studied how fresco painters at Dura-Europos and Rome sought for ways to picture scenes from biblical narratives, such as Moses striking the rock in the desert, Susanna accused by the elders, the good shepherd returning with the saved, and Jesus walking on the waters of the Sea of Galilee. Some of these subjects, like the shepherd, were easily adapted from pagan precedents; others, such as walking on water, required entirely new invention. But all of these scenes were individual dramatic moments taken from a story with one or more characters and a specific setting.

By contrast, the Psalms are poems that express states of feeling through a rich vocabulary of traditional literary images and symbols.[23] In Psalm 69(68):2, for example, the poem's speaker, finding himself in despair, cries out, "I sink in deep mire, where there is no foothold; I have come into deep waters, and the flood sweeps over me." This is not a poem about a shipwreck. It's about a crisis in faith. In trying to convey what he feels, the poet uses the image of being overwhelmed by water and mud to concretize his sense of powerlessness and the imminent danger coming over him, thereby evoking the reader's deep fears of entrapment and drowning. The *Utrecht Psalter*, illustrating this psalm (Figure 47), adopts a solution characteristic of the whole manuscript, which is to create a literal, concrete depiction of the poem's metaphors: we see three boats with high sterns and prows, the prows ornamented in the Viking manner by grotesque heads. In the two flanking boats, enemies of the psalmist menace him as he falls from the center boat toward the water, his hand raised toward God in the heavens, begging help. The same strategy appears in two other poems of despair. Since verse 2 of Psalm 127(126) speaks of the "bread of anxious toil," the *Utrecht* artists literally depict large loaves of bread being distributed to the grieving.

For the beginning of Psalm 130(129), "Out of the depths I cry to you, O LORD," we see the psalmist standing in a pit reading from a scroll of the Law and calling out to God.

Figure 47. Psalm 68(69), *Salvum me fac* (Folio 38v)

These literal transcriptions of poetic metaphors are fairly easy for later viewers to comprehend. But the Hebrew Psalms also employ other, odder images that are clearly a part of a very ancient poetic tradition, and the meanings of some of them are now hard to grasp. For example, the Psalms speak of "the horn" of the righteous, or of the sinner, evidently referring to the traditional use of an animal horn, *cornu*, as a symbol of identity and power. Psalm 75(74):10 asserts "Et omnia cornua peccatorum confringam: et exaltabuntur cornua justi," or "All the horns of the wicked I will cut off, but the horns of the righteous shall be exalted." The north European artists of this Psalter, confronted with this odd imagery, keep to their literalism and picture the psalmist holding a stag's head with a full set of horns and smashing with his rod another stag's head held by the unjust. When describing how his enemies pursue him, the psalmist says in Psalm 56(55):6, "They watch my steps," and so the illustration shows the psalmist raising his right leg and pointing to his heel.

The ambition of the *Utrecht Psalter* is to depict, however, not just one image or symbol from a given psalm, but many, if not most of them, which means that a typical illustration will have various kinds of images collected within its frame. For example, in the well-known Psalm 23(22), "The Lord is my shepherd…," the poet voices his trust in God through a series of metaphors in verses 4–5: "Even though I walk through the darkest valley, I fear no evil; for you are with me; your rod and your staff—they comfort me. You prepare a table before me in the presence of my enemies; you anoint my head with oil; my cup overflows." At the center of the illustration in the *Utrecht Psalter* (Figure 48), we see the psalmist with an angel hovering over him. From one of the angel's hands a vessel pours the holy oil on the psalmist's brow, while from his other hand he extends down the rod or staff of divine help. The psalmist takes this in his right hand; in his left is the cup overflowing. To the left of the psalmist, we see a circular table prepared for a banquet full of serving dishes, and behind it a building that appears over and over in these pictures and represents the Temple of Jerusalem or the sanctuary. It has an open door, and inside we see the altar of sacrifice, though in this picture the building is now Christianized with crosses on the roof. The psalmist is in a valley where goats, cattle, and sheep graze and a running stream crosses in the foreground. God is with him. He is secure. And, what about the "enemies"? Given the way in which this manuscript imagines the Psalms they too must be present, and indeed in the lower right-hand corner of the picture we see a crowd of hostile soldiers shake their spears. One has just shot an arrow toward the psalmist and we see it in midair, but it seems clear that a rocky outcropping will stop it, because God will guard the people of his flock.

Figure 48. Psalm 22(23), *Dominus regit me* (Folio 13r)

Literalism, Jesus' Imagination, and Incarnation

The *Utrecht Psalter*, then, embodies the metaphoric meanings of the Psalms in a remarkably literal fashion, turning analogy and symbol into concrete manifestation. Here instinctively the Catholic artists of the Benedictine Abbey at Hautvillers have adopted the imagination of Jesus as the poet of everyday life; the Jesus who is the poet of the concrete and particular reflected in what is at times a charmingly, naïve literalness. The incarnational instinct of the Catholic imagination here strives literally to embody the abstract ideas and feelings, the elaborate metaphorical language of the psalmist's poetry. Feelings of joy in God, loneliness and abandonment, the longing for community and membership, find direct, literal incarnation in human figures that serve to illustrate on the page the content of the Psalms, just as Jesus expressed his ideas in storytelling of the simplest, most concrete character. The implicit understanding of the artists who fashioned these pictures is that the entire range of experiences that people have in their multifarious relationships with God can be expressed in their bodies and in the things that surround their bodies. Physical gesture, facial expression, clothes, objects such as spears or papyrus scrolls, animals like sheep and goats, falling water, hills—all can directly picture the complex theological and experiential worlds of the Psalms. This is the theology of the incarnation and the aesthetic principle of analogy worked out in the most direct, practical kinds of ways.

The structure of Jesus' teaching also emerges in the structure of these illustrations. Jesus told short tales that very often lack specific place, time, and identity and thus have universal application. Through them he fashioned a cumulative vision by means of the interweaving of a series of sometimes contrasting, sometimes similar tales that the listener must combine into a totality. This technique reappears in these drawings through the combination of individual scenes, often of quite disparate character, that make up the whole picture. The meaning of a given picture comes from the viewer's interpretation of the relationship of the separate images and events to each other, as we have already seen with Psalm 23(22).

This strategy is also evident in the illustration for Psalm 26(25), in which the poet distinguishes between his devotion to God and the folly of evil men: "I do not sit with the worthless, nor do I consort with hypocrites; I hate the company of evildoers, and will not sit with the wicked. I wash my hands in innocence, and go around your altar, O LORD…" (Ps 26[25]:4–6). At the center of the illustration (Figure 49), we see the multiple arches of a Roman aqueduct that splashes water into a large basin where a crowd of nude children are washing themselves. Just to the right of them a nude man is being scourged with sticks while a second one, lying on the ground, is being whipped. Here in literal terms is the righteous one, who washes "in innocence," contrasted with the violence and cruelty of the malignant and the wicked. At the upper left-hand corner of the scene Jesus and his angels appear on clouds, with Jesus holding a large book, perhaps the book recording good and evil deeds described in Daniel's vision of the everlasting king coming in judgment upon humanity in Daniel 7:10.[24] Diagonally across, at the other side of the picture, in the lower right-hand corner devils come out of the sky to apprehend terrified figures, and beneath them the flaming mouth of hell gapes open to receive the wicked. The judgment of God invoked in the very first line of the Psalm, "Vindicate me, O LORD…," is thus exemplified by apocalyptic scenes of the end of time and history. The viewer studying this picture pieces together the meaning of the whole scene by mentally synthesizing the individual images—the figures washing themselves, the figures being punished, Jesus coming on the clouds in judgment, the devils dragging their victims off to hell—into one unified whole, in much the same way as Jesus' first hearers listened to parables about the lost coin, the pearl of great price, the prodigal son, the good shepherd, and came in the end to the conclusion that, as Jesus was arguing through analogy, God loved and cared for them. The story told by this illustration is the narrative of redemption, the innocent purified by the counsel of righteousness that Jesus extends toward them. The people who used the *Utrecht Psalter* would have recognized immediately the sacramental implications of this scene, implications arising from their own life experiences of the sacramental rituals, for example the children washing themselves as suggestive of baptism, just as the anointing of the head of the psalmist in the illustration for Psalm 23(22) might readily have been seen as suggesting the sacraments of initiation.

Figure 49. Psalm 25(26), *Iudica me* (Folio 14v)

Iconic Lexicon

The Psalms use a vocabulary of verbal imagery such as the horn, the oil of anointing, the feast, the enemy. The artists who created the *Utrecht Psalter* created a parallel visual lexicon, a kind of vocabulary of images that reappear over and over, the visual icon being used each time the verbal symbol is evoked in a poem. Just as with our analysis of the teachings of Jesus, or our discussion of the letters of Saint Paul, we can discern, through a consideration of this lexicon of visual images the way in which the *Utrecht Psalter* imagines the world, and this analysis permits us to enter into the imaginative world of this book and to assess in what ways it emerges from the ethos of northern Europe and Frankish military culture, and to what extent that ethos has been comprehended, shaped, and translated by the Catholic imagination.

As with the imagination of Jesus, this world is full of ordinary things, rich with the physical, the natural, but used always as latent with a double meaning, and hence as a visual symbolic language for the thoughts and feelings of the psalmist—a place full of vigor, energy, indeed of prodigality.

Nature and the Transcendent

All one hundred and fifty of the *Utrecht Psalter* illustrations picture scenes set in the open air. As with Prudentius, nature emerges as the language of God. In these skies float the sun, moon, and stars. Personifications of wind and rain sometimes tear up trees and flood the land, as in Psalm 29(28). Scattered through the landscape are rocks, rivers, trees, and a profusion of animals: bulls, sheep, dogs, deer, antelopes, a bear, a lion, a boar; in Psalm 139(138):9, "the farthest limits of the sea" have fish and ducks; and there are also beasts unfamiliar to us but not to the people of the ninth century—unicorns (for example, in the illustration for Psalm 133[132]) and the dragons as alluded to in Psalm 149(148):7.

This natural world is the setting for the interaction between the divine and the human. For the *Utrecht Psalter*, the divine is always immanent, emerging into the natural, the incarnational concept of God as somehow working through created things constantly present. In every one of its skies one can see either God the Father, emblematized by an enormous hand reaching down, or Jesus, who emerges from the clouds usually surrounded by the almond shape known as a *mandorla* and usually accompanied by six angels, three on each side. Sometimes this is Jesus the teacher (in Psalm 94[93], he lectures from an opened book of the Law); sometimes it's Jesus the judge (holding the balances of divine justice in Psalm 111[110]); sometimes the embodiment of God's historical relationship with Israel (extending the scroll of the covenant to the patriarchs in Psalm 105[104]); but only very rarely as the crucified Savior (as in Psalm 89[88]).

Angels not only accompany Jesus, but they also descend to the earth to execute divine will, sometimes, as in Psalm 23(22), aiding the just, at other times using weapons to punish the wicked (for example, in Psalm 110[109] spearing the unjust). Their supernatural rivals appear almost as frequently, demons sometimes with tritons, spears, and whips; in Psalm 141(140) they gather together the damned in a huge net, the "snares" of verse 9. Their destination is the hell-mouth rimmed with flames, which appears regularly in one of the bottom corners of *Utrecht* pictures.

The Psalmist and His World

The supernatural mingles always with human activity. Just as God, Father or Son, is in every picture, so is the psalmist, readily identifiable as a distinct individual and almost always standing by himself. He is the man caught between the divine and the material worlds, and with hands and arms he gestures both upward to God and earthward, directing divine attention toward the needs of the living. Just as there is a distinctly individual voice within the Hebrew Psalms, so there is a distinctly individual person in the *Utrecht Psalter* illustrations. In this way they carry forward the stress upon personal experience and personal choice that we saw in Saint Paul's letters and that, from a Christian perspective, are essential aspects of the idea of redemption.

The psalmist finds himself in the middle of a very human scene. In most of the pictures there are buildings, sometimes small and to the side, sometimes dominating the pictorial space, always made in the same way from squared stone with tiled roofs and sometimes decorated with classical columns. They represent institutions and various forms of human relationship. The temple or tabernacle that we have already alluded to—used for "the congregation" in Psalm 22(21):22 and "the house of the Lord" in Psalm 23(22):6—in the drawing for Psalm 134(133) is pictured as a fantastic palace with late classical features such as colonnades and hanging lamps from Byzantium. Here people publicly give witness to their relationship to God. Frequently we see a citadel: walls, gates, the inner keep. Here people gather for community and safety, and here too warriors fight and die for control. Sometimes the walls of a city stretch across the entire page. Psalm 107(106) pictures a prison. The mansion of one of "those who fear the LORD" appears in Psalm 112(111):1 with a chapel, a throne room where the good man and his wife distribute bread to the poor and the crippled, rooms for his armed retainers and for young, naked children, his "descendents" (in verse 2).

People: Their Nature and Meaning

Inside, around, and moving to and from these structures are what seem to be virtually numberless people pictured as isolated individuals, small groups, or clusters. The drawing renders them with "marked exaggerations—hunched and distorted shoulders, necks stretched forwards, shrugging gestures, curved, jointless fingers, legs spindly-thin and dwindling to threadlike ankles...but full of liveliness, gaiety, and humor...."[25] Their posture is typically balletic and symbolic.

It is usually possible to identify individuals in terms of their occupations. We see businessmen dividing money with balances; farmers (in Psalm 85(84) plowing with oxen, reaping with hand-held scythes, in Psalm 107(106) planting and pruning vines, harvesting grapes and making wine (in Ps 128[127]). Surveyors measure out land with a rod and rope—this is "their land as a heritage" (Ps 135[134]:12). Stonemasons (in Ps 102[101]) are building Sion; in Psalm 118(117):22 they put in place "the stone that the builders rejected [which] has become the chief cornerstone." Hunters are included (for Ps 91[90]:3): "he will deliver you from the snare of the fowler"—a Frankish hunter on horseback draws bow and arrow; his two dogs are pursing a stag. Sailors in Psalm 89(88) using oars propel their boats. Musicians play lutes (Ps 92[91]) and trumpets (Ps 98[97]), while we see women dancing, playing musical instruments and singing in Psalm 150(149). In Psalm 150 people celebrate the Lord with trumpets, psaltery, harps, cymbals, and an elaborate pipe organ played by two musicians (Byzantine pipe organs were just then being imported into Europe).

In the *Utrecht Psalter,* people, whether individuals or social groups, usually represent not only trades and skills but also moral states. In virtually every picture we see the dramatic difference between the just and the unjust. The faithful, frequently wrapped in togas, are in Psalm 105(104): the people of Israel clustered about the psalmist. By contrast, in Psalm 109(108):9, one of the curses on the unjust reads "fiant filii ejus orphani et uxor ejus vidua," or "May his children be orphans, and his wife a widow." In the illustration, three naked children make a kind of begging gesture toward a woman who is reclining and lifting up her skirt to reveal her legs; her breasts are exposed. She appears forced by her situation into being more than just a widow.

Clusters of warriors are perhaps the most frequently seen form of human grouping in the *Utrecht Psalter.* We see them in early medieval fighting dress, in hauberks usually covered by a cape, with lances, battle axes, or bow and arrow, with shields and sometimes a helmet and visor. While most are foot soldiers, there are also cavalrymen on horseback using either lances or bow and arrow. Usually one cluster of soldiers opposes another, and we can thus identify the righteous and their enemies. Usually they are fighting or are about to fight each other.

Figures analogous to Charlemagne, his son Louis the Pious, and the rulers they fought and dominated are also frequently pictured. For Psalm 61(60):6–7—"Prolong the life of the king; may his years endure to all generations! May he be enthroned for ever before God; appoint steadfast love and faithfulness to watch over him!"—we see a colonnaded building inside of which a crowd of warriors stands behind a king who on one knee raises his arms in prayerful supplication to Christ in the heavens, who in turn extends a crownlike wreath to the king. This is clearly illustrating the Carolingian concept of the relationship between divine and earthly power. Psalm 102(101):22 illustrates "when peoples gather together, and kingdoms, to worship the LORD" with a procession of two kings followed by warriors approaching Jesus seated in glory within a mandorla. For 47(46) there is Jesus enthroned in the heavens, the victorious Jewish people singing God's praises from the ramparts of their citadel, and the people who have been subdued kneeling outside the walls looking passively upward.

God and the Warrior

God and Jesus, in these pictures, are just as given to violence and war as the kings they favor. God the Father with his divine hand throws spears at a cluster of cowering men for Psalm 21(20):8, "Your hand will find out all your enemies; your right hand will find out those who hate you." He is aided by armed warriors on the ground who are also assaulting his victims. This is military Christianity justified. This is the God Clovis prayed to, hoping to be saved from his enemies.

Jesus too is a warrior. For Psalm 7(6):13, "he has prepared his deadly weapons, making his arrows fiery shafts," we see Christ with sword, bow and arrow in the heavens. In Psalm 12(11) he leans out of his heavenly mandorla, extending a cross spear to an angel; in Psalm 20(19) he extends a bow to the armed psalmist; in Psalm

144(143) (for verse 1), "Blessed be the LORD, my rock, who trains my hands for war, and my fingers for battle," Jesus bends down from heaven, giving the psalmist a sword and shield; in Psalm 66(65) Christ rides through the heavens on a chariot, and in Psalm 76(75) Christ with a halo spears the wicked. God's angels are usually warriors: in Psalm 129(128) raining down spears and battle axes on the foes of God, and in Psalm 140(139) raining down torches and brimstone on enemy soldiers.

The pages of the *Utrecht Psalter* are full of the horrors that must have been an aspect of the ordinary lives of men in the Frankish army. In the illustration for Psalm 10(9), soldiers kill civilians and devastate towns while triumphant horsemen trample victims. In Psalm 79(78) the bodies of the slaughtered are devoured by animals and birds depicting the Psalm's vision of God's servants whose bodies have been given to beasts and birds by the "the nations" (of verse 1). For Psalm 101(100):8—"Morning by morning I will destroy all the wicked in the land..."—swordsmen outside a wall are stabbing their victims. There are cavalry charges for Psalm 54(53) and Psalm 81(80). Soldiers destroy buildings in Psalm 11(10) and 74(73). The defeated are enslaved; in the pictures for Psalm 14(13) and Psalm 53(52) we see the enslavement of women victims and in Psalm 150 captured kings bound in chains or in the stocks. Peace is represented in Psalm 148 by groups of warriors who have thrust their lances point first into the ground, set their shields down, and now hold palm branches.

Typology and Picturing the Hebrew Psalms

The Carolingian Franks "considered themselves to be replacing the former tribes of Israel in God's special care and protection. This attitude was already implied in their own Lex Salica, and it was a viewpoint flattered by the church and celebrated in literature and art."[26] At the same time it was thought that the "Frankish king began to represent a new type of ruler modeled on David, and like David he was the Anointed of God."[27] It is for these crucial reasons that the Book of Psalms was of particular importance for ninth-century France. The Hebrew Psalms indeed are full of warfare, rife with a vivid sense of enmity toward Israel's foes, and repeatedly they call upon God to destroy the enemies of the Jewish nation—often in

quite grisly ways—and to raise up Israel into a position of domi-
nance. Reading the Psalms, it only made sense for the Frankish warrior class to find themselves on the page and to hear echoing in the
psalmist's phrases their own deepest fears and desires, from the
righteous warrior lying dead on the field of battle his body being
devoured by beasts, to the righteous warrior victorious over his enemies tearing down their citadel, spearing their best warriors, and
enslaving their women and children. The illustrators of the *Utrecht
Psalter* simply put into their pictures what was in the minds of their
era, and what might also be described as a faithful replication of the
warrior ethos of the Hebrew originals.

But of course the creators of the Psalms did not know Jesus.
His emergence on the clouds in *Utrecht* is but the most dramatic
example of how the artists of these pages translated the world of the
ancient poems of Israel into their own times and into their own
visual vernacular, making the Hebrew Psalms into poems that were
a product of the ninth-century Frankish imagination. What we find
in examining the *Utrecht Psalter* illustrations is an intellectually
provocative adoption of the values of militarism from the time of
King David—an ethos familiar to the Frankish army of the eighth
century—and an adaptation of that ethos to a Catholic way of
imagining. And crucial to this discussion is both the quantity and
the characteristic approach of the *Utrecht Psalter* illustrations. First,
there are, as we have noted, a hundred and fifty of them. This means
that the *Utrecht Psalter* contains a remarkably large number of pictures of warfare and military violence. Second, as we have already
seen through long lists of specific examples, the very realism these
artists inherited from Jesus' own imagination means that the Psalter
depicts war with unflinching accuracy of detail. Nothing is held
back and we see indeed much more of the horrific than of the noble
or heroic. Fighting on these pages is not glamorized; instead the
artists report, over and over again on how bad it can get.

Old Testament Poetry Reimagined in Christian Terms

THE KING OF GLORY/JESUS

At the same time, the illustrators of the *Utrecht Psalter* constantly and paradoxically read the Old Testament Psalms in terms
of the New Testament story of Jesus' life, death, and redemptive sal-

vation. This is dramatically illustrated in the picture for Psalm 24(23). This Psalm raises the question of who is worthy to enter God's temple: "Who shall stand in his holy place?" (Ps 24[23]:3). The first answer is, "Those who have clean hands and pure hearts..." (4). Then in celebration the Psalm cries out, "Lift up your heads, O gates! and be lifted up, O ancient doors! that the King of glory may come in. Who is the King of glory? The LORD, strong and mighty, the LORD, mighty in battle" (7–8). This typically Judaic evocation of a warrior God who leads the Jewish people to victory receives in the *Utrecht Psalter* a striking Christian interpretation (Figure 50). On the left side of the picture, we see, coming out of a dense wood, soldiers armed with spears and shields. They are looking about in various directions as if wondering where they are.

Figure 50. Psalm 23(24), *Domini est terra* (Folio 13v)

Stepping away from them toward the right and looking wide-eyed and purposeful we see a haloed Jesus dressed as a warrior, his spear topped with a cross. This is Jesus as warrior-leader. Above Jesus and his army in the heavens angels emerge, and the huge hand of God the Father comes from a cloud in blessing. All of this is on the left-hand side of the picture. On the right we see a walled citadel built of stone. Its towered gate has been flung open, and standing before it two guards welcome Jesus. Standing on the wall above the gate the psalmist also beckons in welcome. Inside the citadel, in an open courtyard, a crowd of the faithful, some holding scrolls that suggest their careful study of scripture and their knowledge of God's covenant with humanity, stand waiting for the arriving warrior-leader. These are the innocent, those with "pure hearts," and just behind them is the Temple of Jerusalem, as it is always pictured in these illustrations, its doorway open, the altar of sacrifice seen just inside. Clusters of people, frequently dressed in loosely flowing togas, express the longing so frequently heard in the Psalms for membership in the community, for the cleansing and redemptive justification that can bring the individual person, often so lonely and outcast, into the warm nurture and spiritual wholeness of the community within the walls of the citadel, which, as in this specific picture, is so clearly welcoming into its midst the Jesus who leads and who saves. This citadel, with these people, is the way in which the Franks imagined the Catholic community. In this picture their consolation and the sign of their unity is not shared religious observance or acts of charity[28] but instead a sharing in the victorious power of Jesus as a general who wins victories for his people.

In many other places within the *Utrecht Psalter* the forms of traditional Jewish religious expression used in the Psalms find similar ingenious interpretation, an interpretation ultimately typological in character. The Carolingian Franks read the Psalms not just as reflecting a warrior ethos similar to their own. They further understood the Psalms to anticipate or even in some crucial cases to predict the coming of Jesus, his redemptive life and death, and the subsequent spread of his church, including the process of expanding that church through warfare. We can see this in the various ways in which Judaic forms of expression are reconceived in the *Utrecht* illustrations.

HELL

For the desperate cry to God in Psalm 16(15):10—"For you do not give me up to Sheol, or let your faithful one see the Pit"—these artists supply a Christian answer to death through scenes of Jesus' resurrection and his rescue of Adam and Eve from their sojourn in hell. When the Psalms address the God of the Jewish people, saying in Psalm 30(29):3, "O LORD, you brought up my soul from Sheol," the *Utrecht Psalter* shows, to the left, the pit of hell as Christians would have conceived it, with devils armed with tritons forcing down the damned while the resurrected Jesus with a cross-staff helps the dead psalmist rise up from his sarcophagus. For Psalm 55(54):23, the psalmist's *puteum interitus* or "lowest pit" becomes a Christian hell-mouth, and in Psalm 73(72), the verse, "You put an end to those who are false to you" (verse 27), is interpreted as a wingless angel with whip and spears driving "those who are far from you" into this same hell—a kind of destruction envisioned not by the Hebrew psalmist but by the Christian tradition.

THE JUST

The sense of injustice inflicted upon the people of Israel and expressed in Psalm 34(33):19—"Many are the afflictions of the righteous, but the LORD rescues them from them all"—becomes, surprisingly, a scene of the early Christian martyrs Saints Peter, Paul, and Lawrence (Figure 51). Peter hangs upside-down from his cross, Paul bends his neck beneath the sword of his executioner, and Lawrence is stretched over the raging fire on his iron grid. Here they represent "the righteous" being afflicted, and each has an angel by his side ready to take him to a Christian paradise.

Figure 51. Psalm 33(34), *Benedicam Dominum* (Folio 19r)

OUR KING

In Psalm 74(73), the phrase "rex noster...operatus est salutem in medio terrae"—"Yet God my King is from of old, working salvation in the earth" (verse 12)—is interpreted not as a Judaic king but rather typologically as anticipating a nativity scene in which

Mary reclines, watching two midwives bathe the infant Jesus. In Psalm 87(86) the identical scene—the midwives, Jesus, Joseph, and the reclining Mary—illustrates verse 6, "The LORD records, as he registers the peoples, 'This one was born there.'" In both cases the illustrations express the typological mindset that passages like these in the Psalms are indeed prophetic of the birth of Jesus. The Jewish tradition of God's care for Israel is thus here reinterpreted in terms of the incarnation.[29]

THE ANOINTED ONE

For Psalm 89(88):39—"You have renounced the covenant with your servant; you have defiled his crown in the dust"—a lament in the Psalms for the whole Davidic dynasty, we see the crucifixion, with two men spearing Christ. Again the Psalm is interpreted typologically, so that the Davidic "servant" anticipates Jesus and his suffering as the one who was "spurned and rejected."

SACRAMENTS

Psalm 116(115), a psalm text used in the eucharistic liturgy, here becomes an occasion for picturing both the crucifixion and the martyrdom of saints. The latter is justified by (verse 15), "Precious in the sight of the LORD is the death of his faithful ones" (in Jerome's Latin, "Mors sanctorum ejus"). The illustration of the crucifixion shows Mary and Saint John looking on from the right. To the left the psalmist captures Jesus' blood in a chalice, which echoes the Psalm's "cup of salvation" (verse 13), while in his left hand he holds a paten with the sacramental bread, echoing verse 17, "Tibi sacrificabo hostiam laudis" or "thanksgiving sacrifice." Catholic sacramentality emerges in the traditional imagery of Jesus crucified as the source of the body/bread and wine/blood of the eucharistic liturgy. In the Psalm the reference is to Jewish rituals of thanksgiving; the Catholic adaptation mirrors Saint Paul in 1 Corinthians 10:16: "The cup of blessing that we bless, is it not a sharing in the blood of Christ? The bread that we break, is it not a sharing in the body of Christ?"[30]

From the earliest days of the apostles, Christians regarded Jesus and his movement as the final phase in the history of redemption that began with God's choosing Abraham as patriarch for his people. From this perspective, the Hebrew Scriptures have always been regarded by Christians as theirs and about them, as well as about the Jewish people. Thus the artists of the *Utrecht Psalter* were able to interpret the images and ideas of the Hebrew poets in terms of their own worldview and in terms of what was understood to be the Christian meaning of ancient Jewish poetry.

Pragmatic Christianity

There can be little doubt that the men and women of the Carolingian court under Louis the Pious found on the pages of the *Utrecht Psalter* an intellectually as well as spiritually satisfying synthesis of the world as they knew it and the ideals of Christianity. Objections to their form of warrior Christianity would certainly have met with the response, "What is one to do faced with a reality recounted, as we saw at the beginning of this chapter in the history of Gregory of Tours, in which 'there were many deeds being done both good and evil; the heathen were raging fiercely; kings were growing more cruel...'?" Charlemagne, by force of arms, brought large tracts of Europe under a single rule, spreading the Catholic faith and a kind of revived classical education. In such a context, turning the other cheek meant finding yourself one in the heaps of the dead and dying. For the Franks, Old Testament warrior culture resonated with their own *Weltanschauung*—their way of comprehending the world in which they lived. Thus understood, the illustrations in the *Utrecht Psalter* constitute a highly important development in the Catholic imagination, a historical point in which elements arguably alien to the gospel teachings about peace are somehow integrated into an ever-expanding way of conceiving the nature of human existence. While on the one hand the pictures in the *Utrecht Psalter* picture God the Father spearing the unjust and Jesus in full battle gear leading his troops into the citadel of Jerusalem, they also graphically depict the horrors of war and in particular the suffering both of the soldiers themselves and of their victims. We see on these pages kings in their citadels receiving the crown of authority from God; yet there is not much in the way of glory for anyone other than God. The *Utrecht Psalter* is singularly devoid of victory parades, heroes on pedestals, heaps of plunder divided among the winners. Hence it can be argued that while this celebrated manuscript does picture Old Testament/Frankish militarism and does understand God to be supportive of that militarism, it takes no great pleasure in the facts of fighting and dying. Rather, it simply shows the world as it is, and God within it somehow, paradoxically, perhaps inscrutably, working there.

Thus the imagination of the victors. Now for the "enemies" they defeated.

CHAPTER TWELVE

Warrior Christianity II
The Saxons and The Heliand

The Saxons

Ptolemy (110?–170?) mentions the Saxons in his *Geography*, the first known reference to this Germanic people who were at the time inhabiting the Jutland peninsula north of modern Germany. During the third and fourth centuries the Saxons migrated south into the Weser River Valley and by 350 were invading Roman-held territory. During the fifth and sixth centuries, as their numbers expanded, some Saxons joined Jutes and Angles in taking over large parts of southern England.

The Germanic Franks, as we saw in chapter 11, were inveterate enemies of the Saxons. Early in the eighth century, Pepin of Herstal (635–714) attacked them, and his illegitimate son and heir Charles Martel (688?–741) did the same. Charlemagne's thirty-three-year campaign against them started in 772.

The Lord of the Gallows

Throughout this period of struggle the Saxons "seemed," as Peter Brown observes, "part of an older Europe. Frisia and Saxony, from the North Sea coast to the Teutoburg Forest, were staunchly pagan."[1] It's difficult now to be certain exactly what the beliefs of these people might have been. Theirs was a culture without alphabetic writing, and in their case conversion to Christianity meant, among other things, systematic efforts at erasing any recollection of past beliefs. But working from the assumption that the Saxons were

252

in some general way a part of a far more widespread culture occupying not only northern Germany but also Anglo-Saxon England and Scandinavia, it is possible to make some educated guesses that are indeed borne out by traces of the old convictions, now translated into Christian terms, found in later Christian documents. In addition there is one celebrated report about the old customs, evidently from eyewitnesses. It comes from the Christian historian Adam of Bremen, who flourished around 1068. His chronicle tracing the spread of Christianity into the north of Europe, the *Gesta Hammaburgensis Ecclesiae Pontificum* (completed sometime around 1072) includes information derived from interviews with King Svend Estridson of the Danes and Archbishop of Adalbert of Bremen and that appears to reflect firsthand reports of pagan practices. Adam describes the temple at Uppsala in Sweden, its nearby sacred tree, and statues of the gods Thor, Frey, and "Wotan, that is the raging one, who wages war and gives man strength against his enemies." (In the wonderful original Latin: "Wodan, id est furor, bella gerit, hominique ministrat virtutem contra inimicos..."). Adam goes on to describe a festival held there every nine years at which dogs, horses, and humans ("canes et equi pendent cum hominibus") were killed and their bodies hung from the sacred tree and left to rot.[2] This account does harmonize with other literary sources that depict Woden as the chief of the Germanic gods, known also as "The Lord of the Gallows." Woden's association with execution and with human sacrifice and with the peculiar phenomenon of hanging bodies in the air links as well with one of the most intriguing stories about him from Germanic myth, in which Woden, to achieve a vision of hidden wisdom, voluntarily chooses to be hung from Yggdrasil, the Germanic tree of life, for nine days and to pierce himself with his own spear. G. Ronald Murphy sees this as a myth of "the god of consciousness... risking an approach to death, hanging on the cosmic tree of life and piercing himself with a spear to gain the hidden power of knowledge."[3] What the legends tell us is that from this painful and heroic act the "Lord of the Gallows" or, to use another of the epithets for Woden, "The Hanged Man" learns nine powerful songs and eighteen runes, mysterious verbal formulae used for spells and to work magic. These, then, are the peculiar and suggestive characteristics of the central god of the pagan Saxons.

The Pagan Saxon Imagination: Loyalty, Fate, Destruction, Renewal

Living for centuries by the North Sea, the Saxons were excellent sailors with "Viking-style longboat(s)"[4] and were familiar with the dangers of a storm at sea. Theirs was a society of small, independent tribes. Within each there was a chieftain or liege lord—the "generous mead giver" of English Anglo-Saxon poetry—who distributed gold, jewels, and drink in his wooden gathering hall.[5] The chieftain's men, frequently called "thanes," owed their *drohtin* or lord a personal, permanent loyalty.[6] It was he who led them into battle. The Saxons thought of themselves as tough fighters, and the highest virtue in Saxon society was to maintain loyalty to the death, symbolized by the archetypal scene of the "embattled warrior group making their last brave stand against a superior enemy force,"[7] the moment when the true hero can demonstrate a "calm acceptance of the unavoidable and submission to the will of God."[8] Defeat came, ultimately, not from one's individual enemies but from *wurd*—fate.[9]

This anticipation of defeat and its collateral cult of stoic bravery links with the German mythic concept of history in which, at the end of time, the forces of evil and chaos will destroy everything that exists: *Ragnarok*, the Twilight of the Gods. This, however, is not the end. Following purgation by fire of men, the gods, and all created things, a new, idyllic world will rise from the sea. Some of the old gods will return. Others will be reborn. Now two progenitors, Lif (life) and Lifthrasir (eager for life) will give birth to a new human race and an era of peace and prosperity will begin in which gods and people will live together in harmony.

The Conversion of the Saxons and the Writing of The Heliand

Although some Saxons accepted an Irish form of Catholicism after missionaries of various kinds, including monks from Columba's monasteries, worked among them, this did not satisfy the Roman popes. When the British Saxon Christian monk Wynfrith (675–754) visited Rome in 719, he was renamed Boniface and "supported by Charles Martel and then by Pippin (the Short), the future king, Boniface received from the popes (between 722 and 739) a series of ever-widening commissions to act as a missionary bishop and supervisor of new churches throughout 'Germany.'"[10] What the papacy, the Frankish kings, and Boniface all sought was a systematic conversion of all the Saxons that would place them squarely under Roman discipline, what G. Ronald Murphy calls the "romanization of the faithful...(with) the Mass...celebrated in a pure form of Latin."[11] This coincided perfectly with the attitude of the Frankish kings, including the post-Boniface Charlemagne. From his point of view, "As subjects, they had to be Christians."[12] Since there was no central ruler for the Saxons, each tribe had to be defeated and "converted" separately, and individual groups might sign a treaty and then renege on their promises. The fighting went on year after year, ending only, as noted earlier, in 804 and leaving the Saxons sullen and rebellious in defeat.

At the beginning of the ninth century, in the heart of traditionally Saxon lands on a tributary of the Weser River stood the Benedictine monastery of Fulda. Boniface had founded Fulda in 744, and Rome had designated it as responsible for the conversion of the Saxons. Decades after the death of Boniface, and shortly before the conversion of the last Saxons, an Abbey church modeled on St. Peter's in Rome was started at Fulda: a large and expensive structure completed in 819. The ambitious symbolism must have been clear to everyone. Rome was now physically taking root in the north. By this time Rabanus Maurus was abbot. Charlemagne was dead, and Louis the Pious was at the head of a Frankish Empire. It was a time of poise and perhaps deeper consideration. Charlemagne's territorial gains had all been made, unity of a sort had been achieved in his new empire, and now artists were able to consider the meaning of what had happened. In Hautvillers near Reims, men were beginning to illustrate the *Utrecht Psalter*. It was in all likelihood at this time and in Fulda that a Saxon-speaking poet, undoubtedly at the bidding of his abbot, wrote the epic that he did not formally name but that became known in the nineteenth century as "Savior"—*The Heliand.*

The poet's aim—one of several—was to tell the Saxons the story of Christ's life in their own terms, and emphatically not in Frankish terms; that is, not simply to translate but to reimagine the gospel narratives as if Jesus were a Saxon warrior-chieftain, in an effort to understand the deepest meanings of faith and commitment and also of defeat and death. In this way, it is quite clear, his aim was to reconcile the Saxons to what had happened to them and to help them understand the paradox that the Christianity that had been forced upon them was, unexpectedly, the best thing that could have happened and, in a way, the most Germanic. Whereas the *Utrecht Psalter* still looks south, using a style of drawing and kinds of imagery that echo Rome and Byzantium, the *Heliand* translates the history of a Jewish savior into northern terms. The Mediterranean is almost entirely forgotten, and we are in the Teutoburg Forest, where, in sporadic bursts of tribal conflict, bands of warriors fight to the death for their chieftains.

The Heliand: Death and the Hero

The Heliand is an epic poem both in its length and in its breadth of conception. Its nearly six thousand lines of German alliterative verse are divided into seventy-one *fitts* or "songs." The author's familiarity with the oral chanting of ancient hero tales that had been a part of the pagan culture of the Saxons may have led to this subdivision. Now he was working from books in the monastic library, using as a source not only the Bible itself but an early Latin retelling of the four Gospels by Tatian called the *Diatessaron* or "through four," which "harmonizes" or collates all four versions of Christ's life into a single, ongoing chronological narrative. Clearly he also consulted books of theology and of biblical commentary.[13] His poem has survived in several manuscript copies, but it's not easy to be sure how widely read it might have been in the ninth and tenth centuries.

Nineteenth-century German scholarship rediscovered and took up the *Heliand* as an early example of an emerging German world vision, and in the past century and a half the poem has been much studied. Indeed, at the moment of writing there are two complete copies of the original text on the World Wide Web. Recent scholarship in English has been dominated by the work of G. Ronald Murphy. His *Saxon Savior* of 1989 is the best short English-language study of the poem, its context, and its meanings, and his translation, *The Heliand: The Saxon Gospel* (1992), is the best contemporary English version. Murphy's work opens up for this study an opportunity to examine a series of important issues that have to do with the continuing vigorous and independent work of the Catholic imagination.

Narrative

In the opening chapters of this study we considered the fundamentally narrative character of the Catholic imagination. Christians believe in a man they understand to be the incarnate Son of God. They base that understanding on the storytelling of the Gospels. There they find the narrative of redemption. Some of the earliest Christian texts, such as the letters of Saint Paul, point to the story of Jesus as the center of their belief (Paul's "clear picture of Jesus Christ crucified") and then go on to tell other, parallel stories, such as the implicit autobiographical narrative of Paul's own life examined in chapter 6. In our study of the growth and evolution of the Catholic imagination, we have been looking at the different ways in which the contact between Christian vision and existing cultures served to alter and, indeed, sometimes to reconceive elements of Christian belief. Here, for the first time in our survey, we take a look at a new narrative.

The poet's use of the *Diatessaron* raises an interesting question. Any attempt to "harmonize" the Gospels, to reshape their contents into a single chronological narrative, can seem to represent an effort to historicize the life of Jesus. Rather than four different, sometimes contradictory tellings (in chapter 5 we described them as "four biographies"), we now have a single chronicle based upon a single point of view and reflecting a coherent and unified set of ideas. Does this then become a "critical biography," in our modern sense of that term, in which conflicting accounts have been assessed and sorted out? The poet of the *Heliand* is indeed very careful with his sources, and he appears to be at pains to conform every element of his book to theological orthodoxy. At the same time, this is not an effort to recover the "historical Jesus" in any traditional way— quite the opposite, in fact. This is a "biography" of Jesus as Saxon warrior-leader that reimagines and reinterprets virtually every element of the Gospels.[14]

Cultural Translation

In fashioning his "biography," the poet of the *Heliand* was working in exactly the manner demanded by Jesus when he taught. When Jesus asked his listeners to "suppose," as we saw in chapter 1, he was asking them to use their imaginations, to enter into the stories that he was telling, and to refashion those stories according to the listeners' own imaginative grasp of the world. This German poem is just such a reimagining, and what is so useful about it is the way in which it connects a cultural world profoundly alien to Jesus' own Palestine with the kernel story of Jesus' life, death, and resurrection. An interesting instance of this is the poet's revoicing of Jesus' teaching known traditionally as the "Beatitudes." What is he going to do, one wonders, with Jesus' celebration of "peacemakers" and the "sorrowful"? In Song 16 (Figure 52), he presents his solutions formulated in terms of the Saxon worldview: a cosmology in which human life is lived in "this middle world" and in expectation of an afterlife "on the meadows of heaven," where the saved will share in a heavenly "banquet"—just as Saxon warriors feasted in the meadhall of their chieftain. Jesus speaks here mysteriously, as if he is a soothsayer, because divine wisdom such as Woden won by hanging on a tree is difficult to attain.

Figure 52
From **Song 16: The Chieftain's Instructions on the Mountain; the Eight Good Fortunes**

Then the Land's Herdsman, God's own Son, sat down in front of the men. He wanted with His talk to teach the people many wise sayings, how they could perform the praise of God in this world-kingdom. The holy Chieftain sat there in silence and looked at them for a long time with tender feelings for them in His mind and generosity toward them in His heart. Then...Christ spoke in wise words to the men whom He had picked to come to His talk, to those men who were of all the inhabitants of earth, of all mankind, the most precious to God—to them He spoke in soothsaying.

He said that those were fortunate here in this middle world who were poor in their hearts through humility, "to them is granted the eternal kingdom in all holiness, eternal life on the meadows of heaven."

He said that those too were fortunate who were gentle people, "they will be allowed to possess the great earth, the same kingdom."

He said that those also were fortunate who cried here over their evil deeds, "in return, they can expect the very consolation they desire in their Master's kingdom."

"Those too are fortunate who desired to do good things here, those fighting men who wanted to judge fairly. With good things they themselves will be filled to satisfaction in the Chieftain's kingdom for their wise actions; they will attain good things, those fighting men who judged fairly here. Nor will any people want to deceive them with secrets when they are seated there at the banquet!"

"Fortunate also are the many people who have cleaned their hearts, they will see Heaven's Ruler in His kingdom."

He said that those too were fortunate "who live peacefully among the people and do not want to start any fights or court cases by their own actions, they will be called the Chieftain's sons for He will be gracious to them, they will long enjoy His kingdom."

He said that fortunate too are the fighting men who wanted justice, "and, because of that, suffer more powerful men's hatred and verbal abuse. To them is granted afterwards God's meadow and spiritual life for eternal days—thus the end will never come of their beatific happiness!"

This and subsequent inset quotations come from *The Heliand: The Saxon Gospel*, translated by G. Ronald Murphy, SJ, copyright © 1992 by Oxford University Press, Inc. Used by permission of Oxford University Press, Inc.

For his warrior audience this poet transforms such gospel beatitudes as "Blessed are the peacemakers, for they will be called children of God" (Matt 5:9) into a presumably more palatable formulation that celebrates the "fortunate 'who live peacefully among the people and do not want to start any fights or court cases by their own actions....'"[15] This seems to suggest that fights will come but that the virtuous Christian will not, at least, start them.

The inculturation of the gospel message into a work like the *Heliand* acts as a form of revelation. While we know that Jesus was not literally a warrior-leader, we can come to realize that imagining Jesus in this way can shed new light on just what he did and who he was. Just as Jesus did with his parables, so, too, the poet of the *Heliand* has developed a series of analogies through his process of interpretation, and each of these analogies invites us to look afresh at crucial elements in the story of salvation. Jesus may not have been a warrior, but in the gospel narratives we see him demonstrating in the face of cruel and sinister opposition, a very particular kind of courage and resolution that compels not only admiration but emulation. If the Germanic warrior anticipated the probability of defeat with stoic calm, that analogy too tells us something about traditional descriptions of Jesus' last hours and the highly serious silence with which he reacted to Judas, the Sanhedrin, and Pilate.

The statements that God's Son "became a man" (the incarnation) and "died to redeem everyone" (redemption) represent an effort to verbalize the incomprehensible. In order to understand such assertions, we consider each of them from varying points of view. God "became a man." How can that be? What was it like? For two thousand years Christians have struggled with this concept, and one way to work with it, whether one is a theologian or an artist, is to explore new, variant analogies. A rational/materialist would describe this as an endless game of self-deception. For a believer, however, it's the ongoing development of understanding directed by the Holy Spirit, the *Creator Spiritus*. In this context, a work such as the *Heliand* constitutes a further development in humanity's efforts to know Jesus, a further opening up of the mystery and the secret of his story. It is in this sense that it is a form of revelation.

Considered in that light, let us look at just a few of the themes and issues that emerge from this long poem, and let us explore how they work both as cultural translation and as a form of analogical thinking.

Saxons and Jews

It is one of the intriguing paradoxes of this era of European culture that both the victorious Franks and the defeated Saxons imagined themselves as the successors to the Jewish people. We have already noted how the Book of Psalms seemed to the makers of the *Utrecht Psalter* a collection of poems about their own experience of life and of religious belief. They saw themselves as the successors to the chosen people of God. But as the poet of the *Heliand* turned to the gospel narratives he too found a parallel, not now with the Israelite nation of David's era but with the Jewish people of Jesus' time. They were, as Murphy notes, "a conquered people," and the author of the *Heliand*

> evokes Saxon empathy with the sons of Israel, "noble-born" and "famous for their strength," subject to a foreign ruler at the whim of Caesar Augustus (Charlemagne's full title, after 800, was: *Carolus Augustus a Deo Coronatus* "Charles Augustus (Caesar Augustus) Crowned by God"), and (this parallel thus) begins setting the stage for the Saxon warrior's eventual identification with Peter and the disciples.[16]

Indeed the parallel applies even in particular details. Consider, for example, how the *Heliand* describes the local representatives of distant Roman imperial power and how it pictures them as analogous to the local Frankish authorities of the poet's own day. Here is the King Herod of Christ's birth: "It was only thanks to Caesar in hill-fort Rome, who ruled the empire, that the descendents of Israel, those fighting men renowned for their toughness, had to obey him (Herod). They were Herod's very unwavering friends—as long as he held power, for as long as he had authority over the Jewish people" (Song 1).[17] The irony of this passage is clear. The Jewish people, enjoying the highest kind of praise this poet can give—tough fighting men—are forced to remain "very unwavering friends" of Herod...as long as Caesar in hill-fort Rome has power over them. What is unstated is that the moment Roman authority deserts Herod, so will his Jewish subjects. This looks very much like the conditions under which Saxon warriors must have lived during the rule of the Franks. The point of the poet, here and elsewhere, is that the Saxons now feel just like the Jews once felt: defeated, imposed upon, ready to rebel when the time was right, but in the meantime "Herod's very unwavering friends...." They know the humiliation of oppression, they feel the denial of their masculine power, they taste the bitterness of a hypocrisy forced upon them by a political situation they hate but must accept. For the Saxons, living in just such a context, the life and death of Jesus make immediate sense. Like them, he too had to face humiliation, powerlessness, the hypocrisy of dealing with leaders unjustly in power. Indeed this Saxon version of his life illuminates the effect of these elements on Jesus.

Phrases such as "very unwavering friends" alert the reader to watch this narrative for unexpected paradox and irony, and to look for a kind of doubleness, even secretiveness, in the writing of the *Heliand* that emerges from a situation in which not everything the writer and his audience might think and feel can be candidly written down.

Language and Power

This secretiveness is a part of the *Heliand* poet's larger understanding of the nature of language and of its uses. He works in accordance with a theory of language deeply connected to Catholic tradition and at the same time formulated in terms of his own Germanic culture.

In the very first words of the *Heliand*, the story of the life of Jesus is described as having a very specific, very unusual character: it is made up of *giruni* or "secret runes" that have lived in the hearts of *manega* or "many."[18] He goes on to describe the four evangelists as the only "heroic sons of men" who have been given, by the "power of God," the ability and the courage to write these runes down, in the process lifting up their voices "to chant God's spell." This spell is made up of the most powerful words on earth. These words can "fell every evil creature or work of wickedness, (and)...withstand the hatred and aggression of enemies" (Song 1).[19]

We have already briefly noted how, in Germanic tradition, many runes function as mysterious, secret verbal formulae of enormous power capable of working magic. These runes can only be learned at great risk and only by the bravest. In the mythic story of Woden, the most powerful god of the Germanic pantheon must hang on the tree Yggdrasil for nine days, pierced with his own spear, before he is able to grasp the secret runes. The poet now draws an explicit parallel: the evangelists now have found something that is in many hearts but that hardly anyone has had the courage to acknowledge or the power to voice, a new runic mystery that is the story of Jesus. This story, which they have now told through words, has the power of earlier runic spells to work against wickedness. The task of the poet as he begins is thus the transmission of these runes to a German-speaking audience.

The connection between language and power links the traditional concept of Germanic runes with the Jewish tradition discussed in chapter 3, which sees God as a poet uttering creation, creating the universe through language. A German pagan would describe this as a "spell." The *Heliand* poet indeed echoes this Jewish tradition in describing the creation of "the whole universe" as coming "with one word," and he goes on to voice the theological tradition that all creation remains fixed or "held in place by the Divine words" (Song 1).[20] Thus for both traditions language has power to create, preserve, and destroy.

The secrecy that surrounds both God's word and runic spells is crucial and necessary because not only is it dangerous to let something so powerful fall into the wrong hands, but in all likelihood no human being could fully understand or control something as mysterious as the divine utterance. God's word is fearful because God's power is incomprehensible. It is for this reason that Jews were forbidden even to utter God's name. What humans have, ordinarily, are replacement terms, verbal substitutions, or what we have been calling analogies.

With the story of Jesus, however, the "secret runes" find voice. Somehow, his incarnation permits the unsealing of at least some of the mysteries and the release of a certain kind of power latent in the story of his life as the evangelists tell it. This theory of language and of the ability of Christianity to voice aspects of divine will and divine power finds an interesting expression in the *Heliand*'s account of Jesus gathering disciples. When he calls them together the poem describes them as "word-wise warriors" (Song 14).[21] The weapons Jesus hands them are not the spears and arrows of the *Utrecht Psalter* illustrations but something quite different. During the Sermon on the Mount the disciples ask Jesus for "the secret runes" (Song 19),[22] and he teaches them the Lord's Prayer. The point of the Germanic interpretation here is that the kind of mysterious power that Jesus can convey to the Saxons so recently defeated by the Franks is a runic power possessed not by physical weapons but by prayer. Murphy notes that the length of the Lord's Prayer in the gospel accounts is "quite similar to that of parallel Germanic spells and prayers."[23] It thus becomes a replacement for Woden's runic charms. The phrase from the Lord's Prayer usually translated into English as "lead us not into temptation" is, in the *Heliand*, "Do not let evil little creatures lead us off to do their will..." (Song 19),[24] a magic spell to hold off the temptations of trolls and faeries. The story of Jesus and the prayers he teaches can thus be understood as new words of power to confront danger and evil—mysterious, to some degree ultimately incomprehensible, but nonetheless efficacious, and something beyond the weaponry of the victorious Franks.

The "Secret of Jesus"

From time to time the original Gospels stress what later biblical scholars have come to call "the secret of Jesus." At moments Jesus solemnly and severely instructs his followers not to tell other people what they have seen and heard, as for example after the Transfiguration, when, Mark tells us, "He warned them to tell no one what they had seen, until after the Son of man had risen from the dead" (Mark 9:9). After preaching to the crowds in parables, which the common people find baffling, the Gospels sometimes show Jesus taking his disciples aside and explaining to them privately what the parables mean. Mark puts this odd strategy very mysteriously: "He did not speak to them [ordinary people] except in parables, but he explained everything in private to his disciples" (Mark 4:34). It may well be that the original gospel writers stressed this theme as a response to skeptical critics who asked why the Jewish people had refused to accept Jesus as the predicted messiah during his life on earth. One answer would be that he wished to baffle them, to maintain his own secret, so that, paradoxically, only the foolish and the outcast would come to believe. Hence in explaining the parable of the seed and the sower Jesus says to his disciples, "To you it has been given to know the secrets of the kingdom of heaven, but to them it has not been given" (Matt 13:11).

This so-called messianic secret clearly fascinated Germanic readers because it connected so immediately with the secrecy of runes and with the theory of the power of verbal spells. The *Heliand* implies to its readers that in the Gospels and in this poem they will now learn the new magic, which is more powerful than the old, and will stand up to the evil of their enemies. But by invoking both the runic mysteries and the verbal power of the Judaic God, the *Heliand* also provides another explanation for the way in which the "secret" of Jesus functions as a way of representing the inadequacy of language itself. As has already been suggested, all language is inadequate to the task of formulating and accounting for God's actions and for Christ's life. It must necessarily be incommensurate with the reality it gropingly tries to articulate. Jesus himself is the secret. His incarnation is the phenomenon, like the runes, that can be glimpsed only by the brave and the fortunate. He is the power or "spell," in fact the "God-spell," that cannot be limited and is adopted only with reverence. No explanation in human words can satisfactorily explain him. At best, the disciples are led to this: simple loyalty to a leader whose commands may not make sense, but who has the absolute right to command.

As if to confirm his stress upon the mysterious power and essential secretiveness of Jesus and Jesus' verbal message, the poet of the *Heliand* consistently describes Jesus' parables as not verbal or linguistic but pictorial. He notes how Jesus "described in pictures what there was in the world-kingdom among mankind that was similar to the heaven-kingdom" (Song 32).[25] The distinction is between language, instrumental and hence secret, and visual images, "pictures, brilliant signs" (Song 32)[26] useful for teaching but without the power of words.

In the story of the prophecy of Simeon the *Heliand* deals with another aspect of secret language, the capacity to articulate the mysteries of the future. In Luke's Gospel, Simeon, an "upright and devout man," is in the temple when Mary and Joseph bring their child to be "purified." Simeon recognizes that Jesus is Messiah, takes him from his parents, and, holding the baby, prophesies his future greatness and Mary's future suffering, saying to her, "This child is destined for the falling and the rising of many in Israel, and to be a sign that will be opposed so that the inner thoughts of many will be revealed—and a sword will pierce your own soul too" (Luke 2:25,34–35). Unlike the account in Luke, Simeon in the *Heliand* "in soothsaying," like a Germanic wizard, speaks "secretly." The *Heliand* poet wishes to stress the dangerous power of prophetic utterance. The Lukan phrase "a sword will pierce your soul" is then translated into a prophecy of Jesus' death, which is imagined as his *wurd* or fate, the death of a warrior, and what it will mean for his mother: "You will suffer pain in your heart when heroes' sons overwhelm Him with weapons. Then your great work will begin: to bear sorrow" (Song 6).[27] The conclusion, a poetic expansion of what is only hinted at in Luke, echoes the ideals of fatalistic courage in Germanic tradition.

Incarnation: The Nativity Story

The incarnation of Jesus as Savior is, in the *Heliand*, the advent of a warrior-leader. This brings with it an exploration of the following problem: In what way can a fighter "save" his people? After thirty-three years of warfare, the Saxons had learned that sword and spear may not achieve this end. But what will? And what will that "salvation" look like? These questions lead to a reconsideration of what Saxon Christians might have understood by the crucial concept of redemption.

THE ANNUNCIATION

In Luke's originating narrative, the message brought by the angel Gabriel to the Virgin Mary is couched in distinctly traditional Jewish terms. Jesus as Messiah is to complete the destiny of the House of Israel by coming as a king: "He will be great, and will be called the Son of the Most High, and the Lord God will give to him the throne of his ancestor David. He will reign over the house of Jacob for ever, and of his kingdom there will be no end" (Luke 1:32–33). The *Heliand* poet discards all of this, as indeed he almost always ignores the allusions to Jewish history and tradition found in the Gospels. His Jesus is coming not to fulfill the messianic promises to the House of David, but to liberate an oppressed people, the Saxons, and it will be his destiny "to free all the clans of people here from evil" (Song 4).[28] This is the "salvation" the poet longs for. Jesus is to achieve this end as a Saxon liege lord. Mary understands this. Her response to Gabriel is in terms of warrior society obeisance: "I stand here ready," she said, "to perform any service He may wish to give me" (Song 4).[29]

JOHN THE BAPTIST

The figure of John the Baptist troubled the writers of the Gospels from the start. He may indeed have, historically, been a rival preacher in Jesus' own day, and the evangelists are at pains to stress his subordination to Jesus. The *Heliand* poet, always concerned with order and hierarchy, takes this interpretation to its logical, Germanic conclusion. His John the Baptist is Jesus' thane, shaped by fate to serve his leader. Gabriel's prophetic explanation to John's father Zachary exemplifies the poet's worldview: "This is the way the workings of fate made him, time formed him, and the power of God as well" (Song 2).[30] He is to be "a warrior-companion of the King of Heaven" (Song 2).[31] His parents are to train him in "loyalty" or (as Murphy notes) *treuwa*, the unflinching fidelity to one's chieftain, especially in battle.[32] Later, when John preaches, he is described as seeking "to announce Christ's coming and powerful strength throughout this middle world" (Song 11).[33] His response to questions from Jerusalem about his own calling is, "I am to clear a road for him— my Lord" (Song 11).[34] The *Heliand* makes it clear that the Baptist recognizes and accepts his subordinate position, and life prepares him to serve. He is the first member of Jesus' new battle formation.

THE NATIVITY

As he begins his account (Figure 53), the Saxon poet pictures the kind of state power all too familiar from Frankish rule, in which a virtually all-powerful central monarch sends out his "messengers" who, notably, are literate—"men who could read and write"—and they use this skill as a kind of power to ensure that "no human being could escape from paying tax...."

Figure 53
From **Song 5: The Chieftain of Mankind Is Born in David's Hill-Fort**

Then there came a decree from Fort Rome, from the great Octavian who had power over the whole world, an order from Caesar to his wide realm, sent to every king enthroned in his homeland and to all Caesar's army commanders governing the people of any territory. It said that everyone living outside their own country should return to their homeland upon receipt of the message. It stated that all the warrior heroes were to return to their assembly place, each one was to go back to the clan of which he was a family member by birth in a hill-fort.

That command was sent out over the whole world. People came together at all the hill-forts. The messengers who had come from Caesar were men who could read and write, and they wrote everyone's name down very carefully in a report—both name and nationality—so that no human being could escape from paying the tax that each warrior had on his head.

The good Joseph went also with his household, just as God, ruling mightily, willed it. He made his way to his shining home, the hill-fort at Bethlehem....

I have heard it told that the shining workings (of fate) and the power of God told Mary that on this journey a son would be granted her, born in Bethlehem, the strongest child, the most powerful of all kings, the Great One come powerfully to the light of mankind—just as foretold by many visions and signs in this world many days before.

At that time it all came to pass, just as wise men had said long ago: that the Protector of People would come in a humble way, by His own power, to visit this kingdom of earth. His mother, that most beautiful woman, took Him, wrapped Him in clothes and precious jewels, and then with her two hands laid Him gently, the little man, that child, in a fodder-crib, even though He had the power of God, and was the Chieftain of mankind. There the mother sat in front of Him and remained awake, watching over the holy Child and holding it. And there was no doubt in the mind or in the heart of the holy maid.

The poet wishes to explore the complex paradoxes inherent in the Christian narrative of Jesus' birth, and so he begins stressing the authority of God and "fate" in what is happening and insists upon seeing the tiny child a "the strongest," "the most powerful," "the Great One...." Thus he is at first reluctant to picture the poverty of Jesus, the fact that there was no room for his parents at the inn of Bethlehem, or that simple shepherds would be the first to hear the good news of his birth. Instead, he speaks only in general terms of Jesus coming "in a humble way," and then at once, as if to get beyond this admission, his mother Mary wraps him "in cloths and precious jewels" (Song 5).[34] But then, exploring the other half of the paradox, the *Heliand* poet in a tender moment adds that she "with her two hands laid Him gently, the little man, in a fodder-crib...."

As the nativity narrative continues (Figure 54), the poet transforms Luke's shepherds into a military leader's "horse-servants [who]...were outside,...men on sentry duty, watching over the horses, the beasts of the field..." (Song 5).[35] God makes sure "the Chieftain of mankind," at least at this moment, is properly guarded. The angelic host resemble the *Utrecht Psalter* angels in serving as God's soldiers: "an enormous number of the holy army, the shining people of God..." (Song 5).[36] In all of these ways the *Heliand* poet demonstrates that the incarnation can be understood analogically through the story of an aristocratic warrior-chief forced by the political oppression of his era to accept a "humble" birth.

Figure 54
From **Song Five**

What had happened became known to many over this wide world. The guards heard it. As horse-servants they were outside, they were men on sentry duty, watching over the horses, the beasts of the field: they saw the darkness split in two in the sky, and the light of God came shining through the clouds and surrounded the guards out in the fields. Those men began to feel fear in their hearts. They saw the mighty angel of God coming toward them. He spoke to the guards face to face and told them that they should not fear any harm from the light. "I am going to tell you," he said, "something very wonderful, something very deeply desired. I want to let you know something very powerful: Christ is now born, on this very night, God's holy Child, the good Chieftain, at David's hill-fort. What happiness for the human race, a boon for all men! You can find Him, the most powerful Child, at Fort Bethlehem. Take what I now tell you in truthful words as a sign: He is there, wrapped up, lying in a fodder-crib— even though He is king over all the earth and the heavens and over the sons of all the peoples, the Ruler of the world." Just as he said that word, an enormous number of the holy army, the shining people of God, came down to the one angel from the meadows of heaven, saying many words of praise for the Lord of Peoples. They then began to sing a holy song as they wended their way through the clouds toward the meadows of heaven.

The guards heard how the angels in their power praised the all-mighty God most worshipfully in words: "Glory now be," they said, "to the Lord-Chieftain Himself, in the highest reaches of heaven, and peace on earth to the sons of men, men of good will, those who because of their clear minds recognize God!"

The herdsmen understood that something great had been told to them—a merry message! They decided to go to Bethlehem that night, they wanted very much to be able to see Christ Himself.

THE MAGI

In the *Heliand*, the Magi are imagined as Germanic wizards or soothsayers. They are able to *rekkien spel godes* or can "interpret God's speech" (Song 7),[38] but notice the crucial term *spel*—they understand the magic that God's words are working, they interpret those words, and so they come to find Jesus. In this respect these "three strong thanes" or "warriors" wish, like the converted Saxons, "to kneel to Him, to go and become His followers—God's (fate-)workings were leading them on" (Song 7).[39] They become figures representing all people who make the journey to find a once-distant Savior and make him their own. When they reach Jesus, "the foreign fighting men fell on their knees to the good Child and greeted Him in the royal manner" (Song 8).[40] Then they "stood there attentively, respectful in the presence of their Lord, and soon received It (the Child) in a fitting manner in their hands" (Song 8).[41] The poet's additions here tell us a great deal. In Matthew's Gospel, the source for this scene, the Magi offer their gifts and then withdraw. In the *Heliand* they take Jesus into their hands "in a fitting manner," clearly a proleptic anticipation of the Mass and the sacrament of the Eucharist. Details such as this one help us understand how this poet's imagination constantly works diachronically, picturing different eras of time simultaneously. Here his Magi in Palestine accept Jesus as the eucharistic sacrament like devout ninth-century Saxons. The body of the infant is simultaneously a sacrament, connecting then and now just as the poet connects them in language.

HEROD AND THE SLAUGHTER OF THE INNOCENTS

The imagination of the *Heliand* poet rarely forgets the conditions in which his Saxon readers lived. Frequently they become a distinct aspect of the world of his poem. The depiction of King Herod for example, as Murphy points out, "seems to point to another determined kingly figure, Charlemagne."[42] This Herod is "slithery-mouthed," a man "who always enjoyed murder" (Song 7),[43] a "slime-hearted king" (Song 9).[44] When Herod asks about prophecies of Messiah, his advisors or "good men...who truly held the most book-power in their breasts" tell him that what is expected is "the mighty Counselor who will rule the Jewish people and who will distribute His gifts generously throughout the middle world to many peoples" (Song 7).[45] The second half of this passage is an addition. It pictures the future adult Jesus as a Saxon liege lord, the "ring giver" of Anglo-Saxon poetry, who in the midst of the meadhall distributes wealth and plunder to his loyal thanes in rituals of interdependence. The idea here that this distribution will include many peoples expands upon the Matthew citation of Micah, which expects a messiah who will only "shepherd my people Israel" (Matt 2:6). As with the earlier promise of liberation, the *Heliand* poet imagines a Jesus whose redemption will embrace not just the Jewish nation, but all peoples.

The description of the slaughter of the innocents stresses the moral indifference of Herod's men, who resemble the Frankish soldiers who had so recently defeated the Saxons: "They saw nothing evil, they saw nothing wrong, the ones who carried out this outrageous crime. With the weapon's edge, they did an enormous work of evil, cutting down many a man in his infancy" (Song 9).[46]

The promise of these *songs* is liberation for an oppressed people brought about by someone prepared by God's will and by fate to take on the most dangerous of battles. In this remaking of the gospel narratives the Germanic poem distances itself from the lingering dreams of Jewish patriarchal hegemony and resolutely turns itself to a vision of universal human redemption. This is the salvation Jesus will bring.

Community: The Public Life

The events of Jesus' public life also take place within a Saxon world familiar to the poet's readers. Here we find the Catholic belief in the centrality of community understood in terms of a warrior tribe. By stressing from the first Jesus as military leader, the poem anticipates his death, the event in his life story that seems to have been of central concern for this poet and that haunts virtually his every page, the event that leads in the end to redemption.

DISCIPLES

In the first days of his public life, Jesus as warlord assembles his band of followers, at once preparing for a campaign. "It became known to all the people, from hill-fort to hill-fort, that the Child of God was assembling companions....It was clear from His words as well as His deed, that He was Chieftain..." (Song 14).[47] He turns to fishermen, whom he finds in a distinctly Saxon setting "sitting up on a sand dune," and he asks them to leave their "nailed ships" (Song 14).[48] The disciples and Jesus never forget their early links with the sea. Withdrawing from the pressing crowds one day, Jesus tells his men he wishes "to take a trip out on the sea (it is on the border of Galileeland)."[49] And so "the weather-wise warriors hoisted up the sail...." But soon, despite all their caution, "the storm wind rose, the waves grew, thickening darkness rushed in, the sea began to move, the wind battled the water! The men were worried, the ocean was so angry...." They wake their sleeping Lord. "Then He spoke to the wind and also to the sea itself, and He told both of them to behave themselves more calmly....The Son of God had saved them from peril, the boat glided onward, the high-horned ship" (Song 27).[50] In scenes such as this we find ourselves in the world of *Beowulf* and of Anglo-Saxon elegiac poems such as "The Seafarer." One can recognize how the details from the Gospels that pictured the apostles as sailors—people just like his own—must have resonated with the *Heliand* poet.

THE MARRIAGE AT CANA

We see the Saxon meadhall too, in the story of the marriage feast of Cana. "The conviviality of the earls in the drinking hall was a beautiful sight, and the men on the benches had reached a very high level of bliss....Then the wine ran out on them: the people had no more apple wine" (Song 24).[51] In keeping both with "the secret" of Jesus and with the Germanic stress upon the secrecy of spells, "God's mighty Child gave His orders very quietly so that a lot of people would not know for sure how He said it with His words" (Song 24).[52] The miraculous change of water into wine, however, becomes an important sign for his followers. "They had more trust in His protection after that, more confidence that He had the power and authority of God in this world. It became widely known to the Jewish people throughout Galileeland how the Chieftain's Son, right there in their country, had changed water into wine" (Song 24).[53]

ENEMIES AND HEROIC RESOLVE

Such demonstrations of power, however, only bring on the kind of opposition that must have been all too familiar in the tribal rivalries of the poet's era. With the achievement of Jesus' early successes,

> the local people, the warriors, began to plot among themselves how they could inflict the greatest pain on the powerful Christ. They called their fighting-men together, their warrior-companions. They wanted to accuse him of sins and evil intentions. His word was of no use to them nor His brilliant spells. (Song 32)[54]

Recognizing what is coming, this Saxon Jesus pictures his future capture and death in warrior terms: "The Jewish earls are still to bind me, though innocent, to torture me at Jerusalem by inflicting astonishing pain with the weapon's edges; with the spear-point to see to it that I age no more, with its sharp edges to take away my life" (Song 37).[55]

The stress upon the spear edge and upon the spear as the weapon that will inflict pain and death is striking, given the fact that the Gospel Jesus was to die from being nailed on a cross. The point of the spearing of Jesus' side in the original gospel narratives is to ensure that he is already dead.[56] But the *Heliand* poet wishes to anticipate the future passion in terms of warrior weapons, not the ignominious cross but rather the heroic spear wound. He was also almost certainly expecting his readers to recall Woden hanging on Yggdrasil, enduring his own self-inflicted spear wound. This poet, whose theology strongly reflects the high Christology of the Gospel of John, will argue that Jesus was so in control of what would happen to him that, like Woden, he elected to receive his wounds, including the wound from the spear-point.

The public life of Jesus is thus understood in this poem to be a preparation for confrontation, battle, and painful death. The redemption Jesus comes to achieve must be won in this way. The poet thus prepares the way for the complex series of paradoxes that summarize his vision.

Redemption: The Passion and Death of Jesus

Fully one-fourth of the *Heliand* is devoted to Jesus' last hours. Song 54, the beginning of this phase of the narrative, is the only song in the whole poem with a title: *Passio* in the Munich manuscript, *Passio Domini* in the London. What does the poet choose to stress in his depiction of Jesus' death? How does he interpret these events in the terms of his own culture? And how, ultimately, does he come to define what he understands about the redemption? Let us find out by considering two of his major themes: betrayal and solitude.

Betrayal

PETER AND THE DISCIPLES

One of the most dramatic aspects of the Christian narrative of Jesus' death is its stress on how Jesus' followers failed him. Indeed the evangelists emphasize that those who had pledged faith and loyalty to Jesus violated their promises and left him to suffer and die at the hands of his enemies. These accounts depict Jesus' chosen principal disciple, Peter, as the worst of all, explicitly and forcefully denying his loyalty to his Lord in reply to questions posed by an unimportant servant.

Loyalty to one's chieftain or leader was, as we have already seen, perhaps the core value of Saxon culture. Jesus as the *drohtin* or "family head and chieftain" (Song 54)[57] had the absolute right to the loyalty of his men, to their *treuwa*, and specifically had the right to expect that they would defend him to the death. In the *Heliand* the disciple Thomas states this Germanic ideal forcefully: "We should continue on, stay with Him, and suffer with our Commander. That is what a thane chooses: to stand fast together with his lord, to die with him at the moment of doom" (Song 48).[58] What the Saxon poet chooses to do, echoing not only the story but the theology of his gospel sources, is to stress the betrayal of Jesus' friends.

ALIENATION

The Jesus of the *Heliand* knows his fate. He can foresee the unavoidable destiny God is shaping for him. At the same time, the poem will insist that Jesus' rank and power make him superior to the old, pagan *wurd*, and that Jesus could choose to defy fate and overturn his destiny but will not, as in the Gospel of John, because of his obedience to his Father's will.

He tells his disciples clearly, "There is no turning away of this....The mighty One will be sold to the massed people, fastened to the cross, and will suffer horrible tortures" (Song 54).[59] Confronting this certitude Jesus moves on. He "knew that He would have to give up these dwelling places and set off on the journey to God's kingdom, to His Father's ancestral homestead" (Song 54).[60] The way in which the poet imagines destiny here suggests how much he conceives of Jesus as a leader far from his real home, which he calls his "ancestral homestead." Later, in a curious exchange, a scornful Pilate will say to Jesus, "I am not a fellow clansman of Yours" and Jesus will reply to him, "I too do not come from this country" (Song 62).[61]

THE LAST SUPPER

At the Last Supper, Jesus quickly turns to the question of loyalty, saying to his disciples, "You devotedly promised Me your thaneship...(but) one of you twelve intends to sneak away from his promised loyalty and sell me to the Jewish clan" (Song 55).[62] He offers the fatal bit of bread to Judas. "As soon as the disloyal traitor took the food and put it into his mouth to eat it, the power of God left him. Cruel things started going into his body, horrible little creatures, Satan wrapped himself tightly around his heart" (Song 55).[63] For this Saxon writer, Judas's central fault is to violate *treuwe*, the loyalty he owes, as thane, to his chieftain, Jesus. When Judas has left, Jesus offers the remaining apostles the first Eucharist. "This body and blood is a thing which possesses power: with it you will give honor to your Chieftain" (Song 56).[64] The theology of incarnation and specifically of Jesus' embodiment in the Eucharist is here forcibly stated. Eucharist is "a thing," a concrete, tactile object and, like the verbal formulae of the runes, it "possesses power." Further, the Eucharist becomes an element, like the other meadhall community celebrations of gift giving, in a ritual of loyalty and dependency. In taking it, the disciples honor their chief.

THE ARREST

Jesus and his men now go out into the night, in every respect like a Saxon leader and his thanes. The relatively inconspicuous little hill called the Mount of Olives becomes, in this Germanic treatment, a full-fledged mountain, and the enemies coming for Jesus a hostile army led by Judas, "the hate-filled man" (Song 58).[65] Like Prudentius in an earlier century, this poet intensifies the details of the gospel stories, making everything larger and, if possible, more dramatic (Figure 55). He knows how significant these events will be for human history and consequently sees them being played out on a grand scale.

Standing on the mountain slope, Jesus the exemplary Saxon warrior-chief remains calm. "He was awaiting the workings of fate, the glorious time" (Song 58).[66] The paradoxes begin. Defeat, humiliation, torture, a bloody death—this will be "the glorious time." For the poet's warrior-audience, explaining paradoxes such as this one becomes a crucial challenge.

Figure 55
From **Song 58: Christ the Chieftain Is Captured;**
Peter, the Mighty Swordsman, Defends Him Boldly

Judas, the hate-filled man, was showing them the way; the enemy clan, the Jews, were marching behind. They were carrying fires with them, bringing lighted lamps and burning torches from the hill-fort, as they moved up onto the mountain for battle. Judas knew the place well to which he was to lead the people....Judas took the lead, ahead of the army, and told them a sign.... "I will go up to Him first," he said, "kiss Him and talk to Him. That person will be Christ Himself, whom you are to capture by the might of the clan, tie Him up, up on the mountain, and bring Him back to the people at the fort. He has forfeited His life by His words."

The warriors marched forward, the grim Jewish army, until they had come to Christ. There He stood with His followers, the famous Chieftain. He was awaiting the working of fate, the glorious time. Judas, the man without loyalty, went up to Him, bowed his head to God's Child, and spoke to his Lord. He kissed the mighty One, keeping his word....The Chieftain of Peoples, the Ruler of this world, bore all that with patience, spoke to Judas in His words and asked him frankly, "Why are you coming to Me like this with an army? Why are you leading these people to Me and selling Me to this loathsome Jewish clan, and with your kiss identifying Me to this crowd?"

Then He went to speak to the other men, the warriors, and asked them in His words why they had come looking for Him at night bringing their warrior-companions with them, "as if you want to cause trouble for someone." The crowd spoke back to Him and said that they had been told that the Healer was up here on the hill, the one who creates mobs among the Jewish people and calls Himself God's Son. "We have come here looking for Him, we are anxious to find Him. He is from Galileeland, from Fort Nazareth." As the rescuing Christ told them in soothsaying that He was the one, the Jewish people became frightened; they were so terrified that they instantly fell backwards and everyone of them was on the ground....They could not stand up to the Word, the voice, of God.

On first glimpsing Jesus, the Jewish warriors recognize his power. They "were so terrified that they instantly fell backwards and everyone of them was on the ground....They could not stand up to the Word, the voice, of God" (Song 58).[67] We are in the midst now of a battle scene in which warring Germanic tribes face off, preparing for the fighting to come. Jesus' enemies don't hold back for very long. Like the Saxons, they let battle rage consume them, relying upon frenzy to carry them beyond fear. "There were some real fighting men among them who...went raging forward in hatred until they had Christ the Rescuer surrounded with their men" (Song 58).[68] At first, "Christ's followers...held their position in front." In their final moment of real loyalty they say to Jesus, "if it should be Your will that we be impaled here on their spear-points, wounded by their weapons, then nothing would be as good to us as to die here, pale from mortal wounds, for our Chieftain" (Song 58).[69] For a moment, even Peter seems to find an opening toward real courage and greatness, when he hacks off the ear of Malchus (Figure 56).[70]

The Saxon poet imagines the leader of Jesus' men as a terrifying swordsman.

Figure 56
From **Song 58**

Then Simon Peter, the mighty, the noble swordsman flew into a rage; his mind was in such turmoil that he could not speak a single word. His heart became intensely bitter because they wanted to tie up his Lord there. So he strode over angrily, that very daring thane, to stand in front of his Commander, right in front of his Lord. No doubting in his mind, no fearful hesitation in his chest, he drew his blade and struck straight ahead at the first man of the enemy with all the strength in his hands, so that Malchus was cut and wounded on the right side by the sword! His ear was chopped off, he was so badly wounded in the head that his cheek and ear burst open with a mortal wound! Blood gushed out, pouring from the wound! The cheek of the enemy's first man had been cut open. The men stood back—they were afraid of the slash of the sword.

Then the Son of God spoke to Simon Peter and told him to put his sharp sword back into its sheath. "If I wanted to put up a fight against the attack of this band of warriors, I would make the great and mighty God, the holy Father in the kingdom of heaven, aware of it so that He would send me so many angels wise in warfare that no human beings could stand up to the force of their weapons. No human army, however huge, could ever stand fast against them nor afterwards still be in possession of their life-spirits. But, the ruling God, the almighty Father, has determined it differently: we are to bear whatever bitter things this people does to us. We are not to become enraged or wrathful against their violence, since whoever is eager and willing to practice the weapon's hatred, cruel spear-fighting, is often killed himself by the edge of the sword and dies dripping with his own blood. We cannot by our deeds avert anything."

He then went up to the wounded man and skillfully put the parts of his body back together, his headwounds, so that the sword-slash was quickly healed.

In another of the paradoxes of this scene, both for the Gospels and for the *Heliand*, it is Jesus who must put a stop to all of this. He recognizes that he must carry out the divine plan and in the *Heliand* he does so in terms of Germanic fatalism saying: "We cannot by our deeds avert anything" (Song 58).[71] In telling Peter to yield to the arrest, "Christ is shown teaching Peter the parallelism of two of the oldest Germanic and Christian religious attitudes: calm acceptance of the unavoidable and submission to the will of God."[72]

The ensuing flight of the apostles was exquisitely unpleasant to the *Heliand* poet and his audience, and so he seeks a way to absolve them of their disloyalty. "His close warrior-companions had run away from Him…not because of any cowardice…but because a long time ago it had been said—the words of the soothsayer—that it would happen in this way. Therefore, they could not have avoided it" (Song 59).[73]

However, he will not let Peter off the hook. In the scene at the courtyard of the "bishop," which is how this poem renders "Caiaphas the high priest" (Matt 26:57), Peter finds himself being questioned by a "clever, nasty woman…a maid-servant of one of the Jewish commanders." The poet judges that here Peter's denial of his master is a failure of courage: "His courage went soft….God's strength, toughness, had gone out of his heart" (Song 59).[74] Again, however, the poet pardons him. "It was supposed to happen that way" (Song 59).[75] He describes Peter's ensuing shame at length: "He was so worried that hot and bloody tears came pouring up from his heart" (Song 59).[76] Murphy comments that for the Saxons, rather surprisingly, "Shame (was)…a sign of mature knightly virtue, demonstrating the presence in the warrior of deeply held feelings of loyalty."[77] Given the contradictions—Peter betrays his Lord, but has been fated to do so and cannot avoid what he does—Peter becomes a tragic figure. "The best of men lamented in deep misery and regret that he had denied his beloved Lord" (Song 59).[78]

THE PARADOXICAL GOOD IN PETER'S BETRAYAL
The poet then gives his own ethical and indeed theological justification for Peter's betrayal—perhaps we might say his own theory of tragedy, and a richly suggestive one at that.

The holy Chieftain intended to make Peter the first man in the leadership of His household, and wanted Peter to realize how much strength there is in the human spirit without the power of God. He let Peter commit sin so that afterwards he would better appreciate people, how all human beings love to be forgiven when they have done something wrong. People love to be freed from their loathsome sins and crimes—just as God, the King of Heaven, forgave Peter the wrong he had done. (Song 59)[79]

Here the *Heliand* poet achieves one of his greatest moments, in which he works out an explanation for the theme of betrayal in the Gospels. The paradox is that Peter and the other disciples must sin so that when they take over the task of leading the new church they will fully understand what it means to be human and so will understand that each person has failed and needs to be forgiven. Each human being needs to be redeemed. As with the notion of the "fortunate fall"—that is, that Adam's sin was paradoxically good because it necessitated the redemption that Jesus came to achieve— here the betrayal of Jesus' disloyal thanes is good because it reveals to them their human limitations and so prepares them to be the apostles of an emerging Christianity.

Judas, unlike Peter, is not so lucky. In his persistent disloyalty he remains the embodiment of the antithetic example, a man who persists in turning away from God, refusing pardon, and betraying his leader and consequently becomes little more than the pitiful victim of Germanic demons.

> He walked along—just as the ferocious sons of the enemy fiends told him to do. They had taken such cruel hold of the man's mind...he made himself a noose...putting his head into the deadly rope to strangle and hang himself, and chose his punishment: the hard oppression of Hel, hot and dark, the deep valley of death—because he had been unfaithful to his Chieftain. (Song 61)[80]

The Solitude of the Hero

Because all of his men betray him, Jesus must face death alone. The Gospels of Matthew and Mark make Jesus' sense of solitude dramatically clear, climaxing in his despairing cry to God the Father, "Why have you forsaken me?" (Matt 27:46; Mark 15:34). The loneliness of the hero facing death without the help of his friends may have been one of the tragic themes of the Germanic oral tradition. It is certainly central to the first written Germanic epic, the Anglo-Saxon poem *Beowulf*, which may be close in time to the *Heliand* and also features a protagonist who must face diabolical foes unaided.

THE AGONY IN THE GARDEN

The *Heliand* poet begins to depict Jesus' loneliness during the scene traditionally known as "the agony in the garden." Here the gospel narratives suddenly and atypically give us an inner view of Jesus' private emotions, Matthew describing him as "grieved and agitated" when he leaves the chosen disciples behind to go on and pray by himself (Matt 26:37). The *Heliand* poet uses this scene as a way into his own Christology and his understanding of the incarnation. He understands Jesus to possess both divine and human natures, and at this moment the poet suggests Jesus' human weakness becomes almost overwhelming. "His mind was clouded and afraid; in his humanness his feelings were upset, his flesh was frightened. His tears fell, his precious sweat dripped down just as blood comes welling out of wounds" (Song 57).[81] Mark describes how Jesus becomes "distressed and agitated" (Mark 14:34), and Luke writes that in the midst of this intensity of fear "his sweat became like great drops of blood falling down on the ground" (Luke 22:44). None of the Synoptic Gospels explicitly has Jesus crying, nor do they give the explanation that he is now "in his humanness." But the *Heliand* concludes, "The spirit and the body were at war in God's Child" (Song 57).[82]

For the Saxon poet, the point of all this is precisely the radiantly courageous way in which Jesus rises above this moment. The very intensity of the anxiety and fear help to dramatically underscore his courage. The poet seizes upon the gospel metaphor in which Jesus, addressing his Father, pleads, "If you are willing, remove this cup from me" (Luke 22:42) and translates the imagery into a gesture of loyalty to God the Father in the form of a mead-hall salute: "I take this chalice in my hand and drink it to your honor, my Lord chieftain, powerful Protector" (Song 57).[83] At this crisis moment, the Jesus of the *Heliand* achieves a Germanic understanding of fate, of God's power, and of his own need to cooperate with the divine plan. "Fate is at hand, so that everything will go just as God the Father in His might has determined it....My flesh is worried, my body is holding Me back, it is very loathe to suffer pain. Despite this, I will still do what My Father wants done" (Song 57).[84] Here Jesus becomes the model for Christian heroic conduct. While his disciples may have run away, he will do what his own chieftain asks of him, right down to the bitter end—not because a pagan fate forces him to do so, but because he freely chooses to accept what the Father asks of him. This is how Jesus accomplishes our redemption, through the paradox of self-abnegation. The second paradox is that he will not seem to others to be heroic at all. This kind of Christian heroism emerges from humiliation, finds victory in being defeated, and experiences the greatest joy in pain and grief. It accords, perfectly, with the humiliation, oppression, and pain of the Saxons.

As he is being arrested, this Jesus confronts the mob of "hostile warriors" with calm irony, speaking fearlessly (Figure 57).

Figure 57
From Song 58

God's Son spoke to the hostile warriors. "It seems very amazing to Me," He said, "that if you wanted to do some harm to Me, why did you not capture Me when I was among your people in the shrine and was soothsaying with My words? There was sunshine then, the precious light of day! You did not want to do any harm to Me then in all that light—and now you bring out your people at night in darkness just as one does when it is a thief one wants to catch, a criminal who has forfeited his life-spirit." The Jewish warriors then grabbed at God's Son, a cruel clan, a hate-filled mob. The angry army of men massed around Him—they did not see their crime—they fastened His hands together with iron handcuffs and His arms with chains.

There was no need for Him to suffer such terrible pain, such horrible hardship and suffering, but He did it for the sake of this warrior clan, because He wanted to save the sons of people, to haul them up from Hel to heaven—to wide-flung happiness! That is why He did not say a thing about what they wanted to do to Him in their spiteful hate.

THE ARREST AND INTERROGATIONS

The Jews, in arresting Jesus, "fastened His hands together with iron handcuffs and His arms with chains" (Song 58),[85] a form of Frankish control seen in the *Utrecht Psalter* in the illustration for Psalm 150, where captured kings are also imprisoned by handcuffs and chains. Jesus continues to experience solitary inner grief: "The Son of God, his hands bound, walked among the warriors down to the valley feeling sad and upset" (Song 59).[86] But the point of being a Germanic warrior, and now of being a Christian hero, is not to betray one's fear or to permit one's enemy to exult in one's suffering. And so though the Jews "hit Him on the cheeks with their hands...," Jesus remains unmoved. "God's Child stood His ground among the enemy....He never flew into a rage over the attacks of these warriors" (Song 61).[87] To Herod's questions, "he did not want to give an answer...not a single word" (Song 63).[88] He maintains a similar inscrutable silence before Pilate.

For this silence the poet has an intriguing explanation.

> He did not want to let all the Jewish people know openly that He was God Himself. For, if they really knew how much power He had over this middle world, their feelings would turn cowardly within their breasts and they would never dare to lay their hand on the Son of God, and then the kingdom of heaven, the brightest of worlds, would never be unlocked to the sons of men. (Song 64)[89]

Jesus' passivity under the hands of his tormentors is thus seen not only as an example of his heroic fortitude but also of his understanding that the redemption he is winning for every human person can only come through his death, and to save him from it would paradoxically be to lose everything he has come to earth to achieve. He chooses to hide his divinity and to accept the coming death.

The poet continues to play with this paradox in telling of the dream of Pilate's wife. In Matthew she sends a messenger to Pilate while he is interrogating Jesus, begging him, "Have nothing to do with that innocent man, for today I have suffered a great deal because of a dream about him" (Matt 27:19). The *Heliand* turns this into a story of demonic interference. Satan has entered the woman's dream as "the deceiver, who was invisible, hidden by a magic hel-

met." He does this in order to "use her words to help Christ..."
(Song 65).[90] But why would Satan try to save Jesus from death?
"Satan knew for sure that Christ wanted to set the whole world free
from the oppression of Hel by his hanging, freeing everyone to go
to God's light." This "gave Satan a feeling of great pain and was
profoundly disturbing to his mind. He immediately wanted to come
to Christ's aid....He wanted Him to remain alive so that human
beings would not become safe and secure from their sins and the
inferno" (Song 65).[91] Again a paradox. Satan tries to achieve for
Jesus the very same rescue from ignominy and death that Jesus had
begged for in the garden. But it is only by Jesus accepting death that
humanity can be saved. Satan's seeming kindness is evil, and his failure to free Jesus from the agony to come is good.

THE CRUCIFIXION

The reference to Jesus' "hanging" in the story of the Satanic
dream is but one of many instances in which the *Heliand* poet
intentionally blends the story of Woden and the death of Jesus.
Woden chose to hang himself on Yggdrasil. His self-willed pain
was important to the *Heliand* poet because it indicated the god-
hero's courage and proved that he was not the victim of others but
that he consciously and freely willed his suffering—a theological
point already driven home in John's Gospel when Jesus says, "The
Father loves me, because I lay down my life in order to take it up
again. No one takes it from me, but I lay it down of my own accord.
I have power to lay it down, and I have power to take it up again.
I have received this command from my Father" (John 10:17–18).
Maintaining the parallel between pagan myth and Christian narrative, the *Heliand* repeatedly makes reference to Jesus on the
"gallows," Jesus "hung," Jesus on a rope. In the *Heliand* the cross
is sometimes called a tree, and this connects both with the Woden
story and with another Christian tradition that goes back to Saint
Paul and that finds a parallel between the tree in the garden of paradise, which is the source of Adam's fall, and the cross/tree on
which Jesus hangs in order to redeem humanity from that sin.[92] In
Christian tradition Jesus' tree of the cross replaces Adam's tree of
guilty knowledge and indeed medieval legends imagined that the
cross had been fashioned out of the wood of that primal tree.

However, in the northern Europe of the *Heliand,* "warrior-heroes use the edges of their battle-axes to make a mighty cross out of a hardwood tree..." (Song 65),[93] and "there on the sandy gravel they erected the gallows, up on a field the Jewish people set it up— a tree on a mountain—and there they tortured God's Son on a cross" (Song 66).[94] At times, as in the mocking challenge of the bad thief, it seems as if the poet pictures Jesus hung not so much by nails as by a noose: "If You are the king...get down from the cross, slip out of the rope" (Song 66).[95] In reply the Good Thief describes their own condition: "Here you are: held to the gallows, broken on the tree" (Song 66).[96] Later, just after Jesus' moment of death, the poet writes, "The Protector of the Land died on the rope..." (Song 67).[97]

Jesus' last hours of suffering define heroic courage, including Christian forgiveness of the enemy. "His blood ran down onto the earth...but He did not want to take vengeance on the Jews for the terrible deed. Instead He asked mighty God the Father not to be angry with the people of the human race, 'because they do not know what they are doing,' He said" (Song 66).[98] In his crisis of despair Jesus seems to be a loyal warrior captured by the enemy, now being tortured and wondering when his Chieftain will come to his rescue. "He stood there fastened by the arms...," and he cries out, "Beloved Chieftain...Why is Your help and Your support so far away? I am here among the enemy being tortured horribly!" (Song 67).[99]

In the end, Jesus freely elects his death. "He said, 'My spirit is now ready to go, ready to travel.' The Chieftain of Mankind then bowed His head, the holy breath escaped from the body" (Song 67).[100] The scene resembles "an escape of a prisoner of war from his captors...,"[101] and when the Jews come to pierce his side with a spear, the wound is "just the way He wanted it and had predetermined beforehand for the benefit of mankind...."[102] "They found Him already gone, His soul had been sent on the true road to the long-lasting light....His life-spirit was far from the flesh" (Song 67).[103]

Immediately, Joseph of Arimathaea begins the reassembly of Jesus' warrior band. He removes the corpse "from the new gallows pole..." and treats the body "as the Chieftain deserved..." (Song 68).[104] (See Figure 58). The church is already beginning.

Figure 58
From Song 68

When the bright sun, together with the heavenly stars, had sunk nearer to its rest on that gloomy day, our Chieftain's thane set off on his way. An intelligent man, he had been a follower of Christ for a long time, although not many people really knew of it, since he concealed it with his words from the Jewish people. Joseph was his name, secretly our Chieftain's follower. He did not want to follow wicked people of the clan into doing anything sacrilegious and so he waited among the Jewish people in holiness for the kingdom of the heavens.

At that moment he was on his way to speak with the military governor, to deal with emperor Caesar's thane. Joseph urged the man earnestly to release Christ's body from the cross on which it now was, dead, freeing the good man from the gallows, and to lay it in a grave, commit it to the earth. The military governor had no desire to refuse what Joseph wanted, and so he granted him the authority to carry it out. From there, Joseph set off for the gallows, walking to the place where he knew that God's Son, the corpse of his Lord, was hanging. He removed it from the new gallows pole and pulled the nails out of it. He took the beloved body in his arms, just as one should with one's lord, wrapped it in linen, and carried it devoutly— as the Chieftain deserved—to the place where they had hewn out the inside of a rock with their hands, a place where no hero's son, no one, had ever been buried. There they committed God's Son, the holiest of corpses into the folds of the earth in the way customary in their country, and closed the most god-like of all graves with a stone. The poor women who had seen all of this man's terrible death sat there crying and distraught. Then the weeping women decided to go away from there—they noted carefully the way back to the grave—they had seen enough of sorrow and overpowering sadness. The poor distraught women were all called Mary. Evening came then, and the night fog.

The Paradox of Christian Heroism

In the midst of despair, when even his Father and Chieftain seemed to have deserted him, this Jesus finds meaning through assent. His heroism emerges from his humiliation. There is a beauty in his sorrow. His victory comes only with his defeat. Alone and in terrible solitude he achieves something for everyone else, the redemption that will liberate not only the Saxons but all people, not from the temporary oppression of the Franks but from sin and death. The paradoxes that in chapter 3 of this study we found a necessary consequence of the vision of two different orders of meaning, the divine and the material, thus become the most significant conceptual structures of the *Heliand* and characteristic of the resolutions of its thematic problems.

We noted earlier how the *Heliand* poet sought to show his audience that, undoubtedly to their surprise, the Christianity imposed upon them by Frankish conquest was the best thing that could have happened to them, and in a way the most Germanic. In his development of this premise the poet reimagined in terms of the incarnation a Jesus like themselves in cultural attitudes and values, a fleshly man whom they, like the Magi before them, could still touch in the sacrament of the Eucharist; a man weak enough to cry, vulnerable to injury and hurt, and at the end of his life feeling at least for a moment the despair of absolute desertion. At the same time his is the story of redemption, a hero narrative in which courageous resolve saves not just one person or one clan but all people through a liberation from sin and death. Throughout this narrative Jesus' responsibility to community never wavers. He is a hero-leader who builds a community, is betrayed by it, and yet goes on to sacrifice himself so that the community might live again, and it begins to do so moments after his death.

In *The Heliand*, the morning of the resurrection dawns when God's power causes light to shine on humanity, the gates of Hel to burst open, heaven to be united with earth, and Christ to rise from his grave (Figure 59). The road between heaven and earth is the rainbow arch, the *bifrost* of Germanic myth connecting the earth with heaven. Jesus builds this road so that the human community can follow him and cross over into that paradise that Germanic myth had foreseen as following Ragnarok and that Christians imagine as "the kingdom" coming beyond the last judgment for all who are saved. Meanwhile Jesus' beloved followers find themselves at the doorway of the empty tomb greeted by the message of an angel: "This place, this grave in the sand, is empty....The Chieftain...is already in Galileeland Himself, where His followers, His warrior-companions, will see Him again..." (Song 69),[106] and so off they go, the new church already forming, "the followers of Christ, the warrior-companions... gathering together" (Song 70).[107]

Figure 59
From **Song 68**

Warriors were picked from the Jewish battle-group for the guard. They set off with their weapons and went to the grave where they were to guard the corpse of God's Son. The holy day of the Jews had now passed. The warriors sat on top of the grave on their watch during the dark starlit night. They waited under their shields until bright day came to mankind all over the middle world, bringing light to people.

It was not long then until: there was the spirit coming, by God's power, the holy breath, going under the hard stone to the corpse! Light was at that moment opened up, for the good of the sons of men; the many bolts on the doors of Hel were unlocked; the road from this world up to heaven was built! Brilliantly radiating, God's Peace-Child rose up! He went about, wherever He pleased, in such a way that the guards, tough soldiers, were not at all aware of when He got up from death and arose from His rest.

The Jewish warriors, the fighting men with their shields, were sitting outside, around the grave. The brilliant sunlight continued to glide upward. The women were on their way, walking to the grave, women of good family, the Marys most lovely. They had traded many jewels, silver and gold to buy salves, and given much wealth to get roots, the best they could obtain, so that they could pour salve on the corpse of their beloved Lord, the Chieftain's Son, and into the wounds carved into Him. The women were very concerned in their minds and some were speaking about who could roll the huge stone off to one side of the grave. They had seen the men lay it over the corpse when they had buried the body in the rock. When the noble ladies had come into the garden so that they could look at the grave itself, an angel of the All-Ruler came down out of the skies above, moving along on its coat of feathers like a roaring wind so that all the ground was set to shaking; the earth reverberated; and the resolve of the earls, the Jewish guards, weakened; and they fell down out of fear. They did not think that they would have their life-spirits—simply be—alive much longer!

Conclusion

Catholic Belief and Artistic Expression

In the second half of this book we have come to see how the initiating imagination of Jesus emerged in the Catholic art of Europe in terms of four defining traits: belief in the incarnation, hope and trust in redemption, a Christian life shaped and nourished by sacramentality, and lived in terms of community. As we looked closely at the nascent autobiography of Saint Paul, the house-church at Dura-Europos, the Greek Chapel in the catacomb of Priscilla, the poetry of Prudentius and Columba, the manuscript pictures and decorations of *The Book of Kells* and the *Utrecht Psalter,* and the heroic epic narrative of *The Heliand* we observed each of those four characteristic traits present, distinctive, and generative.

Incarnation

The Catholic belief in the incarnation, together with its conviction about the constant presence of God and the constant care of God for God's creation; its vision of Jesus as both God and human; and its sense that the divine can intersect with the created at any historical moment established a metaphysic, a way of seeing, understanding, and working with the world. Hence the free confidence with which Christian artists from the earliest days of the church painted visual images of God and of Jesus, such as the Savior walking on the water at Dura-Europos, Jesus breaking bread at the eucharistic table in wall fresco of the catacomb of Priscilla, the images of Jesus teaching and of Jesus arrested in the *Book of Kells,* and the virtually omnipresent drawings of Jesus often as war hero and of God as a mighty hand in the sky seen in the *Utrecht Psalter*. Hence too God reflected in his creation, and particularly in nature: in Paul's defiant assertion to the Romans that God has always been evident to those who will look, in Prudentius's ecstatic celebrations of natural things as simple as a cock crowing or as complex as his vision of every created thing proclaiming its love for God, and Columba's *Altus Prosator* and its astonishment:

> By the divine power of the great God is hung
> The globe of the earth, and the circle of the great
>   deep placed about it,
> held up by the strong hand of almighty God,
> with columns like bars supporting it,
> promontories and rocks as their solid foundations,
> fixed firm, as if on certain immovable bases.

This is a God who can be found in the lives of individual people—in the events of Paul's paradigmatic life, or in the brave defiance of the Hero of the *Heliand*. This is a God who can be found in the church that Jesus began and in its daily life and worship as Prudentius celebrates them; a God present in history—in, for example, the typological parallels between the great events of Jewish and Christian history as defined by Paul and depicted in the Adam and Eve of Dura and the Moses and Susanna of the catacomb of Priscilla.

Redemption

Catholic hope rests always, ultimately, upon the story of a man, the story of redemption. It sees a broken world damaged by sin, haunted by death, and it recognizes that evil is real and active, and yet at the same time it finds consolation in the certainty that God cares about human suffering and that Jesus' redemptive death and resurrection offer salvation to everyone. It sees present reality as a place where good and evil struggle, but Catholics view that struggle in terms of hope, sharing a vision of a world redeemed which gives meaning to history.

The Catholic belief in redemption establishes a primal or kernel narrative, a story with the power to structure time, experience, action, and choice along distinctly Christian lines. It serves to establish a narrative paradigm for how to live and thus gives meaning to every aspect of life. We explored that kernel narrative repeatedly: in the gospel biographies of Jesus, in Paul's narrative of his own life, and in the scriptural narratives that structure the iconographic programs of the early fresco cycles at Dura and at Rome, where, for example, Noah, Abraham, Moses, Susanna, and the faithful Hebrews in the fiery furnace anticipate the Magi before Mary and Jesus, the resurrection of Lazarus, and the redemptive feast of the Last Supper. Prudentius's poetry rejoices in celebrating redemption:

> ...tell His passion's victory,
> tell of the triumphant cross,
> sing of the sign, marked on our foreheads,
> which shines out so brightly.
> Oh, what a new miracle, that wound of His
> astonishing death!
> From His heart flowed waves here of blood, there of water;
> The water, certainly, washing us clean of sin,
> while blood wins the crown of victory.

The most extended version of this kernel story that we considered is the *Heliand* and its careful situating of Christ's life, death, and resurrection within the culture of the Saxon believers for whom it was written.

Sacramentality

Sacraments dominate the lives of Catholics. They constitute the constant presence of God within each person's individual context. In the sacraments the human and the divine cooperate, Catholics believing that God is present, active, and participating in sacramental events when people reach out to him through sacramental ritual. The sacraments involve both individual participation and community action—they are hence simultaneously public and personal. They can take place anywhere, any time; but through the history of the Catholic tradition there has evolved a liturgical calendar, rooted in the Paschal mystery of Christ's saving action, which shapes the lives of individuals, communities, and the entire church, establishing an annual rhythm, structuring the timing and the character of human encounters with the divine and with the community.

Embedded in Paul's Epistles we find both some of the earliest written accounts of sacramental language, such as the words still used in the eucharistic celebration, as well as some of the earliest recorded Christian hymns. The rooms at Dura-Europos reflect in their structure and layout the liturgical and sacramental life of that early community, while the decorations of the room used for baptism employ images of saving water to help church members understand the double vision of Catholic sacramentality—here baptism washing candidates free from past sins, preparing them for a new life in Christ, which in various ways will be analogous to the cripple who can now walk, the doubter who now strides across the waves of the sea, the hopeful women coming to the empty tomb on Easter morning. Prudentius's book of poems suggests ways in which the hours of the day and the seasons of the year were being ordered in the Roman Empire of the early fifth century, the rhythms of his lines echoing the rhythms of the life of his fellow believers. The great, decorated sacred texts—the *Kells* Gospels, the *Utrecht* Psalms—so costly in time and imagination, to say nothing of materials required, for their creation, were made to be used liturgically. The *Book of Kells,* for example, was carried in procession and displayed upon the altar at Iona as a concrete example of the presence of God in the words of sacred scripture and in the ritual prayer life of the monastic community. Here we find art blessing and sanctifying daily experience. In much the same way, the chanting of the Psalms, a core prayer ritual in medieval monastic community life, finds aesthetic embodiment in the *Psalter* at Utrecht and the effort of its artists to help believers see the content and the meaning of the Psalms in the most complex and yet literal visual terms. In those drawings the experience of the people of Israel emerges as a type for the experience of the future Christian community and in many of the *Utrecht* drawings we see the faithful gathering to share in the sacramental life.

Community

The foundational insistence within Christianity upon life centered upon a community established a context for living, giving structure and meaning to the individual self in terms of others. To be, for

Christians, meant to be in relationship with others. To be good, to be happy, to be saved were defined in terms of participation in the body of Christ, the church as Paul defines it in his Epistles and as he lived it as a missionary building communities of faith throughout the Mediterranean region. Within this context Christians soon came to shape the physical character of their surrounding world: constructing buildings of many types in which communities could gather, live, and act, and even at times altering the face of the earth itself to correspond to their communal needs. The house-church at Dura-Europos shows us how early Christians shaped communal spaces useful for their sacramental lives; the catacombs at Rome show us how they understood death and lived in a Christian communal relationship with those who had died. When Prudentius sings, much of the time he uses the pronoun *we*—he sings from and for the community. The *Kells* and *Utrecht* manuscripts emerge from monastic community life and serve its purposes, as, presumably, did the *Heliand,* a poem divided into chapters that appear to have been proportioned for the purposes of recitation before a community.

This then is the theoretical structure promised the reader in this book's first pages. While the terms and their definitions as presented here may be relatively simple, they offer the reader a conceptual framework for thinking about a Catholic imagination and about how that imagination might be discerned in many different works of art. By design the examples considered closely in part 2 come from the early history of the church and are meant to serve as illustrations of some of the ways in which a Catholic imagination first emerged. That is how this book ends. It is, however, the aim of the book to extend its usefulness beyond these pages by enabling the reader to carry on thinking about these topics in terms of other times, other forms of aesthetic expression, and so on. How that might be done will probably vary with each reader's background, enthusiasms, and inclinations. From the sculptures of Michelangelo to Beethoven's *Missa Solemnis,* from Roberto Rossellini's *Open City* to the cathedral at Chartres, from Tintoretto's *Crucifixion* at the Scuola San Rocco to the sonnets of Hopkins, the possibilities are virtually numberless, as are the forms of revelation. If this study helps to incite some of its readers to enter into such further exploration, then all the work that has gone into the making of it will have been well worth it.

Notes

CHAPTER 1 Origins

1. Andrew J. Greeley, "The Catholic Imagination and the Catholic University," *America* 164: 10 (March 16, 1991), 286.

2. Andrew Greeley, *The Catholic Imagination* (Berkeley: University of California Press, 2001), 35. Andrew Greeley's work on the subject of Catholic imagination is central to any discussion of the topic, as the two sources just quoted indicate. His book *The Catholic Imagination* uses "works of high culture" in an effort to define a "Catholic sensibility" that can be validated by sociological study (*Catholic Imagination,* 3). The present work moves in a different direction, beginning with a study of the biblical sources of a Catholic imagination and tracing its later influence.

3. The New Revised Standard Version translation used in the discussion of these lines expresses Jesus' sense that his hearers must use their imaginations through the word *suppose,* which is their way of translating the Greek original "kai eipen pro autou ti ex umown exei filon" more literally translated in the King James Bible as "And he said unto them, Which of you shall have a friend...." *Suppose* directly expresses the two conditional questions that Jesus poses; first, "imagine" the scene itself; second, imagine the outcome of the scene.

CHAPTER 2 Catholic Belief

1. Paul himself records one of the first spats in Galatians 2:6–7. Of course he wins.

2. The Greek *katholikos* means "universal" and is derived from *kata* or "in respect to" and *holos* or "the whole."

3. James A. Kleist, SJ, *The Epistles of St. Clement of Rome and St. Ignatius of Antioch* (Westminster, MD: Newman Press, 1949), 91.

4. Ibid., 54.

5. Ibid., 57.

6. John Clarkson, SJ, et al., *The Church Teaches: Documents of the Church in English Translation* (St. Louis, MO: B. Herder, 1955), 2.

7. Richard P. McBrien, *Catholicism: New Study Edition* (San Francisco: HarperSanFrancisco, 1994), 714–15.

8. In this Bonaventure becomes typical of medieval Christian writers for whom "creation...is seen as a 'voicing,' a kind of narrative...an expression consistent with other expressions [of God's] divine imagination....Of God's glory the created order is, literally speaking, a lively 'translation'..." (David Jeffrey, *People of the Book: Christian Identity and Literary Culture* [Grand Rapids: William B. Eerdmans, 1996], 150).

9. In the following discussion I write about the sacraments as they have been defined by Catholic tradition. In our own time the theological discussion of "sacrament" and "sacramentality" has broadened the understanding of what these terms might mean, leading to a vision parallel to that of Saint Bonaventure, quoted earlier in this chapter, which finds all things as participating in the divine and hence all things as sacraments. From this perspective such things as a tree, a poem that moves us, and the sharing of a moment of physical kindness can be sacraments. Without wishing to deny the cogency or the richness of this theological insight, my discussion here concentrates on Catholic ritual and its traditional concept of sacramentality.

10. In the scene in which a woman caught committing adultery is about to be stoned, Jesus is pictured "writing on the ground with his finger" before he says, "Let anyone among you who is without sin be the first to throw a stone at her" (John 8:7). Modern biblical scholars note the absence of this passage from many ancient copies of this Gospel and find it not to be written in John's characteristic style. None of this was known until recently, however, and Catholics have always read this as a valid account of an episode in the life of Jesus.

CHAPTER 3 **The World of Jesus' Imagination**

1. Gerard Vallee, *The Shaping of Christianity: The History and Literature of Its Formative Centuries (100–800)* (New York: Paulist Press, 1999), 45.

2. Michael Grant, *Jesus* (London: Weidenfeld & Nicolson, 1977), 88.

3. Geza Vermes, *The Religion of Jesus the Jew* (Minneapolis: Fortress Press, 1993), 92–95.

CHAPTER 4 Jesus' Teaching and Catholic Belief

1. In the ensuing discussion I am consciously avoiding the complex question of Jesus' self-knowledge during his lifetime, theories of "high" and "low" Christology, and so on. Centuries of theological debate have not resolved, indeed cannot resolve, this central problem. Because my present concern is how relatively naïve, literal readings of the New Testament led to the development of a Catholic imagination, I write here from that perspective.

2. Raymond Brown et al., eds., *The New Jerome Biblical Commentary* (Englewood Cliffs, NJ: Prentice Hall, 1990), 702.

CHAPTER 5 The First Christian Narratives: Four Biographies of Jesus

1. Pierre du Bourguet, *Early Christian Art* (New York: Reynal, 1971), 22.

2. Saint Paul helped formulate many of these ideas, and in chapter 6 we return to them briefly in the discussion of "A Pauline Theory of History."

Introduction to Part II

1. Pierre du Bourguet, *Early Christian Art* (New York: Reynal, 1971), 136.

2. Ibid.

3. S. G. F. Brandon, *Man and God in Art and Ritual: A Study of Iconography, Architecture and Ritual Action as Primary Evidence of Religious Belief and Practice* (New York: Charles Scribner's Sons, 1975), 294.

4. Archeological discoveries of the twentieth century have unearthed some fascinating exceptions to this rule, examples of Jewish communities that ignored this ban and decorated their synagogues with pictures.

Chapter 6: Saint Paul and Autobiography

1. Paul perhaps remembers Jesus' parable of the woman working yeast into dough when he writes, "A little yeast leavens the whole batch of dough" (Gal 5:9). But this kind of example is unusual.

2. Though it must be said that it anticipates the way Jesus will speak in the Gospel of John, which was written after the Pauline letters.

3. The first time for Christianity. Elements of this vision of history—the coming of a redeemer—can be found much earlier, for example in Isaiah's description of the "suffering servant" who "make[s] his life an offering for sin" and thereby will "make many righteous" by "bear[ing] their iniquities" (Isa 53:10–11).

4. C. A. Patrides, *The Grand Design of God: The Literary Form of the Christian View of History* (London: Routledge & Kegan Paul, 1972) explores this issue in detail.

5. Here we see Paul picking up on Jesus' ironic jokes about the powerful, the rich, the arrogant, which we discussed in chapter 3.

6. Robert Carroll and Stephen Prickett, eds., *The Bible: Authorized King James Version with Apocrypha* (Oxford: Oxford University Press, 1997), 413, note of Paul's life in Acts that it is "the first in a long line of such stories…characteristic of certain forms of religious experience, and its shape has influenced the way many later people have told their own story." The point I wish to make here is that the letters in a very different way constitute the first Catholic autobiography.

CHAPTER 7 The First Churches: Dura-Europos

1. Cited in Rodney Stark, *The Rise of Christianity* (San Francisco: HarperSanFrancisco, 1997), 8–9.

2. Ibid., 10.

3. Jean Lassus, *The Early Christian and Byzantine World* (New York: McGraw Hill, 1967), 9.

4. Stark, *Rise of Christianity*, 39.

5. Peter Brown, *The Rise of Western Christendom* (Oxford: Blackwell, 1996), 25.

6. Ibid., 26.

7. The central reason for Roman persecutions lay in the fact that Rome's official religion included "sacrifice, prayer, and public rejoicing for the welfare and success of the Emperor's Divine Majesty" (Richard Krautheimer, *Early Christian and Byzantine Architecture* [New Haven: Yale University Press, 1986], 25). When Christians refused to take part in these rituals of loyalty, they appeared to threaten not only the religious but also the civil homogeneity of Roman society. Refusing public prayer and worship for the emperor was interpreted by traditional Romans as treason; hence the sporadic persecutions.

8. Krautheimer, *Christian and Byzantine Architecture*, 24.

9. Ibid., 28.

10. Ibid.

11. In later centuries, Christian architects, recognizing that a church as building can be read symbolically as an embodiment of Christ, consciously replicated aspects of Christ's own body in, for example, the overall cruciform plan for the Gothic cathedral.

12. Lassus, *Christian and Byzantine World,* 11. The place name is spelled differently by various authors. Clark Hopkins who helped direct the excavation styles it "DuraEuropos" while Ignacio Pena uses "Dura Europus."

13. Clark Hopkins, *The Discovery of DuraEuropos,* ed. Bernard Goldman (New Haven: Yale University Press, 1979), 93.

14. Krautheimer, *Christian and Byzantine Architecture,* 27.

15. Andre Grabar, *Christian Iconography: A Study of Its Origins* (Princeton: Princeton University Press, 1968), 19.

16. Hopkins, *Discovery of DuraEuropos,* 91.

17. Ibid., 94.

18. Krautheimer, *Christian and Byzantine Architecture,* 27.

19. Brown, *Rise of Western Christendom,* 24.

20. Because early Christianity was in danger both of official persecution and of doctrinal slippage, Brown argues that early Christians exhibited a "ferociously inward-looking quality..." (Peter Brown, *The World of Late Antiquity: From Marcus Aurelius to Muhammud* [London: Thames & Hudson, 1971], 67). Membership in this community came only after elaborate training followed by initiation rituals such as baptism, and each member was kept aware by a "formidable penitential system" of their difference from those who did not belong (Ibid., 68).

21. The contrast with the Jewish synagogue, from which the Christian Church emerged, is striking. There was but a single Jewish Temple, once located in Jerusalem, and only there could sacrifice be offered to God. After the year 70 and the Temple's destruction by the Romans, no other place on earth offered to faithful Jews the sacred recesses of the "Holy of Holies." The synagogue was a place not for sacrifice but only for prayer.

22. Pierre du Bourguet, *Early Christian Art* (New York: Reynal, 1971), 32.

23. Stark argues that this aspect of early Christianity is one of the principle reasons for its rapid growth and development and notes that "Christian values of love and charity had, from the beginning, been translated into norms of social service and community solidarity" (*Rise of Christianity,* 74). He points out that in Christianity there exists a concept "alien to paganism...the notion that because God loves humanity, Christians cannot please God unless they love one another....Indeed they

must demonstrate their love through sacrifice on behalf of one another" (Ibid., 86).

24. Grabar, *Christian Iconography,* 22.

25. Hopkins, *Discovery of DuraEuropos,* 110.

26. Bourguet, *Early Christian Art,* 22.

27. "Symbolism was typical of the entire epoch. Oriental influence, and more particularly the mystery religions, had planted it in every mind." Ibid., 52.

28. "The earliest known representation of Christ…," according to F. van der Meer, *Early Christian Art* (London: Faber & Faber, 1967), 86.

29. "The scene of the Resurrection is a rare version, with no angel and with an enormous closed sarcophagus.…It is more than a half-century earlier than the other representations of the same scene at Rome…" (Grabar, *Christian Iconography,* 21).

CHAPTER 8 Death and Belief:
The Roman Catacombs

1. Richard Krautheimer, *Early Christian and Byzantine Architecture* (New Haven: Yale University Press, 1986), 29.

2. Pierre du Bourguet, *Early Christian Art* (New York: Reynal, 1971), 39.

3. Fabrizio Mancinell, *The Catacombs of Rome and the Origins of Christianity* (Firenze: Scala, 1981), 7.

4. Krautheimer, *Christian and Byzantine Architecture,* 26.

5. Mircea Eleade, *A History of Religious Ideas. Vol. 3: From Muhammad to the Age of Reforms* (Chicago: University of Chicago Press, 1985), 51.

6. Bourguet, *Early Christian Art,* 42.

7. Jean Lassus, *The Early Christian and Byzantine World* (New York: McGraw Hill, 1967), 13.

8. Ibid.

9. Current thinking argues that the villa of a Roman senatorial family named Acilii once stood here, near a stone quarry that had been abandoned after a rock slide closed its entrance. Mancinell, *Catacombs of Rome,* 28.

10. Sandro Carletti, *Guide to the Catacombs of Priscilla* (Vatican City: Pontifical Commission for Sacred Archaeology, 1982), 31.

11. Greek was frequently spoken by educated Romans, and indeed the entire New Testament is written in Greek. There is no reason to think this place was somehow devoted to specifically Greek immigrants to Rome.

12. See Mancinelli, *Catacombs of Rome*, 29. Vincenzo Fiocchi Nicolai more recently suggests dating the catacomb of Priscilla "nei primi decenni del III secolo…" in Vincenzo Fiocchi Nicolai and Fabrizio Bisconti, Danilo Massoleni, *Le Catacombe Cristiane di Roma* (Regensburg: Schnell & Steiner, 1998), 17.

13. Lassus, *Christian and Byzantine World,* 13.

14. Psalm 105 is a useful example of this kind of structure, hymning a long series of episodes from Jewish history as illustrations of God's strength and patience.

15. Which anticipates Saint Francis and his "Canticle of Brother Sun." Thomas of Celano acknowledges the influence of the Book of Daniel on Saint Francis. See Ignatius Brady, OFM, *The Writings of Saint Francis of Assisi* (Assisi: Casa Editrice Francescana, ca. 1983), 20.

16. Carletti, *Guide to the Catacombs of Priscilla,* 25.

17. Ibid.

18. Ibid., 26.

19. Mancinelli, *Catacombs of Rome,* 28.

20. Carletti, *Guide to the Catacombs of Priscilla,* 29.

21. Ibid.

22. F. van der Meer, *Early Christian Art* (London: Faber & Faber, 1967), 92.

23. Ibid., 93.

24. Ibid., 96.

25. Ibid., 97.

26. "The new *Sol Invictus, Sol Salutis, Sol Iustitiae.* The pagan type of the sun-god in his chariot, or apotheosis of an emperor or a hero, has been adapted to the Christian belief in the risen God…" John Beckwith, *Early Christian and Byzantine Art* [Harmondsworth, UK: Penguin, 1970], 8).

27. See Bourguet, *Early Christian Art,* 10 and 53.

28. Ibid., 9.

29. Ibid., 37.

30. Ibid., 23.

31. Ibid., 49.

CHAPTER 9 Beginning Catholic Poetry: Prudentius

1. Peter Brown, *The Rise of Western Christendom* (Oxford: Blackwell, 1996), 22–23.

2. Richard Krautheimer, *Early Christian and Byzantine Architecture* (New Haven: Yale University Press, 1986), 39.

3. Brown, *Rise of Western Christendom*, 35.

4. Ibid., 36.

5. Krautheimer, *Christian and Byzantine Architecture*, 59.

6. Terrot Reaveley Glover, *Life and Letters in the Fourth Century* (New York: Russell & Russell, 1968), 254.

7. H. J. Thomson, trans., *Prudentius* (Cambridge, MA: Harvard University Press, 1949), I, viii.

8. Ibid., I, xii.

9. F. J. E. Raby, *A History of Christian-Latin Poetry: From the Beginnings to the Close of the Middle Ages* (Oxford: Clarendon Press, 1956), 71.

10. Glover, *Life and Letters in the Fourth Century*, 264.

11. Macklin Smith, *Prudentius' Psychomachia: A Reexamination* (Princeton: Princeton University Press, 1976), xi.

12. Thomson, *Prudentius*, I, viii.

13. Ibid., I, 76–85.

14. David R. Slavitt, trans., *The Hymns of Prudentius: The Cathemerinon; or The Daily Round* (Baltimore: Johns Hopkins University Press, 1996).

15. C. E. Bennett, trans., *Horace: The Odes and Epodes*, Odes I, 11 (Cambridge, MA: Harvard University Press, 1914), 33.

16. Odes I, 28. Ibid., 77.

17. Odes I, 25. Ibid., 71.

18. Odes, I, 1. Ibid., 5.

19. Thomson, *Prudentius*, I, 15.

20. Hymnus II, ll. 49–52. Ibid., 14.

21. Ibid., 21.

22. Ibid., 76.

23. Slavitt, *Hymns*, 4.

24. Slavitt, *Hymns*, 1–2.

25. We recall Christ as the sun-god Apollo in Mausoleum M of the Julii in Rome discussed in chapter 5.

26. Hymn XI. Thomson, *Prudentius*, I, 99, 101.

27. Ibid., 85.

28. Hymn VIII. Ibid., 73.

29. Hymn V. Ibid., 45.

30. Hymn III. Ibid., 23.

31. Hymn XII. Slavitt, *Hymns*, 57–58.

32. Bennett, *Horace*, 39.

33. Hymn VI, 57. Thomson, *Prudentius*, 52.

34. Hymn XII, 183–84. Ibid., 112–113.

35. Hymn V. Slavitt, H*ymns*, 18–19.

36. Hymn III. Ibid., 8.
37. C. H. Lawrence, *Medieval Monasticism,* 2nd ed. (London: Longman, 1989), 3.
38. Ibid., 8.
39. Ibid., 14.
40. Ibid., 16.
41. Slavitt, *Hymns,* 2.
42. Ibid., 3.
43. Thomson, *Prudentius,* I, 87, 89.
44. Hymn III, ll. 201 and 205. Ibid., I, 30.
45. Ibid., I, 3.
46. Ibid., I, 23.
47. Ibid., I, 92.
48. Ibid., I, 97.
49. Hymn V, ll. 1 and 4. Ibid., I, 39.
50. Hymn II. Ibid., I, 109.

CHAPTER 10 The Celtic North and *The Book of Kells*

1. Nigel Pennick, *The Celtic Cross* (London: Blandford, 1997), 13–14.
2. Ibid., 14.
3. Bernard Meehan, *The Book of Kells* (London: Thames & Hudson, 1994), 10.
4. Tomas Owen Clancy and Gilbert Markus, *Iona: The Earliest Poetry of a Celtic Monastery* (Edinburgh: Edinburgh University Press, 1995), 6.
5. Peter Brown, *The Rise of Western Christendom* (Oxford: Blackwell, 1996), 205.
6. Clancy and Marcus, *Iona,* 11.
7. The *Altus Prosator,* following long-standing Christian tradition, sees this as Satan's "second" fall. Ibid., 47. His first, from proudly refusing to follow divine commands, is also described earlier in the poem; Ibid., 45.
8. Ibid., 47.
9. Ibid.
10. Ibid.
11. Ibid., 49.
12. Ibid., 58.
13. Ibid., 46.
14. Ibid., 47.
15. Ibid., 59.
16. Ibid., 45.

17. Ibid., 44.

18. Ibid., 49.

19. Ibid., 47.

20. Ibid., 53.

21. Meehan, *Book of Kells,* 10–14.

22. Ibid., 9.

23. G. Frank Mitchell et al., *Treasures of Irish Art: 1500 BC–1500 AD* (New York: Knopf, 1977), 101.

24. Meehan, *Book of Kells,* 9.

25. C. R. Dodwell, *Painting in Europe: 800–1200* (Harmondsworth, UK: Penguin Books, 1971), 5.

26. Quoted in Meehan, *Book of Kells,* 89.

27. Brown, *Rise of Western Christendom,* 296.

28. Meehan, *Book of Kells:* 22. Based upon "a faith…in the validity of visual images as signals from man to God, no less acceptable than prayer" (George Henderson, *From Durrow to Kells: The Insular Gospel-Books: 650–800* [London: Thames & Hudson, 1987], 198). Note unexpected stress: picture is a prayer addressed to God, not a visible message of God's meaning.

29. Each page or folio of the manuscript is given a number. The first side of the page is called the "recto" and signified by "r," while the second side is the "verso" signified by "v."

30. Dodwell, *Painting in Europe,* 4.

31. Meehan, *Book of Kells,* 48.

32. Henderson, *From Durrow to Kells,* 153.

33. Meehan, *Book of Kells,* 41.

34. M. Swanton, *English Literature before Chaucer* (London: Longman, 1987), 87.

35. Quoted in Meehan, *Book of Kells,* 89.

36. Meehan, *Book of Kells,* 29.

37. Clancy and Marcus, *Iona,* 49.

38. Mitchell, *Treasures of Irish Art,* 101.

39. Meehan, *Book of Kells,* 64, reads these flames as Christ declaiming the word of God.

CHAPTER 11 Warrior Christianity I: The Franks and the *Utrecht Psalter*

1. Flavius Claudius Julianus (331?–363), later crowned emperor (reigned 361–363). Raised a Christian, he later reverted to paganism and so became known to Christian historians as Julian the Apostate.

2. His conversion came during a crucial battle in which Clovis called on the Christian god for help. His prayer, as reported by Gregory of Tours, illustrates the kind of reasoning typical of early Frankish monarchs: "Jesus Christ, whom Clotilde declares to be the son of the living God, who art said to give aid to those in distress, and to bestow victory on those who hope in thee, I beseech the glory of thy aid, with the vow that if thou wilt grant me victory over these enemies and I shall know that power which she says that people dedicated in thy name have from thee, I will believe in thee and be baptized in thy name. For I have invoked my own gods, but, as I have found, they have withdrawn from aiding me; therefore I believe they possess no power, for they do not help those who obey them. Now I call upon thee, desire to believe in thee—only let me be rescued from my adversaries" (Gregory of Tours, *History of the Franks*, trans. E. Brehaut (New York: Norton, 1969), 40.

3. Gregory of Tours, *History of the Franks*, 1.

4. C. R. Dodwell, *Painting in Europe: 800–1200* (Harmondsworth, UK: Penguin Books, 1971), 2.

5. Peter Lasko, *Ars Sacra* (Harmondsworth, UK: Penguin, 1972), 33.

6. John Beckwith, *Early Medieval Art: Carolingian, Ottonian, Romanesque* (London: Thames & Hudson, 1996), 29.

7. Including Rabanus Maurus (776–856), later archbishop of Mainz and the probable author of the hymn, "Veni, Creator Spiritus."

8. Beckwith, *Early Medieval Art*, 11.

9. Brown, *Rise of Western Christendom*, 277.

10. Beckwith, *Early Medieval Art*, 27.

11. Ibid., 30.

12. Lasko, *Ars Sacra*, 33.

13. The dates are debated. These come from Beckwith, *Early Medieval Art*, 43.

14. Dodwell, *Painting in Europe*, 30, guesses between 816 and 823; Beckwith, *Early Medieval Art*, 44, "the third decade of the ninth century."

15. Under the directorship of Koert van der Horst and Frits Ankersmit. All of my subsequent references to the *Utrecht Psalter* come from this source, including its Latin transcript of the Gallican version of the Vulgate Psalms. The English translation of the Psalm texts in my text come from the NRSV, as elsewhere in this book. In my discussion I refer to the number of the Psalm in question (see note 23), that number then referring to the "page" of the CD-ROM where a digitized version of the whole page of the *Utrecht Psalter*, a transcription of the Latin text as well as an English translation, and a commentary on the images can all be found.

16. David Diringer, *The Illuminated Book: Its History and Production* (London: Faber & Faber, 1967), 206.

17. Beckwith, *Early Medieval Art,* 43–45.

18. Lasko, *Ars Sacra,* 35.

19. Dodwell, *Painting in Europe,* 31.

20. Ibid., 30.

21. Dirniger, *Illuminated Book,* 205.

22. Beckwith, *Early Medieval Art,* 44.

23. The numeration of the Psalms differs within different editions, the original Hebrew text, the King James Version, and most modern translations using one system of numbering; the Greek Septuagint and the Latin Vulgate, which was commonly used in the Catholic Church during this period, using another. Because the *Utrecht Psalter* reproduces the Vulgate Latin text and yet most modern translations of the Bible use the original Hebrew version, I cite both numbers, first the Hebrew/modern, second the Septuagint/Vulgate. Hence the famous twenty-third Psalm, "The Lord is my shepherd," is here numbered 23(22). Readers should keep in mind that the *Utrecht Psalte*r always uses the Vulgate number, that is, the second number to appear in each of my citations.

24. I'm grateful to James Walsh, SJ, for drawing my attention to this probable reference.

25. Diringer, *Illuminated Book,* 197.

26. Dodwell, *Painting in Europe,* 21.

27. Beckwith, *Early Medieval Art,* 9.

28. It must be pointed out that individual acts of charity do appear. In Psalm 72(71), for example, for v. 12—"For he delivers the needy when they call, the poor and those who have no helper"—we see a rich man distributing grain to a crowd of children and adults, their hands extended begging, while in Psalm 112(111), "those who fear the Lord" distribute bread to widows and orphans and to cripples leaning on staffs.

29. Images of the Virgin Mary are rare in the *Utrecht Psalter,* perhaps simply because the Psalms do not offer many instances in which such typological anticipations could be found.

30. In chapter 6 we saw Prudentius elaborating the same point in his Hymn IX.

CHAPTER 12 Warrior Christianity II: The Saxons and *The Heliand*

1. Peter Brown, *The Rise of Western Christendom* (Oxford: Blackwell, 1996), 258.

2. Capitulum 26–27. See G. Ronald Murphy, SJ, trans., *The*

Heliand: The Saxon Gospel (New York: Oxford University Press, 1992), 200.

3. G. Ronald Murphy, SJ, *The Saxon Savior: The Germanic Transformation of the Gospel in the Ninth-Century Heliand* (New York: Oxford University Press, 1989), 77.

4. Murphy, *Saxon Savior,* 66.

5. Ibid., 62.

6. Ibid., 17.

7. Ibid., 95.

8. Ibid., 107–8.

9. Ibid., 34.

10. Brown, *Rise of Western Christendom,* 265.

11. Murphy, *Saxon Savior,* 15.

12. Brown, *Rise of Western Christendom,* 273.

13. Murphy, *Saxon Savior,* 27.

14. Ibid., 4.

15. Murphy, *Heliand,* 146.

16. Murphy, *Saxon Savior,* 20.

17. Murphy, *Heliand,* 5–6. Consistent with his own image world, the *Heliand* poet refers to urban centers not as cities but as "hill-forts."

18. Ibid., xvii.

19. Ibid., 3–4.

20. Ibid., 4.

21. Ibid., 40.

22. Ibid., 54.

23. Ibid., 55.

24. Ibid.

25. Ibid., 86.

26. Ibid., 87.

27. Ibid., 19.

28. Ibid., 12.

29. Ibid., 13.

30. Ibid., 7.

31. Ibid., 7–8.

32. Ibid., 8. This is the root of our modern word *truth.*

33. Ibid., 31.

34. Ibid., 33.

35. Ibid., 16.

36. Ibid.

37. Ibid., 17.

38. Ibid., 22.

39. Ibid., 21.

40. Ibid., 25.

41. Ibid., 26.

42. Ibid., 29.

43. Ibid., 21.

44. Ibid., 27.

45. Ibid., 24. The "middle world" is the Germanic way of describing the earth, Midgard, as John the Baptist's preaching "to announce Christ's coming and powerful strength throughout this middle world" (Ibid., 31).

46. Ibid., 28.

47. Ibid., 42.

48. Ibid., 41.

49. Ibid., 74.

50. Ibid., 75.

51. Ibid., 67.

52. Ibid., 68.

53. Ibid., 69.

54. Ibid., 87.

55. Ibid., 101.

56. This detail, from John 19:34, was read from the early days of the church as a symbolic foreshadowing of the sacraments of baptism and of the Eucharist—springing directly from the fatal spear wound in Christ's side.

57. Ibid., 148.

58. Ibid., 130.

59. Ibid., 146.

60. Ibid., 148.

61. Ibid., 172.

62. Ibid., 150.

63. Ibid., 152.

64. Ibid., 153.

65. Ibid., 158.

66. Ibid., 159.

67. Ibid.

68. Ibid.

69. Ibid., 160.

70. Ibid.

71. Ibid., 161.

72. Murphy, *Saxon Savior,* 107–8.

73. Murphy, *Heliand,* 162.

74. Ibid., 163.

75. Ibid., 164.

76. Ibid., 165.

77. Ibid.

78. Ibid.
79. Ibid., 166.
80. Ibid., 170.
81. Ibid., 156.
82. Ibid., 157. It is at moments such as this that the influence of later theological developments on the poet of the *Heliand* is evident.
83. Ibid., 157.
84. Ibid.
85. Ibid., 162.
86. Ibid.
87. Ibid., 168.
88. Ibid., 174.
89. Ibid., 177.
90. Ibid., 179.
91. Ibid.
92. See also Deuteronomy 21:22 for a much earlier version of the tree of execution.
93. Ibid., 182.
94. Ibid.
95. Ibid., 184.
96. Ibid.
97. Ibid., 187.
98. Ibid., 183.
99. Ibid., 186.
100. Ibid.
101. Murphy, *Saxon Savior,* 110.
102. Murphy, *Heliand,* 188.
103. Ibid.
104. Ibid., 189.
105. Ibid.
106. Ibid., 193.
107. Ibid., 195.

Bibliography

Anon. *Latin Psalter in the University Library of Utrecht.* London: Spencer, Sawyer, Bird, n.d.

Arasse, Daniel et al. *Botticelli and Fillipino.* Milan: Skira, 2004.

Augustine of Hippo. *City of God.* Henry Bettenson, trans. London: Penguin, 1984.

———. *Confessions.* R. S. Pine-Coffin, trans. London: Penguin, 1961.

Bann, Stephen. *The True Vine: On Visual Representation and the Western Tradition.* Cambridge, UK: Cambridge University Press, 1989.

Bataille, Georges. *Eroticism: Death and Sensuality.* San Francisco: City Lights Books, 1986.

Beckwith, John. *Early Christian and Byzantine Art.* Harmondsworth, UK: Penguin, 1970.

———. *Early Medieval Art: Carolingian, Ottonian, Romanesque.* London: Thames and Hudson, 1996.

Beckwith, Sarah. *Christ's Body.* London: Routledge, 1993.

Bennett, C. E., trans. *Horace: The Odes and Epodes.* The Loeb Classical Library. Cambridge, MA: Harvard University Press, 1914.

Blunt, Anthony. *Artistic Theory in Italy.* Oxford: Clarendon Press, 1940.

Bonaventure. *The Soul's Journey into God.* Ewert Cousins, trans. New York: Paulist Press, 1978.

Bossy, John. "The Mass as a Social Institution 1200–1700." *Past and Present* 100 (Aug 1983): 29–61.

Bourguet, Pierre du. *Early Christian Art.* New York: Reynal, 1971.

Brady, Ignatius. *The Writings of St. Francis of Assisi.* Assisi: Edizioni Porziuncola, ca. 1983.

Brandon, S. G. F. *Man and God in Art and Ritual: A Study of Iconography, Architecture and Ritual Action as Primary Evidence of Religious Belief and Practice.* New York: Charles Scribner's Sons, 1975.

Brown, George Hardin. "Old English Verse as a Medium for a Christian

Theology." In Phyllis Rugg Brown et al., *Modes of Interpretation in Old English Literature.* Toronto: University of Toronto Press, 1986.

Brown, Jonathan. *The Golden Age of Painting in Spain.* New Haven: Yale University Press, 1991.

Brown, Peter. *The Cult of the Saints: Its Rise and Function in Latin Christianity.* Chicago: University of Chicago Press, 1981.

———. *The Rise of Western Christendom.* Oxford: Blackwell, 1996.

———. *The World of Late Antiquity: From Marcus Aurelius to Muhammud.* London: Thames and Hudson, 1971.

Brown, Raymond et al., eds. *The New Jerome Biblical Commentary.* Englewood Cliffs, NJ: Prentice Hall, 1990.

Carletti, Sandro. *Guide to the Catacombs of Priscilla.* Vatican City: Pontifical Commission for Sacred Archaeology, 1982.

Carroll, Robert and Stephen Prickett, eds. *The Bible: Authorized King James Version with Apocrypha.* Oxford: Oxford University Press, 1997.

Clancy, Tomas Owen and Gilbert Markus. *Iona: The Earliest Poetry of a Celtic Monastery.* Edinburgh: Edinburgh University Press, 1995.

Clarkson, John et al. *The Church Teaches: Documents of the Church in English Translation.* St. Louis, MO: B. Herder, 1955.

Cornini, Guido. *Botticelli.* Florence: Giunti, 2004.

Cunningham, Lawrence. *Saint Francis of Assisi.* San Francisco: Harper and Row, 1981.

Cyril of Jerusalem. *The Works of St. Cyril of Jerusalem.* 2 vols. Leo P. McCauley et al., trans. Washington, DC: Catholic University Press of America, 1969.

Dante. *The Divine Comedy of Dante Alighieri: Purgatorio.* Allen Mandlebaum, trans. New York: Bantam Books, 1984.

———. *The Inferno.* John Ciardi, trans. Introduction by Archibald T. MacAlister. New York: New American Library, 1954.

———. *The Paradiso.* John Ciardi, trans. Introduction by John Freccero. New York: New American Library, 1970.

———. *The Purgatorio.* John Ciardi, trans.. Introduction by Archibald T. MacAlister. New York: New American Library, 1957.

Deimling, Barbara. *Botticelli.* Cologne: Benedikt Taschen Verlag, 2000.

Dihel, Patrick S. *The Medieval European Religious Lyric: An Ars Poetica.* Berkeley: University of California Press, 1985.

Diringer, David. *The Illuminated Book: Its History and Production.* London: Faber and Faber, 1967.

Dodwell, C. R. *Painting in Europe: 800–1200.* Harmondsworth, UK: Penguin Books, 1971.

Drabkin, William. *Beethoven: Missa Solemnis*. Cambridge, UK: Cambridge University Press, 1991.

Eckehard, Simon, ed. *The Theatre of Medieval Europe: New Research in Early Drama*. Cambridge, UK: Cambridge University Press, 1991.

Egan, M. Clement. *The Poems of Prudentius*. 2 vols. Washington, DC: Catholic University of America Press, 1962.

Eliade, Mircea. *A History of Religious Ideas. Vol. 2: From Gautama Buddah to the Triumph of Christianity*. Chicago: University of Chicago Press, 1982.

———. *Vol. 3: From Muhammad to the Age of Reforms*. Chicago: University of Chicago Press, 1985.

Ellrodt, Robert. *Seven Metaphysical Poets: A Structural Study of the Unchanging Self*. Oxford: Oxford University Press, 2000.

Enders, Jody. *The Medieval Theater of Cruelty: Rhetoric, Memory, Violence*. Ithaca: Cornell University Press, 1999.

Evans, G. Blakemore et al. *The Riverside Shakespeare*. Boston: Houghton Mifflin, 1974.

Ferrua, Antonio. *Le Pitture della nuove catacomba di via Latina. Monumenti di Antichita Cristina*. II. Serie VIII. Citta del Vaticano: Pontifico Instituto di Archeologia Cristina, 1960.

Finnegan, Jack. *The Archeology of the New Testament: The Life of Jesus and the Beginning of the Early Church*. Princeton: Princeton University Press, 1969.

Gallagher, Tag. *The Adventures of Roberto Rossellini*. New York: Da Capo, 1998.

———. *John Ford: The Man and His Films*. Berkeley: University of California Press, 1986.

Geza, Vermes. *The Religion of Jesus the Jew*. Minneapolis: Fortress Press, 1993.

Gilbert, Katherine Everett and Helmut Kuhn. *A History of Esthetics*. New York: Dover, 1972.

Gill, Michael. *Image of the Body: Aspects of the Nude*. London: Bodley Head, 1989.

Glover, Terrot Reaveley. *Life and Letters in the Fourth Century*. New York: Russell and Russell, 1968.

Godden, Malcom and Michael Lapidge, eds. *The Cambridge Companion to Old English Literature*. Cambridge, UK: Cambridge University Press, 1991.

Grabar, Andre. *Christian Iconography: A Study of Its Origins*. Princeton: Princeton University Press, 1968.

Grant, Michael. *Jesus*. London: Weidenfeld and Nicolson, 1977.

Greeley, Andrew J. *The Catholic Imagination.* Berkeley: University of California Press, 2000.

———. "The Catholic Imagination and the Catholic University." *America* 164:10 (March 16, 1991): 285–88.

Greene, Graham. *The Power and the Glory.* London: Penguin, 1980.

Gregory of Nazianzus. *Three Poems.* D. M. Meehan, trans. Washington, DC: Catholic University Press, 1987.

Gregory of Tours. *History of the Franks.* E. Brehaut, trans. New York: Norton, 1969.

Hardison, O. B. Jr. *Christian Rite and Christian Drama in the Middle Ages.* Baltimore: Johns Hopkins University Press, 1965.

Healy, Thomas F. *Richard Crashaw.* Leiden: E. J. Brill, 1986.

Hellwig, Monika K. *Understanding Catholicism.* 2nd ed. New York: Paulist Press, 2002.

Henderson, George. *From Durrow to Kells: The Insular Gospel-Books: 650–800.* London: Thames and Hudson, 1987.

Herrin, Judith. *The Formation of Christendom.* Princeton: Princeton University Press, 1987.

Homza, Lu Ann. *Religious Authority in the Spanish Renaissance.* Baltimore: Johns Hopkins University Press, 2000.

Hopkins, Clark. *The Discovery of DuraEuropos.* Bernard Goldman, ed. New Haven: Yale University Press, 1979.

Hopkins, Keith. *A World Full of Gods: The Strange Triumph of Christianity.* New York: Plume, 2001.

Horst, Koert van der and Frits Ankersmit. *The Utrecht Psalter: Picturing the Psalms of David.* Utrecht: Utrecht University Library, 1996. CD-ROM.

James, Mervyn. "Ritual, Drama and Social Body in the Late Medieval English Town." *Past and Present* 98 (Feb 1983): 3–29.

Jeffrey, David Lyle. *People of the Book: Christian Identity and Literary Culture.* Grand Rapids: William B. Eedrmans, 1996.

John of Damascus. *On the Divine Images.* David Anderson, trans. Crestwood, NY: St. Vladimir's Seminary Press, 1980.

John of the Cross. *The Poems of St. John of the Cross.* Roy Campbell, trans. London: Harvill, 1951.

Kelley, J. N. D. *Early Christian Creeds.* New York: David McKay, 1960.

Kleist, James A. *The Epistles of St. Clement of Rome and St. Ignatius of Antioch.* Westminster, MD: Newman Press, 1949.

Knipping, J. B. *Iconography of the Counter-Reformation in the Netherlands: Heaven on Earth.* 2 vols. Leiden: B. de Graaf, 1974.

Krautheimer, Richard. *Early Christian and Byzantine Architecture.* New Haven: Yale University Press, 1986.

Lasko, Peter. *Ars Sacra*. Harmondsworth, UK: Penguin, 1972.

Lassus, Jean. *The Early Christian and Byzantine World*. New York: McGraw Hill, 1967.

Lawrence, C. H. *Medieval Monasticism*. 2nd ed. London: Longman, 1989.

Low, Anthony. *Love's Architecture: Devotional Modes in Seventeenth-Century English Poetry*. New York: New York University Press, 1978.

Lynch, W. F. *Christ and Apollo: Dimensions of the Literary Imagination*. New York: Sheed and Ward, 1960.

Mancinelli, Fabrizio. *The Catacombs of Rome and the Origins of Christianity*. Firenze: Scala, 1981.

McBrien, Richard P. *Catholicism: New Study Edition*. San Francisco: HarperSanFrancisco, 1994.

Meehan, Bernard. *The Book of Kells*. London: Thames and Hudson, 1994.

Meer, F. van der. *Early Christian Art*. London: Faber and Faber, 1967.

Meer, F. van der and Christine Mohrmann. *Atlas of the Early Christian World*. London: Thomas Nelson, 1958.

Meyer-Baer, Kathi. *Music of the Spheres and the Dance of Death: Studies in Musical Iconography*. New York: Da Capo, 1984.

Mitchell, G. Frank, et al. *Treasures of Irish Art: 1500 BC–1500 AD*. New York: Knopf, 1977.

Morgan, David. *Visual Piety: A History and Theory of Popular Religious Images*. Berkeley: University of California Press, 1998.

Muir, Lynette R. *The Biblical Drama of Medieval Europe*. Cambridge, UK: Cambridge University Press, 1995.

Murphy, G. Ronald, trans. *The Heliand: The Saxon Gospel*. New York: Oxford University Press, 1992.

———. *The Saxon Savior: The Germanic Transformation of the Gospel in the Ninth-Century Heliand*. New York: Oxford University Press, 1989.

Murray, Linda. *Michelangelo*. London: Thames and Hudson, 1980.

Nichols, Aidan. *The Art of God Incarnate: Theology and Symbol from Genesis to the Twentieth Century*. New York: Paulist Press, 1980.

Nicolai, Vincenzo Fiocchi and Fabrizio Bisconti, Danilo Massoleni. *Le Catacombe Cristiane di Roma*. Regensburg: Schnell and Steiner, 1998.

O'Connell, Robert J. *Art and the Christian Intelligence in St. Augustine*. Cambridge, MA: Harvard University Press, 1978.

Padovan, Richard. *Proportion: Science, Philosophy, Architecture*. London: E. and F. N. Spon, 1999.

Pagels, Elaine. *The Origin of Satan*. New York: Vintage, 1996.

Paolucci, Antonio, ed. *Il Battistero di San Giovanni a Firenze*. Modena: Franco Cosimo Pannini Editores, 1994.

Patrides, C. A. *The Grand Design of God: The Literary Form of the Christian View of History*. London: Routledge and Kegan Paul, 1972.

Pena, Ignatio. *The Christian Art of Byzantine Syria*. [no city given]: Garnet, 1996.

Pennick, Nigel. *The Celtic Cross*. London: Blandford, 1997.

Pseudo-Dionysius. *The Complete Works of Pseudo-Dionysius*. Colm Luibheid, trans. New York: Paulist Press, 1987.

Raby, F. J. E. *A History of Christian-Latin Poetry: From the Beginnings to the Close of the Middle Ages*. Oxford: Clarendon Press, 1956.

Rossellini, Roberto. *Open City*. Excelsa Films, 1945.

Rothschild, E. F. and E. H. Wilkins. "Hell in the Florentine Baptistry Mosaic and in Giotto's Paduan Fresco." *Art Studies* 6 (1928): 31–35.

Sachs, Curt. *World History of the Dance*. New York: Norton, 1937.

Saint-Saens, Alain. *Art and Faith in Tridentine Spain: 1545–1690*. New York: Peter Lang, 1995.

———. *Religion, Body and Gender in Early Modern Spain*. Lewiston: Edwin Mellen, 1991.

Saslow, James M., trans. *The Poetry of Michelangelo*. New Haven: Yale University Press, 1991.

Scarry, Elaine. *The Body in Pain: The Making and Unmaking of a World*. New York: Oxford University Press, 1985.

Screech, M. A. *Laughter at the Foot of the Cross*. London: Allan Lane, the Penguin Press, 1997.

Sendler, Egon. *The Icon: Image of the Invisible*. Torrance, CA: Oakwood, 1988.

Sherry, Norman. *The Life of Graham Greene. Vol. 1: 1904–1939*. New York: Viking, 1989.

Simson, Otto von. *The Gothic Cathedral*. Princeton: Princeton University Press, 1974.

Skrine, Peter. *The Baroque: Literature and Culture in Seventeenth-Century Europe*. London: Methuen, 1978.

Slavitt, David R., trans. *The Hymns of Prudentius: The Cathemerinon; or The Daily Round*. Baltimore: Johns Hopkins Universirty Press, 1996.

Smith, E. Baldwin. *The Dome: A Study in the History of Ideas*. Princeton: Princeton University Press, 1950.

Smith, Macklin. *Prudentius' Psychomachia: A Reexamination*. Princeton: Princeton University Press, 1976.

Snow-Smith, Joanne. "Michelangelo's Christian Neoplatonic Aesthetic of Beauty in his Early *Oeuvre*: The *nuditas virtualis* Image." In Francis

Ames-Lewis and Mary Rogers, *Concepts of Beauty in Renaissance Art*. Aldershot, UK: Ashgate, 1998.

Solomon, Maynard. *Beethoven*. New York: Schirmer Books, 1977.

———. *Beethoven Essays*. Cambridge, MA: Harvard University Press, 1988.

Stark, Rodney. *The Rise of Christianity*. San Francisco: HarperSanFrancisco, 1997.

Stoichita, Victor I. *Visionary Experiences in the Golden Age of Spanish Art*. London: Realdion Books, 1995.

Swanton, M. *English Literature before Chaucer*. London: Longman, 1987.

Thomson, H. J., trans. *Prudentius*. 2 vols. Cambridge, MA: Harvard University Press, 1949.

Tronzo, William. *The Via Latina Catacomb: Imitation and Discontinuity in Fourth-Century Roman Painting*. University Park, PA: Penn State University Press, 1966.

Underhill, Evelyn. *The Miracles of Our Lady Saint Mary*. London: William Heinemann, 1905.

Vallee, Gerard. *The Shaping of Christianity: The History and Literature of Its Formative Centuries (100–800)*. New York: Paulist Press, 1999.

Vermes, Geza. *The Religion of Jesus the Jew*. Minneapolis: Fortress Press, 1993.

Warnke, Frank J. *European Metaphysical Poetry*. New Haven: Yale University Press, 1961.

Waterworth, J., trans. *The Canons and Decress of the Sacred and Oecumenical Council of Trent*. London: C. Dolman, 1853.

Wilkins, E. H. "Dante and the Mosaics of His 'bel San Giovanni.'" *Speculum*, 2, 1(927): 1–10.

Wills, Garry. *St. Augustine*. New York: Viking, 1999.

Wittkower, Rudolf. *Architectural Principles in the Age of Humanism*. New York: Norton, 1962.

Study Guide

CHAPTER 1 Origins

1. What is the relationship of imagination to the teaching of Jesus, as that teaching is described in the Gospels?

2. Why, as a religious teacher, might Jesus have been led to use imagination so frequently? What could he avoid by not arguing as a philosopher or a theologian?

3. Although the Jesus of the Gospels never said anything about the arts, the church emerged as one of history's most important patrons of artistic creation. Three plausible explanations for this development are adaptation, imitation, and inspiration. How do these three explanations differ from one another?

4. Because of Jesus' way of teaching, the second explanation (imitation) made Catholic art inevitable. How did Jesus' manner of teaching constitute a generative example that became a model for imitation to be used by Christian artists for two millennia?

CHAPTER 2 Catholic Belief

1. *Catholic* and *Christian*—what does each of these words mean to you?

2. Is it a good or a bad idea to try to strike a clear distinction between these two words? What gains and losses will result if one insists upon that difference?

3. Is clarity on this issue bought at too great a price in terms of alienating non-Catholic Christians from all the other things this book has to say?

4. Discuss the meaning and some of the implications of the terms *incarnation, redemption, sacramentality,* and *community.*

CHAPTER 3 The World of Jesus' Imagination

1. How do you picture Jesus during the years when he was teaching? What did he look like? How did he address other people? Who would have been the members of his usual audience? What would their reactions have been?

2. From what you know of Jesus' recorded teachings, what does Jesus imagine, and what does he ignore? How would that have had an impact upon his first listeners, and upon the generations to follow?

3. Why might Jesus' ways of imagining and speaking have remained accessible to the amazing range of people throughout the world and throughout time who have listened to his teaching?

4. Jesus was a Jewish teacher, and he thought and spoke within the framework of a Jewish theory of language that sees important connections between God and words. Discuss the concept of God as a user of language, and God as, in some ways, "the Word." What implications does this have for you who are, individually, a user of language?

5. In what ways does Jesus speak as a poet? Can you cite specific instances of any of these ways in Jesus' words as recorded in the Gospels? OR give examples from your favorite poets?

6. Following are the expressive strategies with which Jesus worked. His teaching and preaching are based upon them, and consequently they entered into the way Catholics have thought and imagined ever since. What does each term mean?

- Analogy

- Parable

- Paradox

- Irony and joke

- Division

- Typology

CHAPTER 4 Jesus' Teaching and Catholic Belief

The Gospels, which were written within a few decades after Jesus' death, anticipate what is to come. They depict Jesus during his public life on earth but already anticipating all that was yet to happen.

1. How do the four central traits of Catholic belief—incarnation, redemption, sacraments, community—appear in the Gospels and in Jesus' teaching? In other words, how are the Gospels already functioning as witnesses of Catholic belief?

   - How, for example, could Jesus talk about redemption even before his redeeming death on the cross?

   - How could he talk about the sacraments and the church before there was a church?

2. How is Jesus' teaching about God as Father also read as Jesus' description of himself (God as Son) in examples such as that of the good shepherd?

3. How does Jesus' use of typology help prepare the way for an understanding of redemption? How does it anticipate church, with its community and its communal sacraments?

4. In what ways does analogy—for example, the church as the body of Christ and Jesus as the bread of life—continue to be essential to Catholic thinking? What other analogies form part of the basic structure and the everyday experience of Catholic life?

CHAPTER 5 The First Christian Narratives: Four Biographies of Jesus

Christianity is rooted in a person, and the story of that person's life and death is the core meaning of Christianity and of Catholicism.

1. Consider the implications of this fact.

2. In what ways does this biographical character of Christianity make it different from Judaism, Islam, or Buddhism?

3. What might be some of the factors that led the earliest Christians, in telling the kernel story of Jesus, to focus on his death? Why is death, and that death in particular, central to Christianity?

4. Consider how our Western concepts of history, time, and change have been shaped, at least in part, by the characteristic linearity of the Christian concept of time. How has that helped to condition the ways we think about our own lives, about history, and about the past and future?

CHAPTER 6 Saint Paul and Autobiography

1. How does Paul's way of imagining his world seem to differ from that of Jesus?

2. How does Paul act in a complementary way to Jesus? How might he be understood to be filling in, in some ways, aspects of mind and of human experience not so dominant in Jesus' world?

3. How, on the other hand, do forms of expression already present in Jesus' teaching recur, sometimes with a different emphasis, in Paul's writings?

4. In Paul's letters there emerges the outline of the first Catholic autobiography, one that will serve as a model for later thinking about how each Christian relates to

God. What do you consider to be a crucial element in this autobiographical paradigm?

5. Can you recall later examples of Christians who were to follow Paul's lead in shaping their own lives—in such moments as the crucial decision to choose to join a Christian church, in facing opposition and danger, or in relying upon Christian hope to carry one through difficulties?

6. Catholic trust in redemption is central to Paul. How does Paul voice his own trust in that redemption? How did he find it validated by his own personal experience?

CHAPTER 7 The First Churches: Dura-Europos

1. What would you personally consider to be the irreducible minimum elements of a Catholic church? Would the house-church at Dura-Europos have satisfied your needs? What would you have found missing?

2. What stories did these early Christians choose to decorate the walls of this church? Why would they find these particular episodes from the Old and New Testaments so important?

3. What do their choices suggest to us about the things they believed in? To what degree do modern Catholics continue to share in those same beliefs?

4. To what degree do the people who painted these early frescoes participate in the way in which Jesus imagined? That is, in what ways do they show the inevitable, organic development of a Catholic way of imagining?

5. In what ways does the Dura-Europos house-church suggest to us the meaning of community in early Catholic belief? In what ways does it testify to how it felt to be a part of the Catholic community in this town early in the third century?

CHAPTER 8 Death and Belief: The Roman Catacombs

1. In what ways does the Catholic understanding of the meaning of death, and of the relationship of the living to those who have died, reflect characteristic Catholic belief in incarnation and redemption?

2. How might Jesus' words, "The child is not dead, but asleep," serve as a way into explaining the differences in this regard between Catholicism and other forms of religious belief and disbelief?

3. How did Jesus' imagined world help influence the iconography of the fresco decorations of the catacombs? In particular, discuss: (a) the importance of typological thinking not only to Jesus but also to these early Christians; (b) their frequent use of stories from the Hebrew Scriptures to picture their own trust in baptism; (c) their persistent reliance upon God's aid in times of trial and danger; (d) their deeply personal investment in the sacrament of the Eucharist.

4. How does the imagination picture belief through stories about people? How did the early church rely upon such picturing to express its faith and its hope?

CHAPTER 9 Beginning Catholic Poetry: Prudentius

Prudentius reconceived such traditional poetic themes as love, heroism, and beauty in a newly Christian way.

1. What themes from pagan literature did Prudentius choose to transform through the emerging Catholic imagination?

2. Catholic belief in incarnation plays a vital role in this process of transformation. How does Prudentius, at the beginning of the fifth century, express the view that God's

love and creative power are reflected in the beauty of the world as we find it?

3. Development of Catholic belief and understanding did not stop with the writing of the New Testament. How, thanks to the ongoing presence of the Holy Spirit, does our understanding of God, incarnation, redemption, and community continue to grow and develop?

4. Prudentius takes the poetic liberty of imagining himself back into scenes from scripture such as the "Slaughter of the Innocents." Do you think his elaborations on biblical scenes is an excessive or a permissible exercise in imaginative extrapolation?

5. How have the church year and the church day shaped time?

6. How has the singing or chanting of poetry been a constant feature of Catholic life?

CHAPTER 10 The Celtic North and *The Book of Kells*

1. What differences do you note between southern and northern Europe, in reference, for example, to food, clothing, and the characteristics of houses? How does the poem by Saint Columba, the *Altus Prosator,* reflect the northern world from which it comes? How does that cause interesting shifts in Catholic imaginative vision?

2. What implications are latent in the way such figures as Jesus, Mary, and angels are imagined in the *Book of Kells*—for example, Jesus as blond-haired and blue-eyed; Mary as stiff and powerful, an authoritative ruler?

3. What do you think of the "fantastic" images in *Kells,* such as the figures used to represent the four evangelists? Do you find them silly or intriguing?

4. Why do we find complexity and minuteness coupled with bold and dark framing on some of the pages of the *Kells* manuscript?

5. Does the *Kells* way of envisioning the character of God's creation resonate with the way the world looks to you? Or, if you were illuminating a manuscript, would you take a quite different approach?

Chapter 11 **Warrior Christianity I: The Franks and the *Utrecht Psalter***

1. The ninth-century Franks produced a manuscript of the Hebrew Psalms that illustrated the world as they saw it. What were some of the most pronounced elements of that worldview?

2. The *Utrecht Psalter* contains drawings that depict soldiers and their leaders, fighting, the horrors of war, and the suffering of the defeated. In what ways could such scenes enter into a work of the Catholic imagination?

3. How could these ninth-century Franks locate themselves in the poetry of the people of Israel?

4. How could the Jesus of the Gospels, and the God of both the Jews and the Christians, be understood within the world of the warrior?

5. How, in our own day, does the Catholic imagination deal with issues of war and peace, of power and subjection?

6. How are feelings, ideas, relationships, and ethical norms represented in Catholic culture in our own time? What are the dominant visual symbols of the contemporary Catholic imagination as it pictures our world, and how do they work?

CHAPTER 12 Warrior Christianity II: The Saxons and *The Heliand*

1. What does "cultural translation" mean?

2. The *Heliand's* imaginative retelling of the Gospels discerns within the life of Jesus elements not originally stressed by the evangelists. Do you agree that the poet succeeded in clarifying and illuminating the story of Jesus to the point of achieving a kind of further revelation? Why or why not?

3. Does picturing Jesus as a warrior leader of a Saxon tribe help us to understand his life and death in new and valid ways?

4. What does this poet's imagination suggest as he reinvents such scenes as the nativity, the visit of the wise men, the slaughter of the innocents, and the crucial events of Jesus' passion and death such as Peter's betrayal and Jesus on Calvary?

5. The Germanic tradition includes runes and the concept of language as mysterious but also magical and instrumental, having the power to make and to change things. How, in our own culture, do we continue to see examples of the power of words and verbal formulae such as oaths, adjudications, laws, and political slogans as instrumentally powerful?

6. Paradox is a crucial conceptual structure in the Catholic imagination. How does the *Heliand* poet see Jesus' humiliation and death as somehow heroic?

Index